"In this outstanding book, Lee Beach in ology of exile, forged in the experience of Israel and the early church. But he also challenges an increasingly marginalized church in the West to come to terms with its own situation of exile. Lee Beach argues persuasively that the biblical motif of exile can help Christian communities to reimagine their identity and mission. For Beach, exile is a place of reorientation and hope, which demands an adventuresome faith. Academically sound, but with a strong practical orientation, this timely book has the potential to revitalize how we live out God's mission in a new cultural landscape. Christian leaders and local congregations alike need to hear and heed its challenge."

Dean Flemming, MidAmerica Nazarene University, author, *Recovering the Full Mission of God: A Biblical Perspective on Being, Doing and Telling*

"Instead of pining for a lost Christendom, Lee Beach offers the North American church a deeply biblical model for ecclesial identity and mission that is addressed to our contemporary situation of 'exile.' His nuanced exegesis of Old Testament diaspora tales, his exploration of the mission of Jesus in the context of Second Temple Judaism and his profound analysis of 1 Peter speak powerfully to the church in a post-Christian context. We have much to learn from Beach's insights about holy, missional and hopeful Christian living from the margins."

J. Richard Middleton, Northeastern Seminary, Roberts Wesleyan College

"With profound biblical scope and theological depth, Lee Beach provides wise counsel for a church in exile. Rooted in a serious re-engagement of the biblical motif of exile, Beach engenders an exilic imagination that suggests creative ways for the church to find its identity anew. Here we find a biblical scholarship in service of the church and a church in service of the creation-wide renewal of the world. Exile is both a deep threat and an opportunity for the most creative theological reflection and communal praxis. Beach helps us to navigate these treacherous waters with a compelling pastoral sensibility."

Brian Walsh, Christian Reformed Church campus minister, University of Toronto

"This is a realistic yet profoundly hope-filled account of contemporary, post-Christian, fragmented society and the nature and role of the church in its exilic state. Grounded in thorough biblical exposition, Beach normalizes this state, and in fact suggests that the church is most healthy and most true to its missional identity when it 'digs the ground' it is on! Lee Beach has made a significant contribution to the 'church in exile' literature by fleshing out what it means for said church to live into its true identity. All church leaders should have this book in their arsenal!"

Ross Hastings, Regent College, author of *Missional God, Missional Church: Hope for Re-Evangelizing the West*

"Moving from the center to the margins is an increasing reality for the church in the West. Beach develops a thoughtful theology and praxis of what it means to live as the people of God in exile. If you desire to be a community that is 'intrinsically missional,' then apply the wisdom Beach gives us in developing a prophetic imagination, a responsive theology and an exilic identity as we engage our context in light of God's future."

JR Woodward, national director, V3 Church Planting Movement, author, *Creating a Missional Culture*

The Church *in* Exile

Living in Hope After Christendom

LEE BEACH

Foreword by WALTER BRUEGGEMANN

IVP Academic

An imprint of InterVarsity Press
Downers Grove, Illinois

InterVarsity Press
P.O. Box 1400, Downers Grove, IL 60515-1426
ivpress.com
email@ivpress.com

©2015 by Lee Beach

InterVarsity Press˚ is the book-publishing division of InterVarsity Christian Fellowship/USA˚, a movement of students and faculty active on campus at hundreds of universities, colleges and schools of nursing in the United States of America, and a member movement of the International Fellowship of Evangelical Students. For information about local and regional activities, visit intervarsity.org.

All Scripture quotations, unless otherwise indicated, are taken from the Holy Bible, Today's New International Version˚ Copyright © 2001 by International Bible Society. All rights reserved.

Cover design: Cindy Kiple
Interior design: Beth McGill

Images: Broken stained glass window: St Mary's on the Hill
*   Landscape: Early Morning in the Wilderness of Shur by Frederick Goodall, © Guildhall Art Gallery, City of London / The Bridgeman Art Library.*

ISBN 978-0-8308-4066-3 (print)
ISBN 978-0-8308-9702-5 (digital)

Printed in the United States of America ∞

Library of Congress Cataloging-in-Publication Data
Beach, Lee, 1964-
  The church in exile : living in hope after christendom / Lee Beach.
      pages cm
    Includes index.
    ISBN 978-0-8308-4066-3 (pbk. : alk. paper)
    1. Christianity—21st century. 2. Religious refugees—Biblical teaching. I. Title.
    BR162.3.B43 2015
    270.8'3—dc23

P 23 22 21 20 19 18 17 16 15 14 13 12 11 10 9 8 7 6 5 4 3 2 1

Y 34 33 32 31 30 29 28 27 26 25 24 23 22 21 20 19 18 17 16 15

To my wife and best friend, Joanne, my children, Joshua and Alexandra,

my mother, Gwen, and in memory of my father, Jim.

This has been a family journey.

Contents

Acknowledgments

Sometimes a life-changing moment is nothing more than making an impulse purchase at a bookstore. So it was with me. Sometime in 2001 while browsing through the bookstore at Tyndale Seminary in Toronto, I decided to purchase a collection of Walter Brueggemann's essays titled *Deep Memory, Exuberant Hope*. I cannot recall exactly why I was drawn to the book, but when I started to read it, I was instantly taken in by Brueggemann's insight into culture, the place of the church in culture, and his use of Scripture as a guide to how the church should respond. Primarily I was captured by the connections that Brueggemann made between the exile of Israel and the situation of the church in North America today. His suggestion that the metaphor of exile had relevance to the contemporary church was compelling to me and ultimately changed me in numerous ways and led to the writing of this book. I am most grateful that he agreed to write the foreword for the book, as his generative influence on its formation cannot be overstated.

This book has passed through a number of iterations but was significantly formed in close conversation with my colleague and doctoral supervisor, Michael Knowles. His influence on the content of this work runs throughout. Michael has been a mentor, spiritual director and good friend. His imprint on my life will last for as long as I live.

I also thank Mark Boda, who also served on my doctoral committee. He is a unique scholar, broad in his knowledge of a diverse range of subjects but deep in his ability to analyze an argument and see where it needs further work. His work in the formative stages of this volume, especially in the Old Testament sections, was decisive.

Furthermore, I want to thank Richard Middleton, Rebecca Idestrom and Stanley Porter, all of whom have played a significant role in various ways in the bringing of this book to publication. On that note I also want to thank InterVarsity Press and its great staff, particularly David Congdon, who supported this project and brought it to fruition. Thanks are also due to three former teaching assistants, Bruce Worthington, Jason White and Justin Roberts, who each offered help with the preparation of the manuscript.

On a more personal note, I want to thank my family. My in-laws, Bob and Louella Gould, have provided consistent support and encouragement, including a place to write for extended periods when I needed to get away from the demands of home life in order to focus and get lots of writing done. My mother, Gwen Beach, has always been a tremendous support. She and my father, Jim, provided a foundation for life that I will always be thankful for, and throughout the writing of this book my mom (my dad passed away a number of years ago) has been a constant source of practical help around our house. Her presence in our lives is a genuine gift from the Lord. My children, Josh and Alexandra, kept me grounded and reminded me that there are more important things in life than book writing. I am very proud of the people they are becoming.

I used to be a bit cynical when I would read at the beginning of a book the mention of the spouse at the conclusion of the acknowledgments. It seemed that it was the thing that everyone did as an almost-expected ritual. That was, until I actually wrote a book of my own. Now I understand why such an acknowledgment is absolutely necessary and appropriate! My wife, Joanne, has made this whole project possible. She is my best friend, and I cannot imagine having a more perfect partner to share life with than her.

Foreword

Lee Beach has written an evocative, suggestive book that will reward careful attentiveness. His argument about the future of the church concerns a convergence of social analysis, biblical exegesis and practical theology. His social analysis outlines "the end of Christendom" and the displacement of influence and privilege for the church in the conventional Christianity of North America. Much of his data and illustrations are drawn from Canadian experience, but of course the same pertain in the United States as well.

Beach offers a rich exegetical foray into Old Testament and New Testament texts that concern the notion of "exile as displacement" as an experience in the Bible that serves as a metaphor that may illumine the loss in the contemporary church. He offers an extensive inventory of texts for Israel's exile and then considers especially the first epistle of Peter, where the theme of the church in exile is voiced. He draws the conclusion that "the people of God are by nature exilic" (p. 24).

Midway through his exegesis, however, there is a notable shift of gears that Beach does not acknowledge—a shift that is, in my judgment, altogether commendable. By consideration of the narratives of Esther, Jonah and Daniel, Beach takes up texts that are in fact from the subsequent Diaspora of Israel and not from the usual period of exile. The segue from exile to Diaspora made here is a critical one, one that many interpreters, including this commentator, are making. The difference is that the theme of "exile" leads to an expectation of a return home to normalcy. By contrast "Diaspora" is a practice of life and faith among those who are far from home, who settle in new contexts that become home, with no serious expectation of "returning home" or returning to an old normalcy. The matter is decisive for getting on with ministry. "Exile" might be a hope of "recovery" for the way the church used to be, whereas "Diaspora" is a recognition that there will not be any return home and there will not be a recovery of any old normalcy.

Diaspora as distinct from exile requires finding a new way for theology, church and ministry. The matter is put succinctly by Beach: "[This] leadership will seek to help engender hope in the life of a congregation by cultivating an imagination within them that fuels a missional vision for its future existence" (p. 153).

The key terms are *hope*, *imagination* and *missional vision*.

The book, then, is an extended and bold articulation of practical theology that considers what is now required and permitted for a church that is not "going home." Much of Beach's reflection concerns the holiness of the church. In exile Israel had to focus on being "a holy people to the Lord," which led to the punctilious provisions of Leviticus. And then the church, in the Epistles, is to be a holy people amid the Roman Empire:

> But you are a chosen race, a royal priesthood, a holy nation, God's own people, in order that you may proclaim the mighty acts of him who called you out of darkness into his marvelous light.
>
> Once you were not a people,
>   but now you are God's people,
> once you had not received mercy,
>   but now you have received mercy. (1 Pet 2:9-10 NRSV)

Beach shrewdly sees that a different kind of holiness is urgent and is required in context. He shakes off an older essentialist notion of holiness that had its settled habits. It must now be, rather, a relational, narrative holiness that issues in bold nonconformity. And surely it is the case, that to be gospel-free the urgency of nonconformity has always been crucial for the church as it has shaken off the assurances and expectations of establishment society.

As a card-carrying "progressive" Christian, I have often reflected of late on the fact that many evangelical Christians (by no means all!), including Beach, seem more ready to engage the new, disordered openness of the postmodern context of the church with more energy and expectation than are some fatigued progressives. And when I ask why that is the case, what becomes clear is that there is the well-grounded hope that is rooted in God's own fidelity that is the warrant for fresh initiatives. It is that good hope that makes Beach's argument serious and makes it need to be taken seriously.

More than once his argument returns to the narrative in Acts 10–11. That narrative reports on the way in which Peter is led by the Spirit to new notions of holiness that move past old precisions about purity and cleanness. This new holiness, as Beach views it, is highly contextual, a learning that was most demanding for Peter. His new context in the presence of Gentiles determined that Peter must be adventuresome in his faith and apostolic calling. What is required and permitted for God's holy people is largely determined by context. This kind of Spirit-led faith invites the church to go where it has never been and has never thought to go. The new context for the church is in the midst of radical otherness, as radical as the Gentiles were to Jewish Christians in the first century. Beach's assessment is surely correct. His book invites church leaders to recognize where God has now put the church. The work of new leadership—in terms of hope, imagination and missional vision—is to be about the business of "defining reality" in ways that violate, subvert and transgress all old definitions of reality. Specifically this means to contradict the dominant definitions of reality that oppose gospel truth. Such leaders will anticipate that such new definitions of reality will be vigorously contested, outside the congregation and within it. Anything less than that work will end in irrelevance and despair. This book is a rich exercise in hope!

Walter Brueggemann
Columbia Theological Seminary
August 19, 2013

Introduction

EXILE AND LIFE IN A
POST-CHRISTIAN WORLD

July 1, 1967, was a beautiful summer day in Ottawa, Ontario, Canada, as a crowd of 25,000 people gathered in the nation's capital for the country's centennial birthday celebration. As Canada turned one hundred years old, the festivities began with a prayer service, which was carried on national television and was a centerpiece of the day's events. The crowd waited excitedly as various dignitaries arrived for the service, including all of the main political leaders of the day, the prime minister, members of the cabinet and members of the Senate. When the guest of honor, her majesty Queen Elizabeth, arrived, accompanied by her husband, the duke of Edinburgh, they were greeted by eight members of the clergy, who escorted them to their respective places on the dais. The service consisted of readings from the Bible, including a reading by then–Prime Minister Lester B. Pearson himself, who read from 1 Peter 3:8-14. Hymns from the Christian tradition were sung, and prayers, including a prayer of confession for the sins of the nation and a recitation of the Lord's Prayer, were offered. A litany was recited, and those gathered were invited to respond with the words "We rededicate ourselves, O Lord." The service was a clear nod to the role that the Christian church had played in the first hundred years of the nation's development. The message was that Canada was a religious country, a country whose religion was decidedly Christian.[1]

Similar scenes would not have been uncommon in the United States or in countries all around Western Europe at that time and certainly in years prior. In most of the Western world the Christian religion helped to form the overall ethos of the country and held a certain pride of place in many public celebrations and gatherings.

However, for many of us, the scene that I have briefly recounted is hard to imagine now. Such a public display of Christian faith is rare if not nonexistent in many places where faith once played a major role. The extent of this social evolution may be captured in another snapshot taken of another public service in Canada's capital thirty-four years after the centennial service of 1967. On September 14, 2001, a gathering took place in front of the Parliament buildings three days after the attacks on the World Trade Center in New York City and the Pentagon in Washington on September 11. A crowd estimated at close to 100,000 people gathered on Parliament hill for a day of mourning to commemorate the lives that had been lost in the attacks. While the reason for the gathering could not have been more different and the tone more distinct than the one in 1967, the proceedings were telling in terms of demonstrating the sea change that had taken place in Canadian cultural life.

While representatives from several religions were seated on the dais that day, no Christian clergy (or leader of any religion) was invited to participate in any way. The memorial service, which lasted half an hour, was a quiet one that included brief remarks by Prime Minister Jean Chretien, American ambassador Paul Celucci and Governor General of Canada Adrienne Clarkson. No Scripture was read, no prayers were offered, and no hymns were sung. The only remark that could be considered the least bit religious was the prime minister's words that in a time like this "we cling to our humanity and our common goodness and above all to our prayers."[2]

---

[1]For a more detailed description of the prayer service as well as some fine insight on its significance, see Garry Miedema, *For Canada's Sake: Public Religion, Centennial Celebrations, and the Re-Making of Canada in the 1960s* (Montreal and Kingston: McGill-Queens University Press, 2005), pp. xi-xvi.

[2]See Debra Fieguth, "Rallying in the Face of Horror," *Christian Week*, October 2, 2001. Also see "Further My God," *National Post* editorial, September 18, 2001, p. A7.

The contrast between the 1967 gathering and the 2001 gathering could not be clearer. Each ceremony represented the Canada of its era, and the two together demonstrate how Canada had dramatically changed as a nation, and in fact how drastic those changes had been in a single generation. If the Canada of the early to mid-twentieth century was one decisively shaped by its Christian religious heritage, the Canada of the twenty-first century is one in which no one religious faith of any stripe, let alone Christianity, takes center stage at times of national gathering. In fact, even in a time of national mourning religion was not seen as a necessary part of the grieving process. If such national gatherings provide insight into the ethos of the nation, then in thirty-four years Canada had moved from a nation in which the church played a major role to one in which it was no longer included at all.

While this scenario is drawn from my experience in my own home country, the displacing of Christian faith from countries throughout the West is a shared story. People in the UK, France, Germany, Spain and many other European countries could share similar experiences. Even in the United States, where Christian faith continues to play a more prominent role in national affairs, one can easily find anecdotal evidence of how Christianity is slowly moving from the center of culture to a more peripheral role in many parts of national life. An example of this is in the US's own 9/11 memorials. Three days after the horrible events of September 11, 2001, a memorial service held in Washington offered a distinctly Christian perspective, including Rev. Billy Graham as guest preacher. However, another memorial service was held shortly thereafter at Yankee Stadium in New York City, and this service was hosted by Oprah Winfrey and included a variety of religious traditions. This was a signal of the shifting religious landscape of America, telling those present and those watching around the country that Christianity, while still a part of American life, no longer held the exclusive place that it once did in times when the nation came together and looked to religion for answers. Furthermore, while the dependable Billy Graham was looked to for pastoral care, it was clear that when in national crises the person who would be called on to guide the nation through its grief was a television celebrity known for her eclectic approach to spirituality.

This evolution in the religious orientation of the country would be made even clearer on the tenth anniversary of 9/11, when another service was held at Yankee Stadium. Controversy swirled because the planners chose to completely exclude clergy and prayer as part of the service of remembrance. This drew great ire from many members of the clergy and some members of the media. For some this was indicative of what was happening in the country at large, as religion in general and Christianity in particular were increasingly pushed to the peripheries of the culture.[3]

A survey released by the Pew Research Center's Forum on Religion and Public Life in June 2011 reported that most evangelical Protestant leaders who live in the Global South (58 percent) say that evangelical Christians are gaining influence on life in their countries. However, most leaders who live in the Global North (66 percent) say that evangelicals are losing influence in their countries. United States evangelical leaders are especially negative about the future of evangelical Christianity in American society; 82 percent say evangelicals are losing influence in the US today, while only 17 percent think evangelicals are gaining influence. Overall in the Global North, 54 percent of evangelical leaders say that the overall influence of the church will either stay the same or worsen in the next five years.[4]

Because of this shifting of religious orientation, these are unique days for the church in the Western world. Western culture is in a time of tremendous change. Perhaps the only thing that does not change today is the fact that things are always changing. Representative of this reality is the place that the church occupies in Western culture. At one time the church played a significant role in the shaping of culture and the daily lives of its citizens. As has already been mentioned, for the most part in

---

[3]Laurie Goodstien, "Omitting Clergy at 9/11 Ceremony Prompts Protest," *New York Times*, September 9, 2011, p. A1, www.nytimes.com/2011/09/09/nyregion/omitting-clergy-from-911-ceremony-prompts-protest.html?pagewanted=all.

[4]Pew Research Center's Forum on Religion & Public Life, "Global Survey of Evangelical Protestant Leaders," June 22, 2011, http://pewforum.org/Christian/Evangelical-Protestant-Churches/Global-Survey-of-Evangelical-Protestant-Leaders.aspx.

decades past life in North America and parts of Europe was highly conducive to Christianity in its many expressions.[5]

This can no longer be considered true of the contemporary setting for the church in the West. The place of the church is shifting significantly as the culture in which we find ourselves increasingly wrestles with, and is at times even hostile toward, distinctive Christian values.[6] By this I do not mean that there is overt anger toward or persecution of Christian beliefs, although that may occur at times. Rather, when examined—even in a cursory way—it is clear that the norms of Western culture often move in a direction that challenges the church and its identity within the culture. Christianity, which at one time stood at—or at least near—the center of Western culture and could presume for itself a privileged voice, has witnessed that center unravel and watched as its place at the center has ceased to exist.

Walter Brueggemann's observations concerning American culture reflect on the ramifications of this shift:

> There was a time . . . when a Christian preacher could count on the shared premises of the listening community, reflective of a large theological consensus. There was a time, when the assumption of God completely dominated Western imagination, and the holy Catholic Church roughly uttered the shared consensus of all parties. That consensus was rough and perhaps not very healthy, but at least the preacher could work from it.[7]

Brueggemann's comments present a fair picture of the contrast between former days and the situation as it now stands. With the lack of anything close to a Christian cultural consensus, the church must continue to wrestle with ways to define itself and engage the culture of which it is a

---

[5]For evidence of this see Mark Noll, *A History of Christianity in the United States and Canada* (Grand Rapids: Eerdmans, 1992); and Hugh McLeod and Werner Usterof, *The Decline of Christendom in Western Europe, 1750-2000* (Cambridge: Cambridge University Press, 2003).

[6]Defining the term *culture* is difficult; however, my use of the term here and throughout the book, unless otherwise specified, is broad and refers to the range of things that characterize a society such as its customs, modes of behavior, beliefs, social practices, social structures and the arts. See Jonathan Vance, *A History of Canadian Culture* (Oxford: Oxford University Press, 2009), pp. vii-viii.

[7]Walter Brueggemann, *Deep Memory, Exuberant Hope: Contested Truth in a Post-Christian World* (Minneapolis: Fortress, 2000), p. 1.

part. Some church traditions are consciously aware of this need. Others may be less aware that something has changed, and even if they are aware may not feel overly compelled to respond. However, many who are serious about the future of the church are looking for new ways to understand how better to express the uniqueness of Christian faith in our current cultural context.

In considering how to do this, it may be that the motif of exile offers one of the most provocative and potentially fruitful ways for the church to define itself in this particular historical epoch. There is an emerging conviction that the situation of the contemporary church may be similar to that of ancient Israel or the early church in their respective, and distinctive, focus on exile.[8]

EXILE AS A POTENTIAL MOTIF FOR THE CHURCH

Perhaps exile is the way that the people of God should understand themselves at all times in their history.[9] Christendom, it can be argued, is an anomaly that produced mixed results for the church's mission and identity.[10] In light of this it could be that the recovery of an exilic paradigm as a means of self-definition is absolutely necessary for the church in postmodern, post-Christian times.

In order to appreciate the full potential of this motif we must under-

---

[8]For example see Brueggemann, *Cadences of Home: Preaching Among Exiles* (Louisville, KY: John Knox, 1997), and Brueggemann, *Deep Memory, Exuberant Hope*. In both of these books Brueggemann works from a perspective that exile is the best motif for understanding the place of the Christian church in contemporary Western culture. Richard J. Middleton and Brian J. Walsh utilize this theme throughout their book *Truth Is Stranger Than It Used to Be: Biblical Faith in a Postmodern Age* (Downers Grove, IL: InterVarsity Press, 1995). Ralph Klein also concludes his study *Israel in Exile: A Theological Interpretation* (Philadelphia: Fortress, 1979) with reflection on how the motif aptly connects with the Western church in contemporary culture; see pp. 149-54. See also Michael Frost, *Exiles: Living Missionally in a Post-Christian Culture* (Peabody, MA: Hendrickson, 2006).

[9]See Robert P. Carroll, "Exile! What Exile?: Deportation and the Discourses of Diaspora," in *Judaic Religion in the Second Temple Period*, ed. Lester Grabbe (London: Routledge, 2000), pp. 66-67, where he discusses the idea that exile is *the* biblical story. Also see Jacob Neusner, "Exile and Return as the History of Judaism," in *Exile: Old Testament, Jewish and Christian Perspectives*, ed. James Scott (Leiden: Brill, 2001), p. 221, where he states, "The paradigm of exile and return contains all Judaisms over all times, to the present."

[10]Bryan Stone, *Evangelism After Christendom: The Theology and Practice of Christian Witness* (Grand Rapids: Brazos, 2007), p. 11.

stand that the concept of exile entails more than the stereotypical definition of being displaced from one's native country as a result of forced expulsion or voluntary separation. Exile implies much more than simple geographical dislocation; it can be a cultural and spiritual condition as well. It is the experience of knowing that one is an alien, and perhaps even in a hostile environment where the dominant values run counter to one's own.[11]

In other words, one can experience exile even when one returns to or remains in one's homeland. Well beyond the sphere of religious identity, this observation is confirmed by the experience of artists, poets, political dissidents, philosophers and religious leaders in countries throughout the world. In his important study on the experience of exile, Paul Tabori has reflected on the concept of "inner exile," that is, the experience of "being an outcast within one's own country."[12]

From a cultural and sociological perspective Tabori's work reveals the possible extent of exilic experience and how it includes but should not be limited to physical displacement. He underscores the fact that one can be "in the land" and yet still be in exile. Exile is, in its very essence, living away from home.[13] This is at the heart of Christian faith, as we live away from our ultimate eschatological community. Furthermore, exile is a result of understanding ourselves as a distinct people, strangers in the world. This distinction is defined by our relationship with the supreme God and is rooted in God's call for us to live our lives in accord with this relationship, often in ways that will come into conflict with the dominant culture. This sense of exile is experienced by anyone who feels alienated, cast adrift or marginalized by their inability or unwillingness to conform to the tyranny of majority opinion.[14] Simply put, Edward

---

[11]Brueggemann, *Cadences of Home*, p. 115.

[12]Paul Tabori, *The Anatomy of Exile: A Semantic and Historical Study* (London: Harrap, 1972), p. 32.

[13]See Susan Robin Suleiman, "Introduction," in *Exile and Creativity: Signposts, Travelers, Outsiders, Backward Glances,* ed. Susan Rubin Suleiman (Durham, NC: Duke University Press, 1996), p. 1. Suleiman expands the traditional definition of exile by stating that exile "designates every kind of estrangement or displacement, from the physical to the geographical to the spiritual" (p. 2).

[14]Wendy Everett and Peter Wagstaff, "Introduction," in *Cultures of Exile: Images of Displacement,* ed. Wendy Everett and Peter Wagstaff (New York: Berghahn, 2004), p. x.

Saïd writes that exile is "the perilous territory of not belonging."[15]

For Christians in the West this experience of general cultural marginalization may be compounded by the postmodern ethos that permeates culture today, leading to what Saïd characterizes as an experience of dislocation or "rootlessness."[16] Postmodernism is intrinsically a cultural ethos that tends to leave its citizens feeling homeless. At its heart it is a culture that rejects any universal narrative or collective ethic that might offer a sense of common foundation to its inhabitants, as the Christian story once did for North America and large parts of Europe.

This is because postmodernism is ultimately a reaction to modernism and as such is a deconstructive movement rather than a reconstructionist one. Postmodernism is, by definition, a tearing down of former beliefs and patterns of life. It produces not a new order of things but rather a new "disorder." Brian Walsh and Sylvia Keesmaat explain that the postmodern ethos that questions former assumptions, entertains multiple possibilities and posits few conclusions is a culture of fragmentation. They write, "When one is accustomed to toying with a multiplicity of perspectives, identities, and worldviews it is not surprising that life starts to feel fragmented."[17] Such an outlook produces a fragmented culture and potentially a fragmented self, which can be an isolating experience. In postmodernism the self can slip into a form of isolation as a result of loss of connection with stabilizing community.[18] This destabilizing cultural ethos is compounded all the more when one's social group was once at the center of cultural power and is now increasingly at the margins, as is the case with Christianity in North America and Europe. In such a situation, exile becomes a useful way of self-understanding for the church in the Western world.

---

[15]Edward Saïd, *Reflections on Exile: and Other Literary and Cultural Essays* (London: Granata Books, 2001), p. 177. For a thorough overview of the range of potential uses of exile and how it is being explored within biblical studies and practical theology today, see Pamela, J. Scalise, "The End of the Old Testament," Perspectives in Religious Studies 35, no. 2 (2008): 163-78.

[16]Ibid.

[17]Brian J. Walsh and Sylvia C. Keesmaat, *Colossians Remixed: Subverting the Empire* (Downers Grove, IL: InterVarsity Press, 2004), p. 25.

[18]Michael P. Gallagher, *Clashing Symbols: An Introduction to Faith and Culture* (London: Darton, Longman and Todd, 1997), p. 92.

While *exile* is a complex term that can be understood in a number of ways, for the purposes of this book it will be applied to the church today through the lens of theo-sociological exile. This acknowledges that our exile encompasses both theological and social aspects. As we will see, exile is a deeply theological experience for Israel, and continued to be so for Second Temple Jews. Even in the New Testament, exile is a theologically charged idea that has implications for the ministry of Jesus and the early church. In this study we will see demonstrated that the Western church continues to share a theological kinship with such people. Furthermore, we will explore how our experience of being decentered within Western culture also places us in sociological kinship with Israel, Second Temple Jews and the early church in such a way that the resources they produced can inform our contemporary experience.

It must be said that when appropriating a motif such as exile one must do so cautiously and with deep respect for the seriousness of the term. Exile has been a terrifying experience for many, and glorifying the idea of being stripped of cultural power may seem romantic on the surface, when it does not actually infringe on personal rights, but it is far less appealing when it results in actual violence, forced removal and disenfranchisement. Some will be quick to embrace a post-Christendom identity and its subsequent outsider status for the church. However, Sze-kar Wan warns that when truly stripped of power, exiles experience a longing to regain power rather than to celebrate its loss.[19] Caren Kaplan writes about using the exilic motif in a "faddish" way and thus divesting it of any serious meaning.[20] In the same vein, Edward Saïd wonders, "If true exile is a condition of terminal loss, why has it been transformed so easily into a potent, even enriching motif of modern culture?"[21] These critiques must be heard, and we have to be sensitive in our appropriation of the exilic motif for the church today. However, its legitimacy

---

[19]Sze-kar Wan, "Does Diaspora Identity Imply Some Sort of Universality? An Asian American Reading of Galatians," in *Interpreting Beyond Borders*, ed. F. F. Segovia (Sheffield: Sheffield Academic, 2000), p. 119.

[20]Caren Kaplan, *Questions of Travel: Postmodern Discourses of Displacement* (Durham, NC: Duke University Press, 1996), p. 63.

[21]Saïd, *Reflections on Exile*, p. 137.

comes in part from the fact that exile is not a new motif for the biblical people of God.

In biblical perspective, the people of God are by nature exilic. Throughout history, those who worship the God of Abraham, Isaac and Jacob have often perceived themselves to be a threatened minority, struggling to preserve their particular identity and beliefs. From the original couple being cast out (exiled) from the Garden, to the wanderings of Cain, to the nomadic journeys of the aforementioned patriarchs, to slavery in Egypt, to the constant threats of enemies throughout the period of the monarchy (including both the northern and southern kingdoms' final period where both kings were essentially vassals to Mesopotamian power), to conquest by the Assyrians (eighth century), by the Babylonians (sixth century) and to Israel's subsequent existence under Persian, Greek and Roman rule, the people of Israel never had the pleasure of living with a permanent sense of national security. Neither did the Christians who made up the first generations of the church. Thus the people of ancient Israel, Second Temple Jews and early Christians were plunged into cultural situations where *who* they were and what they were called to be was at odds, sometimes drastically so, with *where* they found themselves.

This experience can aptly describe the situation of the church in the West today, and just as the ancient Israelite, Jewish and Christian communities understood their exile in a variety of ways similar to those delineated above, they responded to their exilic existence with a variety of resources. In fact, exile was for Israel a time of immense creativity, as it was also for the early church. For the community to thrive in exile would take more than simply going back to former practices. A fresh interpretation of faith would be necessary not only to sustain the community but also to meet the challenges of a new life setting. For ancient Israel exile provoked theological creativity that produced new understandings (the Hebrew canon) and new practices (Judaism).[22]

Walter Brueggemann elaborates on this idea by stating that "exile

---

[22]Brueggemann, *Cadences of Home*, p. 115. Ralph Klein also comments, "Exile was and is a catalyst for translating the faith" (*Israel in Exile*, p. 153).

evoked the most brilliant literature and the most daring theological articulation in the Old Testament."[23] In similar terms, Michael Frost speaks directly to the challenge at hand for the contemporary Western church when he suggests that the work of exile is to rediscover the teachings of Jesus and the practices of the early church and to apply them to life on the soil of a post-Christian empire.[24]

Indeed, exile tends to infuse communities with new creative energy that rises to meet the challenges of new cultural circumstances.[25] Accordingly, the responses to exile that are offered by the communities depicted in Scripture provide resources to the contemporary church and its own formation as an exilic people. That is, exile is an appropriate motif for the Western church's understanding of itself and its mission in its current setting; a robust biblical and practical theology rooted in both the Old Testament and New Testament visions of exile can inform the contemporary church's self-understanding and mission.

In this book I will attempt to help us begin to consider both a biblical theology of exile and some of the ways that the church can appropriate this theology in its practice as a church on the margins. In order to do this, we will start by offering a brief consideration of some of the cultural realities that make exile a legitimate paradigm for the church to appropriate as a way of understanding its place in Western culture today. From there we will examine the exilic story of Israel as it is offered to us through the Old Testament. Several major themes that defined Israel's response to their dramatically new circumstances, when they were defeated by the Babylonians and remained in captivity in one form or another for many subsequent centuries, can be identified. In particular we will consider

---

[23]Brueggeman, *Cadences of Home*, p. 3.

[24]Frost, *Exiles*, p. 26.

[25]For an exploration of how exile is an impetus to creativity see Zygmunt Bauman, "Assimilation into Exile: A Jew as a Polish Writer," in *Exile and Creativity*, p. 321, where he writes, "in exile, uncertainty meets freedom. Creation is the issue of that wedlock." Also, Susan Robin Suleiman asks rhetorically, "Is this distance a falling away from some original wholeness and source of creativity, or is it on the contrary a spur to creativity?" ("Introduction," in *Exile and Creativity*, p. 1). Finally, this theme is also explored by Lucia Ann McSpadden in "Contemplating Repatriation to Eritrea," in *Coming Home: Refugees, Migrants and Those Who Stayed Behind*, ed. Lynellyn D. Long and Ellen Oxfeld (Philadelphia: University of Pennsylvania Press), p. 46, as she writes about the way that exile allows one to critique one's own country or established patterns.

three biblical narratives that depict the potential of exilic life. The stories of Esther, Daniel and Jonah are a particular kind of exilic literature that offers a hopeful vision and compelling model of life in exile. These "diasporic advice tales," as they are sometimes called, offer the same kind of generative vision to contemporary exilic communities as they did to the ancient ones to which they were first directed.

Following our consideration of Israel's exile we will briefly trace the development of the exilic theme in Second Temple (or intertestamental) literature. While exile continued to be an important orienting idea during this period of history, we will consider it in an abbreviated form because it helps to introduce exile as a theme in the ministry of Jesus and the early church. Here, particularly through a focus on the epistle of 1 Peter, we will see how Israel's response to exile and Second Temple Jews' continued development of the idea resonated with the author of 1 Peter, and how he appropriates what were even then ancient approaches for his contemporary (first-century) audience. A study of 1 Peter will demonstrate a consistency of ideas between Old and New Testament exilic experiences and will offer compelling suggestions for our own appropriation of this paradigm.

The final section will offer an application of this ancient wisdom for the twenty-first-century church. Specifically we will look at how a biblical theology of exile can apply to the practice of ministry in the areas of leadership, theology, holiness, mission and eschatology. These are not random categories; rather, they are the very categories that the Bible itself identifies as central to exilic practice. An exploration of them in our contemporary context will empower us to appropriate their potential for guiding our ministries as we seek to be the church in exile.

It is almost universally agreed on that the church in the Western world is in decline. After having played a central role in the development of Western culture, the church now finds itself on the sidelines, wondering how it can make a valid contribution to society. My own perspective on this is rooted in my experience as a Christian and a church leader in Canada. While Canada has a distinct story in terms of its move into post-Christendom, and the Canadian church has its own story of marginalization as a result, the experience of responding to this reality may prove informative to Christians in other contexts, in particular the United States, who are "behind" Canada in terms of their cultural experience of exile but who are clearly moving in that direction. The goal of this book is to contribute to the necessary and ongoing conversation around the church's identity in changing times by offering a biblically informed reflection on who the church is and how an exilic self-understanding can put us in touch with life-giving resources essential for renewal, with the hope that the church can continue to have influence in our world, albeit from a very different position in society. As exile was for Israel a time for self-evaluation and reorientation, so it can be for the church. The way forward is to look around and understand our context, to look back and gather the resources that our Christian faith offers us, and then to look forward with a clear vision of how the church ought to and can function as God's people in contemporary exile. In this study I will seek to help inform all three aspects of that necessary process in the hope that the mission of the church will be renewed from its current "home" on the margins of culture rather than from its former home at the center.

While exile was devastating for Israelite life and faith, and life for the early church was a continual challenge, their circumstances proved to be a time of development that generated a better future for both. As Ephraim Radner eloquently states regarding Israel's exile, "Exile is also a movement by which our Lord delineated deliverance. As such, it can hardly be a cause for fear."[26] This can also be the case for the Western church in the twenty-first century if we are willing to learn from the wisdom of our ancestors in the faith.

---

[26]Ephraim Radner, "From Liberation to Exile: A New Image for Church Mission," *Christian Century* 30, no. 18 (1989): 934.

Part One

A Theology of Exile

1

Exile as a Motif for
the Church Today

In the early fifth century Romans reclined in their villas in the south of England feeling secure that their world was intact and would remain that way for many years to come. Yes, the army was busy, always off somewhere to put down an uprising here or a barbarian raid on the frontier there. But the roads still bustled with commerce, the public baths were still operating, and the harvest was under way. The citizens of England were oblivious to the fact that the Saxons were already crossing the English Channel with designs on the land that once seemed to be the eternal possession of the mighty Roman Empire. Soon they would invade, pillage and plunder Roman Britain. It took less than one generation for Roman Britain to vanish. The villas were ransacked and some of the people were killed; others were sold as slaves or driven away. The physical structures were still there, roads, villas and buildings largely intact, but the society as it once stood was completely gone. The Roman world seemed stable, even unshakable. Rome had existed for a thousand years. But times change, and sometimes it doesn't take long.

The story of Romans living in England has relevance for the church in the West today. The world as it existed for a long time has undergone a change that is almost as drastic as the one just described. Ways of life, ideals, positions of power and influence that have long been established, no longer exist the way that they once did. There was a time when the church's place in society was central to the culture, and it may have been hard to imagine things any other way. However, those of us who have lived in North America or parts of Western Europe in the past few decades have an understanding of how things can indeed change in a very short period of time.

Before we can appropriate the wisdom of ancient Israel and the early church and its potential benefit for the church in contemporary Western society, we need to further consider our own circumstances and determine how or even whether exile is a legitimate way for us to understand our place in the current culture. As we briefly explored in the introduction, exile is not an idea that should be appropriated in a flippant manner.[1] Its painful effects on millions are far too severe for us to engage it as a faddish new idea for innovative ministry practice in our comfortable middle-class churches. However, as we examine the realities of our culture and the changing place of the church within it, we can begin to identify ways in which an exilic perspective could help the church identify itself and its place in the Western world today. The key concept that we must look at to make this connection is the demise of what is often referred to as "Christendom." Understanding the significance of this cultural trend will help us to appreciate how the motif of exile is useful as an orienting paradigm for the church today. Thus we will briefly look at Christendom's demise and the development of a post-Christendom cultural experience in the Western world today.

THE DEMISE OF CHRISTENDOM

As we considered in the introduction to this book, there was a time in the history of most Western nations when Christianity held court as the de facto religion of the empire, and the church stood at or near the center of political power. In this cultural setting the church had a significant role to play in the shaping of culture and the determining of the overarching moral structures of society. The demise of this former cultural

---

[1]"To think of exile as beneficial, as a spur to humanism or to creativity, is to belittle its mutilations. . . . Think instead of the uncountable masses for whom UN agencies have been created, of refugees without urbanity, with only ration cards and agency numbers" (Daniel Smith-Christopher, *A Biblical Theology of Exile* [Minneapolis: Fortress, 2002], p. 21, quoting from Edward Saïd, "The Mind of Winter: Reflections on Life in Exile," *Harpers* [September 1983]: 50).

reality has actually been quite rapid and has received extensive treatments by a number of authors.[2] Each of these studies confirms what many of us already know to be true, that Christianity has been gradually losing its status as the lingua franca in Western culture for some time and has increasingly tended to become a local language used only by those who are professing Christians, not understood by others.[3]

Christendom is a term given to the religious culture that has dominated Western society since the fourth century C.E. when Emperor Constantine issued the Edict of Milan, which declared imperial toleration of Christianity in the Roman Empire. From here the emperor offered several more edicts that were favorable to Christianity and that eventually led to Christianity being equated with the religion of the state. This held true and was largely unchallenged for at least the next fourteen to fifteen centuries, as the church and the state stood as pillars equally supporting the overarching cultural milieu. Christianity was an official part of the empire, and in some countries the leader of the country was also head of the church, and citizens of the country were often baptized in state churches and assumed to be Christians simply because of their citizenship.[4] Even in countries where there was not a state church, such as Canada or the United States, Christianity was by default the religion of the nation in its early formation.

This slowly began to change in many older Western nations in the seventeenth and eighteenth centuries as the Enlightenment, or the "Age of Reason" as it is often called, began to emerge and call into question many of the assumptions of Western culture, including its religious ones. As the Enlightenment project grew, the modernist era developed and the foundations of Christendom slowly began to crack. As the twentieth century dawned, Western culture was going through a tremendous up-

---

[2]Some highly accessible volumes include Malcom Muggeridge, *The End of Christendom* (Grand Rapids: Eerdmans, 1980) and Douglas J. Hall, *The End of Christendom and the Future of Christianity* (Eugene, OR: Wipf and Stock, 2002).

[3]Hugh McLeod, "Introduction," in *The Decline of Christendom in Western Europe, 1750-2000,* ed. Hugh McLeod and Werner Ustorf (Cambridge: Cambridge University Press, 2003), p. 11.

[4]Michael Frost, *Exiles: Living Missionally in a Post-Christian Culture* (Peabody, MA: Hendrickson, 2006), pp. 4-5.

heaval in its self-identity. While an in-depth analysis of the particulars is outside the scope of this chapter, Phyllis Tickle chronicles some of the main contours of this immense transition in her book *The Great Emergence*. Tickle calls attention to the world-changing developments in science, economics, political structure, technology, the role of women, family life and morality that began to germinate during the Enlightenment but found serious traction during the twentieth century.[5] All of these contributed to a reevaluation of religion, both in terms of its content and its role in society, that led to its increasing privatization and diminishing role in public life.

While church attendance and expressed religious affiliation do not tell the whole story, they still offer us a window into the reality of how things have changed when it comes to the overall population's relationship to Christianity. A 2008 Pew Forum religious landscape survey revealed the seismic shift that is taking place within the religious beliefs of American people today. The massive Pew survey on more than 35,000 people reports that the US is on the verge of becoming a minority Protestant country for the first time in its history (only 51 percent claim to be Protestant). Catholic Christians make up only 24 percent of the population; however, the survey also reported that 31 percent said they were raised Catholic. The fastest-growing religious affiliation is "unaffiliated." This number is rising most rapidly with younger generations, as one in four Americans aged eighteen to twenty-nine identify themselves as having no religious affiliation. This includes atheists, agnostics and "nothing in particulars."[6] The report offers an analysis of its data by reflecting on the fact that there is an unprecedented amount of religious movement taking place in the US overall, and those reporting no affiliation are the group that best exemplifies this trend. The survey found that 3.9 percent of the adult population reports being raised without any particular religious affiliation but later in life began to affiliate with a religious group.

---

[5]Phyllis Tickle, *The Great Emergence: How Christianity is Changing and Why* (Grand Rapids: Baker, 2008), ch. 5.

[6]The Pew Forum on Religion and Public Life, "U.S. Religious Landscape Survey," February 2008, http://religions.pewforum.org/pdf/report-religious-landscape-study-full.pdf, pp. 5-6.

However, more than three times as many people (12.7 percent of the adult population) were raised in a particular faith but have since become unaffiliated with any religious group. This migration away from religious affiliation reflects a significant trend in American life.[7] If these trends continue at their current pace, religious "nones," as they are often called, will outnumber Christians by 2042.[8]

Even basic belief in God is waning. A 1960 Pew survey asked Americans whether they believed in God. A whopping 97 percent answered "yes" to that query. In 2008 only 71 percent were "certain" that God or a "universal spirit" existed. That represents a 26 percent decline in American religious certainty. Even though the questions were worded slightly differently and different options were offered for the response, the trend is clear.[9]

In Canada similar trends are easily detected; in fact, they are occurring at an even more rapid rate. The work of sociologist Reginald Bibby reveals that 47 percent of Canadian teenagers report that they "never" attend religious services.[10] Bibby's survey, which he has done every four years for more than twenty-five years, demonstrates the way religious affiliation has shifted among younger people in Canada. In 1984 85 percent of Canadian teens reported that they were either Protestant or Catholic. By 2008 only 45 percent reported the same. Dramatically, 32 percent reported themselves as "nones" in terms of affiliation (up from 12 percent in 1984), and 16 percent reported themselves as affiliated with some kind of non-Christian faith (up from 3 percent in 1984).[11] Bibby's stats show that Canada is rapidly becoming a different place religiously than it was only twenty-five short years ago, and the fact that these changes are happening among younger generations signals that these changes are only beginning. Their full effect is yet to fully be felt throughout Canadian culture.

As we enter into the twenty-first century and the dust from the cul-

---

[7]Ibid., p. 25.

[8]Diana Butler-Bass, *Christianity After Religion: The End of Church and the Birth of a New Spiritual Awakening* (New York: HarperCollins, 2013), p. 46.

[9]Ibid., p. 45.

[10]Reginald Bibby, *The Emerging Millenials: How Canada's Newest Generation Is Responding to Change and Choice* (Lethbridge, AB: Project Canada Books, 2009), p. 185.

[11]Ibid., p. 176.

tural upheaval of the previous century begins to clear, it is apparent that the church no longer functions at or near the center of things any more. The new reality for Christianity is that it is no longer fully integrated into the culture, and this reality will only grow more acute as the next decades unfold. The church must now function within a framework that precludes any kind of cultural authority.[12]

This new cultural milieu has been described by pollster Michael Adams as "a winding journey from the death of God and traditional notions of family and community, to a highly individualistic population focused on personal control and autonomy, to a new embryonic but fast-growing sense of human interconnectedness with technology and nature."[13] For some these developments offer liberation from former cultural norms that inhibited human growth.

Adams's analysis captures the evolution of Western culture and the ongoing shifting that leads the culture further and further away from its past allegiance to Christian beliefs. The question as to what led to this change is certainly valid, and the answer is complex, but several significant developments can be considered central to this shift in cultural ethos. The following analysis offers some insight into how Western culture changed so dramatically in such a relatively short period of time.

A growing affluence in the population. A primary development that led to these cultural shifts is the unmistakable growth in national affluence in the postwar years, particularly in North America. There was a boom in manufacturing as factories that had been established to help in the war effort were turned into production facilities for consumer goods. The advent of the suburbs, just on the outskirts of large cities, provided opportunities for young, middle-class families to buy homes and establish themselves in subdivisions populated by other families who, like themselves, were seeking to build their postwar lives in a way that assured that their children would "have it better" than they did.

---

[12]Terrence Murphy, "Epilogue," in *A Concise History of Christianity in Canada*, ed. Terrance Murphy and Roberto Perin (Toronto: Oxford University Press, 1996), p. 369.
[13]Michael Adams, *Sex in the Snow: Canadian Social Trends at the End of the Millennium* (Toronto: Viking, 1997), p. 200.

Despite times of recession, affluence was a dominant theme of cultural discussion in the 1950s and '60s. Even though the Cold War presented many complexities, affluence was taken as a normal condition, and the struggles of the Depression and the travails of the World War II period were now a distant memory, with minimal hold over the new generation of baby boomers.[14] The economic abundance produced by the postwar manufacturing boom was also a catalyst for a rise in the technology sector. These developments brought about overall state growth and an increase in individual wealth.

The rise of material security and comfort, and the freedom of choice that came with them, cannot be overlooked as contributing factors to the overall secularization of the US and Canada, as it led some to abandon any sense of need for religious consolation. While these nations had enjoyed a certain amount of affluence for most of their history, and the pursuit of affluence was certainly not something new in the evolution of human history, it occurred in an unprecedented way in the postwar years and saw a significant rise in the 1960s. The advent of new affluence for many brought changes to their lives and the lifestyles that they chose. These choices affected their participation in certain traditional practices, some-times including religious ones. It also provoked them to question some societal standards that had long been in place, as they sought to use their newfound affluence to enjoy a variety of worldly possibilities. This adven-turous spirit was to some extent inspired by the fact that many North Americans returned from the war having been exposed to other cultures and having acquired a taste for things that up until then had either been foreign or were considered taboo. Once back, they insisted on the oppor-tunity to access some of these things at home. Thus, in many parts of postwar society, a growing lenience arose on things like social drinking, sexual mores and Sunday as a day of "rest." The new consumers were eager to surround themselves with products that contributed to a lifestyle of refined living. Former, more puritanical ways of living were condemned as restrictive of natural human freedoms. As the twentieth century pro-

---

[14]Doug Owram, *Born at the Right Time: A History of the Baby Boom Generation* (Toronto: University of Toronto Press, 1996), p. 183.

gressed, the advent of new products and new technologies, greater in-
comes as a result of two-income homes, and a growing appetite for con-
sumption added fuel to the consumptive fire that roared through major
parts of North American culture. Consumerism and the comforts of material possessions contributed to the dissipation of spiritual appetites.

Secularization. At an even deeper level, these changes drew their life
from the momentum found in the movement of secularization that had
begun to emerge early in the nation's life yet took firmer hold in the
post–World War II years. A brief examination of secularism and its influence on North American life is necessary if we are to forge a basic
understanding of how exile becomes a viable paradigm for the church to
understand itself in the twenty-first century.[15]

In the early years of the twentieth century the forces of secularization
were already beginning to encroach on public life all throughout the
Western world. Thus it is wrong to assume that the process of secularization was a late-twentieth-century phenomenon. However, both the
United States' and Canada's development as nations had a strong religious tone, and it was only after World War II that the overt influences
of secularizing forces began to take their tangible grip on North American
culture. However, on close scrutiny, it is not hard to discern how the
secular trends of the West as a whole were echoed in the evolution of
North American society.

McGill University professor Charles Taylor, who has written extensively on the issue of secularism, identifies the many nuances that mark
it as both a philosophy and as a movement. He offers a partial definition

---

[15]It must be noted that secularism as a philosophy and secularization as a social movement are
multifaceted and not simply defined. A thorough analysis of these forces in Western culture is
beyond the purview of this current work. What follows here is a tracing of the major contours
of both as they affected (and continue to affect) everyday life in North America. For an interesting delineation of these terms offered by someone writing at the time that Canada was coming
to grips with the swirling winds of secularizing forces, see Mark R. Macguigan, "Unity in the
Secular City," in *One Church, Two Nations?* ed. Philip Leblanc and Arnold Edinborough (Don
Mills: Longmans, 1969), pp. 149-50. For a brief but helpful comparison of various understandings of secularization in contemporary thought as it pertains to its effect on religion in Western
Europe (and also indirectly to Canada and the United States) see the essay by Jeffrey Cox,
"Master Narratives of Long-Term Religious Change," in *Decline of Christendom in Western Eu-
rope, 1750-2000*, pp. 201-17.

when he writes that the shift to secularity consists, among other things, in "a move from a society where belief in God is unchallenged and indeed, unproblematic, to one in which it is understood to be one option among others, and frequently not the easiest to embrace."[16] Similarly, historian Ramsey Cook defines it simply as "the shift from a religious explanation of man's [sic] behaviour to a non-religious one."[17] This shift increasingly took place throughout Western culture as it moved from being a collective of nations that valued religion, and Christian religion in particular, as a central part of national identity to a culture that was no longer inclined to give preference to any one religion.[18]

Paul Bramadat identifies the two broader cultural forces that converge in the secularization process as rationalism (the process of organizing life around scientific and logical principles) and disenchantment (the gradual disempowerment of ideas or institutions associated with magic or religion).[19] The forces that drove secularism were rooted in scientific and religious studies. The growing acceptance of Darwinian evolution provided a scientific explanation for the world that no longer necessitated belief in God or at least made belief in God less compelling to those who were disinclined toward belief in the first place. The emergence of more sophisticated scientific theories, such as Albert Einstein's theory of relativity and the quantum mechanics theories of Werner Heisenberg, pushed the scientific envelope and opened up fresh ways of understanding the

---

[16]Charles Taylor, *A Secular Age* (Cambridge, MA: Harvard University Press, 2007), p. 3.

[17]Ramsey Cook, *The Regenerators: Social Criticism in Late Victorian English Canada* (Toronto: University of Toronto Press, 1987), p. 4.

[18]This is not to insinuate that the idea of religious neutrality was brand-new to Canada. Many influential leaders in early Canada were not overly religious or insisted that one religion (or denomination) should never be preferred over another. In certain ways it can be argued that this was the founding view of Canadian society. As J. R. Miller notes in "Unity/Diversity: The Canadian Experience: From Confederation to the First World War," in *Readings in Canadian History: Post-Confederation*, 7th ed., ed. R. Douglas Francis and Donald B. Smith (Toronto: Nelson, 2006), John A. Macdonald's founding vision was one of "unity in diversity" (p. 71). The prominence of Christian belief came about as a matter of fact, simply because most of the early citizens of Canada were practicing Christians. The valuing of religion, then, was more an intrinsic value than one that was legislated. See David B. Marshall, *Secularizing the Faith: Canadian Protestant Clergy and the Crises of Belief 1850-1940* (Toronto: University of Toronto Press, 1992), pp. 22-24.

[19]Paul Bramadat, "Beyond Christian Canada," in *Religion and Ethnicity in Canada*, ed. Paul Bramadat and David Seljak (Toronto: Pearson-Longman, 2005), p. 4.

functions of the universe. The boom in technology that prevailed during and after the two world wars provoked a growing optimism in humankind's ability to innovate and create solutions to universal problems.

In terms of religious studies, the advent of historical criticism in biblical studies in the nineteenth century, as well as the emerging field of comparative religion, provided a religious critique of long-held Christian beliefs and gave people alternative ways of thinking about Christian faith. The late nineteenth century and early twentieth century brought about questions regarding the "historical Jesus." Was the Jesus of the church's faith the same as the Jesus of history? German scholars such as Hermann Samuel Reimarus and Albert Schweitzer published influential books that openly explored this question and inspired a generation of scholars to continue to question the foundations of Christian thought that had been held true for centuries. The conclusions of these scholars brought many traditional interpretations of Scripture into doubt and in many ways allowed for a relaxation of formerly central beliefs.[20] Religion was reframed as something from a "premodern" era that needed to function as a private matter as opposed to an overarching, guiding cultural narrative.

A move away from Christian adherence also allowed for an increase in beliefs and practices that had often been considered taboo by the religious establishment. As noted, this was epitomized by the move toward consumerism. The consumeristic impulse that we have already considered is a part of any developing society and is accepted as a natural part of life. That said, some theorize that the movement of secularization was ultimately more driven by the "internal decay" brought on by consumerism than it was by the "external attacks" delivered by Darwin or the German biblical scholars with the historical criticism that they espoused.[21] Reiterating this view is sociologist Steve Bruce, who acknowl-

---

[20]For a concise overview of the influence of Darwin and historical criticism see Brian Clarke, "English Speaking Canada from 1854," in *Concise History of Christianity in Canada*, pp. 317-22. Also, L. B. Kuffert traces the movement of science and technology in the shaping of the consciousness of Canadian society in chapter three of *A Great Duty: Canadian Responses to Modern Life and Mass Culture 1939-1967* (Montreal and Kingston: McGill-Queens University Press), 2003.

[21]George A. Rawlyk, *Canadian Baptists and Christian Higher Education* (Montreal and Kingston: McGill-Queens University Press, 1988), pp. 36-37.

edges that science has certainly undermined Christian faith in the Western world but says that the real issue is not science's overt intellectual conflict with religion as much as its empowerment of a rationalistic worldview. Bruce suggests that the primary secularizing effects of science did not come from its direct refutation of religious ideas but rather from the general encouragement toward a rationalistic orientation to the world that science offered. Specifically he notes this orientation embodied a rationalistic outlook in bureaucracy as the dominant form of social organization, and the role of technology in increasing our sense of mastery over our own fate.[22]

Whether these analyses are correct or not, they nonetheless remind us that numerous secularizing forces were at work and were slowly but steadily changing the complexion of North American life. A rationalistic, scientific worldview was replacing the Christian one as North American society evolved into an urban-industrial society in which there were multiple indications of decline in the moral authority of churches and in religious commitment among its citizens.[23] This shift developed in a way that has slowly led North American citizens away from ecclesiastical authority and toward individual authority and the individual's ability to pursue personal fulfillment without regard to any particular set of religious beliefs or codes. For the most part, this process has been slow and gradual, at times almost imperceptible.

However, as the process unfolded, the prospect of a society in which religious beliefs and institutions were in decline brought about much consternation for many Christians in Canada, in the United States and in other formerly "Christian" nations in the Western world, as Christianity had been considered foundational to each nation's moral life and social order.[24]

However, the reality of secularization was not only felt by the church— some would say it was perpetuated by the church. Some historians argue that the religious crises engendered by Darwinism and historical crit-

---

[22]Steve Bruce, *God Is Dead: Secularization in the West* (Oxford: Blackwell, 2002), p. 73.
[23]Marshall, *Secularizing the Faith*, p. 16.
[24]Ibid., p. 4.

icism of the Bible encouraged religious people to make Christianity into
an essentially social religion. Thus in certain dominant streams of Christianity there was a substituting of sociology for theology, and as a result
the church increasingly came to represent a religion that sought to appeal
to the public on essentially secular grounds.[25]

Although unintentionally so, this move toward the secularization of
the church was assisted in large measure by the rise of the social gospel
movement. The social gospel as it was conceived and popularized by
American theologian Walter Rauschenbusch and New York City pastor
Harry Emerson Fosdick made its inroads into the mainstream of North
American religion. At its core the social gospel movement sought to take
seriously Jesus' teaching on the kingdom of God and apply it to the realities of modern social life. It tried to instill a social conscience into the
Christian church, urging the church to take seriously its role in responding to the plight of the marginalized in the same way that Jesus
had done. It seemed apparent, especially to many mainline clergy, that
those who had traditionally been influencers of public policy demanded
a response that called for a reformulation of Christian social teaching.
The thinking was that if Christianity could be translated into a message
of social reform and good citizenship, its relevance could be maintained.[26]
Therefore the social gospel sought to integrate Christian principles into
the life of urban-industrial society and thus foster a new Christianity,
one that took seriously the challenges presented by an increasingly
secular nation and an increasingly marginalized church. The thinking
was that this kind of Christianity would not only be faithful to the essence of the gospel but could also provide the Protestant church with the
ability to thrive in a modern society.[27] Furthermore, ecclesiastical leaders
were worried about the decreasing willingness of people to listen to them
on matters that were perceived to be better handled by experts in the

---

[25]Cook, *The Regenerators*, p. 4.
[26]Ibid., pp. 229-30.
[27]See Richard Allen's *The Social Passion: Religion and Social Reform in Canada 1914-28* (Toronto:
University of Toronto Press, 1990) for an in-depth analysis of the social gospel movement and
its development in Canadian society.

social sciences.[28] In response, programs and projects were developed by mainline churches that demonstrated their accommodation to liberalism, egalitarianism and diversity.[29]

Inevitably, many historians argue, this accommodation led the church to become less influential and more accommodated to the prevailing culture. Those denominations that had formerly been so much a part of the shaping of culture were now desperately trying to remain in dialogue with a culture that was rapidly changing. However, in many ways the die was already cast because of what was happening in the culture at large. By urging Christians to emphasize the social utility of the church and to downplay or ignore doctrine, the advocates of a more socially oriented Christianity were in fact making the church irrelevant in a world in which other institutions were better equipped to perform the role that the church once fulfilled in North American society.[30]

Others would argue that the demise of the church was perpetuated not by its adoption of cultural norms but instead by its inflexibility to shifting cultural realities. While the response of the church to secularization is a debated point, what is unquestionably clear is that in the second half of the twentieth century the Christian church lost its place at the center of Western culture, with no sign of the slide abating. Perhaps what is most apparent is that times were rapidly changing and the church was struggling to keep its former place, or at least to find its new place within the newly emerging Western culture.

In the post–World War II period, fewer people were willing to privilege the place of the Christian church and endorse Christianity as the religion of choice in national life. Furthermore, people became increasingly suspicious of hierarchy, authority and exclusive truth claims.

---

[28]Garry Miedema, *For Canada's Sake: Public Religion, Centennial Celebrations, and the Re-Making of Canada in the 1960s* (Montreal and Kingston: McGill-Queens University Press, 2005), p. 50.

[29]Ibid.

[30]Cook, *The Regenerators*, p. 6. It must be noted that this point is contentious among historians. Nancy Christie and Michael Gauvreau claim that the idea that the church aided the advance of secularism is much overblown. See their introduction in *A Full Orbed Christianity: The Protestant Churches and Social Welfare in Canada, 1900-1940* (Montreal and Kingston: McGill-Queens University Press), 1996.

Younger people were less inclined to turn to the institutions that had long determined national life and indeed began to turn away from them and the social norms for which they stood. The result for the church, all sectors of it, was that its role as a social guarantor was in grave decline.[31]

A shifting social context. Also contributing to the changing shape of Western culture was the shifting of immigration laws and patterns. Immigration patterns in North America rose sharply following World War II. As new immigrants began to flow into the United States and Canada, long-standing immigration patterns began to change. For many years prior to World War II, immigration largely came from Western and Eastern Europe. This continued in the early postwar period; however, not much later immigration began to flow increasingly from other regions. Some of the most notable increases came from Southeast Asia, the Middle East and India.[32] In 1971 Canada's prime minister, Pierre Trudeau, acknowledged the government's vision for welcoming people from non-Caucasian ethnic groups when he announced a federal government policy that reflected the new realities of Canadian culture by enshrining "multiculturalism within a bilingual framework" as the guiding philosophy of Canada's approach to immigration. This policy would include assistance to all cultural groups to help them interact with other cultures.[33] Such a policy was a significant contribution to Canada's departure from a Christian monochrome to a religious kaleidoscope during the second half of the twentieth century.[34]

In the United States, 1965 marked the passing of the Immigration and Nationality Services Act, which went directly against an 1882 congressional ban on immigration from China. The new law reflected the desire of the majority of Americans to offer access to immigration and the

[31]Miedema, *For Canada's Sake*, p. 39.

[32]In Canada census statistics demonstrate that between 1972 and 2000 immigration from Europe, Australia and North and Central America dropped off considerably while immigration from Africa and Asia grew exponentially. See J. M. Bumstead, *Canada's Diverse Peoples: A Reference Sourcebook* (Santa Barbara, CA: ABC-Clio, 2006), p. 282.

[33]Ibid., p. 253.

[34]Robert Choquette, *Canada's Diverse Religions* (Ottawa: University of Ottawa Press, 2004), p. 378.

privileges of citizenship to a vast array of potential new immigrants.[35] These changes, which also were part of the evolution of postwar society in European countries as well, influenced and shaped the cultural contours of the nations in significant ways. New immigrants brought with them new fashions and cuisines, which further affected consumer habits and opened up new options for adventurous shoppers and diners. Immigrants from non-European countries also brought new ideas. These included cultural customs and religious beliefs alike. No longer were "foreign" religions like Islam, Hinduism or Buddhism ideas that were relegated to far-off places; now, increasingly, it was possible that one of these was the religion of your neighbor or coworker. If one took the time to get to know them, it was not hard to see that their faith was as meaningful to them as Christianity was to many Americans or Canadians. Also, it soon became evident that while their customs and beliefs were distinct from one's own, they were "good" people with many similar concerns: family, friends, economic prosperity and so on.

Furthermore, as immigrant populations settled, they increasingly desired and even demanded that their particular views be recognized and accepted as legitimate in the public life of their adopted nation. While many came to their new countries prepared to adapt to its ways, they also wanted to be able to retain some of the native culture and have opportunities to express it publicly as well. All of these realities contributed to the shifting place of Christianity as the de facto religion of North American life. As countries became more tolerant of diversity and more accepting of the many new ideas and customs that were being introduced, old traditions were eroded. The world opened up, new practices sprouted, Christianity was being challenged, and the world did not crumble. In fact people began to realize there was potential for fruitful new ways of living within a reordered society. New cultures and new ideas needed to be embraced and included, not simply relegated to some unseen margin.[36]

---

[35]Tickle, *Great Emergence*, pp. 94-95.
[36]It must be acknowledged that this section is a vast oversimplification of the struggle that both indigenous and immigrant populations have faced in this time of transition in North America

CONCLUSION

This is the reality of life in the post-Christian era. While the church once helped define various forms of empire in the Western world, its influence has abated, and there is within contemporary culture a deconstruction of former beliefs, patterns of life and conventions that defined the world for many generations but no longer do. This tearing down of the structures of modernity is akin to a revolution that strips power away from those in control and dismantles the systems that perpetuated their power. As in a political revolution, it leaves those who enjoyed a place at the table of power scrambling to discover where they now fit within a new cultural and social reality. In the post-Christian revolution, it is fair to say that the church is one of those former power brokers who once enjoyed a place of influence at the cultural table but has been chased away from its place of privilege and is now seeking to find where it belongs amid the ever-changing dynamics of contemporary culture.

This brief analysis provides an initial introduction to the social reality in which the Western church finds itself today. Clearly this is a new cultural and philosophical empire whose overarching contours run in opposition to much of what defines the Christian faith. This does not mean to imply that all of contemporary culture stands against the church and its beliefs, or that the things that traditional Christianity stood for were infallible expressions of the gospel and should thus be endorsed by the broader population. Furthermore, it is not to ignore the ways in which Christendom itself contributed to the emergence of the cultural realities that we have considered in this chapter. It is simply to assert that in a former day the culture was friendly to and largely shaped by a church that was, in imperfect ways, trying to express an explicitly Christian vision in society.

While these changes are difficult for many to accept, they also offer a certain prospect of hope. They offer to us a chance to reevaluate what the

---

and places such as Britain. However, the prevailing cultural reality in the West has been toward (sometimes slowly) acceptance and integration of differing cultures. There is no suggestion here that this is a bad trend; I simply want to acknowledge how the presence of new cultures, ideas and practices has affected the fabric of Western culture.

church is supposed to be and where it fits in a highly non-Christian society. It may be that the reality of life in a post-Christian culture serves as a therapeutic opportunity for the church as it provokes a time of deep reflection and self-analysis. As Hugh McLeod optimistically reminds us while reflecting on the decline of Christendom in Western Europe, "Christendom is no more than a phase in the history of Christianity, and it represents only one out of many possible relationships between the church and society."[37] Even church historian John Webster Grant, writing in 1972, saw the potential for renewal in the church as it became increasingly marginalized. He too chose the motif of exile to express his thoughts:

> The church grew and permeated Graeco-Roman society for centuries in the face of official hostility and mob hatred, and there are many who regard its adoption by Emperor Constantine as its greatest misfortune. A period of exile to the periphery of power might well release Christian energies that have been smothered for centuries.[38]

This is when the end of pseudo-Christendom and the advent of postmodern culture can offer a therapeutic voice to the church as it calls us to define it with an exilic mindset.

From this analysis of our cultural location, we can begin to see that to live faithfully as followers of Jesus in these days will demand that we determine how to make an informed response to these new cultural realities. While the church has sometimes been guilty of capitulation to culture, its calling is most often to stand apart from culture and offer an alternative way of life. There are times that the church must see itself as an alien within the host culture. For the church today, this requires an orientation that understands that while once we were at "home," this is no longer the case. Our situation of having moved from the center to the margins is indeed a form of exile.

Of course, exile is not a new experience for the people of God. The Hebrew Scriptures, literature from the Second Temple period and the

---

[37]McLeod, *Introduction*, p. 2.
[38]John Webster Grant, *The Church in the Canadian Era*, 2nd ed. (Burlington: Welch Publishing, 1988), pp. 216-17.

New Testament record our spiritual ancestors' experience of exile and thus offer us a rich resource to draw from as we consider how we can approach our own exile. It can not only inspire us to survive but to be renewed in the midst of this daunting social reality. In an exilic situation, the church must return to its founding narrative—the story of God's people as recorded in Scripture—and there find the resources it needs to recover its identity. There above all we are reminded that we are not the first generation to have faced exile; others have also been there before us and have left us a textual legacy to draw from. It is to these texts that we now turn.

2

Exile in the Old Testament

As a resident of Jerusalem in 587 B.C.E. you would have witnessed a marauding Babylonian army coming into your city and completely overrunning it. You may have witnessed friends, neighbors and perhaps even family members put to death, injured or violated. Perhaps homes around you were destroyed, people's possessions taken from them and important symbols of the city desecrated. Most significant in this latter category would have been the temple itself, the central religious symbol of the nation, the place where God himself dwelled in a unique way. In 587 the Babylonians completely destroyed the Jerusalem temple in an act that physically demonstrated their total control over Judah and spiritually indicated that their god, Marduk, had prevailed over Israel's God, Yahweh. Shortly after the siege of Jerusalem, you may have been forcibly transported away from the only land that you knew, the land that was your home, to a foreign land. There, as a subjugated foreigner, you would live among a people who spoke a different language and practiced strange customs, some of which included things that you had been brought up to deplore. It was here that you would now live, as far as you knew, for the rest of your life.

Exile was a defining experience for the nation of Israel. While scholarly debate over the extent and nature of the captivity as well as the subsequent return continues, the impact of this experience plays a highly formative role in the national life of Israel, even to this day.[1] Can the exilic

---

[1]For example Robert Carroll, "Exile! What Exile?: Deportation and the Discourses of Diaspora," in

experience of an ancient people really inform our own experience as Christians in contemporary Western culture? If so, we need to have some understanding of Israel's experience of exile and how the people responded to it. We will consider a brief history and sociology of the exile and Israelite life during the Babylonian and Persian periods.[2] We also need to consider some of Israel's primary theological responses to exilic life. By understanding these two things, we will gain fresh insight into how the contemporary church can forge its identity as an exilic people in Western society today.

A BRIEF HISTORY OF THE EXILE

As already mentioned, it may be accurate to note that the experience of exile began for God's people with the original couple in the Garden of Eden. Their failings are an archetype for humanity. Their sin led to their being cast out of their home to live in a place that was foreign to them. This may have provided a precedent and a model for Israel to reflect upon as it faced its own exile as a result of its particular infidelity to Yahweh in its own specific historical context. Adam and Eve's banishment from the Garden helped to establish Israel's identity as a people who were always wrestling with God and thus were susceptible to the judgment that came as a result.[3]

The history of Israel was a turbulent one. The northern kingdom,

---

Judaic Religion in the Second Temple Period, ed. Lester Grabbe (London: Routledge, 2000), pp. 66-67, expressly calls the exile a "myth" while at the same time recognizing its ideological potency in shaping the identity of the Jewish nation. Conversely, Peter Ackroyd, *Exile and Restoration* (London: SCM Press, 1968), pp. 237-38, argues for the historicity of the exile, while admitting that its "precise description in detail is a matter of great difficulty." Despite any murkiness in historical detail, he is unequivocal that the experience of exile is decisive in the theological thought of Israel. Also, prolific Jewish scholar Jacob Neusner states that "the paradigm of exile and return contains all Judaisms over all times, to the present" ("Exile and Return as the History of Judaism," in *Exile: Old Testament, Jewish and Christian Perspectives*, ed. James Scott [Leiden: Brill, 2001], p. 221).

[2]For the purposes of this study *Israel* will be employed to refer to the nation as a historic people. This includes both the northern kingdom of Israel and the southern kingdom of Judah. *Judah* will be employed when referring exclusively to the southern kingdom.

[3]Henri Blocher alludes to the paradigmatic nature of the couple being cast out of the garden as a motif for Hebrew and Jewish identity in *In the Beginning: The Opening Chapters of Genesis* (Downers Grove, IL: InterVarsity Press, 1984), p. 187.

Israel, went into exile under the Assyrians first in 734 B.C.E., with a second deportation in 722 B.C.E. The southern kingdom, Judah, went into captivity almost a century and a half later at the hands of the Babylonians. The Babylonian king, Nebuchadnezzar, and his general, Nebuzaradan, forcibly intruded on Judah and Jerusalem three times, in 597, 587 and 581.[4]

The invasion was the culmination of an ongoing Babylonian threat against Jerusalem that began in 605. In the course of the three invasions, evidence indicates that all or virtually all of the towns in the heartland of Judah incurred serious damage.[5] This included the city of Jerusalem, which was destroyed, including the temple, in the second invasion.[6]

While archaeological evidence is inconclusive, and thus the exact history of the exilic period remains to a large degree uncertain, it is hard to believe that any experience of displacement including subjugation by a longtime oppressor and dispersement from one's homeland can be understood as anything other than tremendously difficult. In his studies on this period Daniel Smith-Christopher cites modern exilic experiences as being, without exception, traumatic for those who must live through them.[7] Furthermore, the biblical text provides evi-

---

[4]Bruce Birch et al., *A Theological Introduction to the Old Testament* (Nashville: Abingdon, 1999), p. 322. For a concise overview of the history of the exile that weaves biblical and extrabiblical sources together see Jill Middlemas, *The Templeless Age: An Introduction to the History, Literature, and Theology of the "Exile"* (Louisville, KY: Westminster John Knox, 2007), pp. 9-27. For an extended treatment see Rainer Albertz, *Israel in Exile: The History and Literature of the Sixth Century B.C.E.* (Atlanta: SBL, 2003).

[5]For an overview of the fall of Jerusalem and the destruction of surrounding villages in Judah see Oded Lipschits, *The Fall and Rise of Jerusalem* (Winona Lake, IN: Eisenbrauns, 2005), pp. 36-97.

[6]The result of these actions is of some debate. This stems from the paucity of information available from this period of ancient Israelite history. Some scholars have cast doubt on the historicity of the exile; for a concise review of the scholarly debate around the extent of the exile see Charles E. Carter, *The Emergence of Yehud in the Persian Period: A Social and Demographic Study* (Sheffield: JSOT, 1999), pp. 39-50; Hans Barstad, *The Myth of the Empty Land: A Study in the History and Archaeology of Judah During the "Exile" Period* (Oslo: Scandinavian University Press, 1996); Lester L. Grabbe, *Leading Captivity Captive: The Exile as History and Ideology* (Sheffield: Sheffield Academic Press, 1998); and P. R. Davies, *In Search of Ancient Israel* (Sheffield: Sheffield Academic Press, 1992). All share doubt as to the historical accuracy of the biblical account of the exile. Daniel Smith-Christopher, *A Biblical Theology of Exile* (Minneapolis: Fortress, 2002); Albertz, *Israel in Exile*; and Bustney Oded, "Judah and the Exile," in *Israelite and Judean History*, ed. J. M. Miller and J. H. Hayes (Philadelphia: Westminster, 1977), pp. 435-88, offer more sympathetic responses.

[7]Smith-Christopher, *Biblical Theology of Exile*, pp. 15-21.

dence of the severity of the experience of exile by using graphic language to describe it. The book of Lamentations speaks dramatically: "Judah has gone into exile with suffering and hard servitude" (Lam 1:3 NRSV); "All her people groan as they search for bread; they barter their treasures for food to keep themselves alive" (Lam 1:11). In response to other scholars' opinions that the exilic experience was not especially severe, Smith-Christopher protests that "the poetry of Lamentations is about horrific devastation."[8] Equally dramatic is the description of Jerusalem's fall by the prophet Jeremiah: "On the ninth day of the fourth month the famine became so severe in the city that there was no food for the people of the land" (Jer 52:6 NRSV). The psalmist reflects on these same events by moaning, "They have given the bodies of your servants to the birds of the air for food. . . . They have poured out their blood like water all around Jerusalem" (Ps 79:2-3 NRSV; see also Ps 44:13).[9] In chapter 10 of his prophecies Ezekiel graphically describes, through a vision, the overwhelming significance of the exile and its spiritual implications for the nation. He speaks of God's departure from the temple: "On a vehicle not unlike the chariot throne of chapter 1, the glory moved to the threshold of the temple, then on to its east gate (Ezek 10:19), and finally to the Mount of Olives (Ezek 11:23). One senses in this hesitant departure a grieving over the destruction it symbolized."[10]

For the people of Judah these events must have had devastating consequences. Their experience of exile, like that of modern-day exiles, was one of horrific displacement, powerlessness and painful memory. "To read these texts without some sense of trauma of exile is tantamount to blaming the victim at the very least, and perhaps grossly misunder-

---

[8]Ibid., p. 47.

[9]There are four psalms that can be dated with reasonable certainty to the time of exile: Ps 44; 74; 79; 89. Psalm 137 also contains overt reflection on exilic experience. See Thomas Raitt, *A Theology of Exile: Judgment/Deliverance in Jeremiah and Ezekiel* (Philadelphia: Fortress, 1977), p. 87. Others would include Pss 102; 106; on the list, see Middlemas, *Templeless Age*, p. 36.

[10]Ralph Klein, *Israel in Exile: A Theological Interpretation* (Philadelphia: Fortress, 1979), p. 76. A further source for understanding the consequences of Babylonian captivity comes from nonbiblical evidence that points to the reality of harsh treatment by the Babylonians toward those they conquered, including Judah. See Daniel Smith-Christopher, "Reassessing the Historical and Sociological Impact of the Babylonian Exile (597/587/581)," in *Exile: Old Testament, Jewish and Christian Perspectives*, ed. James Scott (Leiden: Brill, 2001), pp. 23-25.

standing much of the power of the text in its social context."[11]

While it is outside the scope of this book to examine the various arguments over the exact nature of the Babylonian exile in detail, we will proceed on the assumption that the exile had major consequences for the national life and identity of the people of Israel and Judah.

At least three major symbols were taken from Israel with the demise of the nation at the hands of the Babylonians: land, king and temple. Perhaps these three things more than anything else were signs of God's presence and his unique relationship with Israel as his people. The land was his promise to them as part of their exodus from Egypt. It was a symbol of God's faithfulness, and it allowed Israel to establish itself as a people in a specific place of their own. The Davidic kingship was another sign of the covenant between God and his people, as it symbolized God's leadership among his people. And the Jerusalem temple was the place where Israel believed God's presence was particularly immediate. The temple was the center of religious ritual and a reminder that Yahweh was reigning with and over his covenant people. With the exile all three of these symbols were gone. No more land meant no more place to call their own; no more king meant no more political autonomy; no more temple meant no more place to gather to participate in the unique rituals of Yahweh worship. Most poignantly it meant that the things that God had given them as signs of his covenant were now gone. Did this mean that the covenant was over? Were they no longer God's chosen people? Had Yahweh abandoned them? These were the questions that exile presented.

LIVING IN EXILE

While the triumph of the Babylonians had traumatic consequences, there is archaeological, biblical and extrabiblical evidence that also points to the fact that for some, once the trauma of the initial captivity had subsided, life did settle into a certain pattern that included the undertaking of normal human activities for both those in Babylon and for those left in the land. The fact that exile was a mixed experience for

---

[11]Smith-Christopher, *Biblical Theology of Exile*, p. 104.

various people within Israel meant that there were a variety of responses from within the community.

The sociology of Israel in exile, including the Babylonian and Persian captivities,[12] is a rich, multifaceted cultural matrix that warrants extended consideration. For our purpose, however, that of connecting Israel's ancient experience of exile with that of the contemporary Western church, a brief review of some significant social contours will be sufficient to offer some suggestive linkages between ancient history and today's situation.

The Bible is ambiguous regarding the exact number of people who were deported from the land of Judah to Babylon during the three invasions that took place between 597 and 581 B.C.E. Jeremiah 52:28-30 records a total of 4,600 being taken from the land in the course of three distinct deportations. Second Kings reports that in the eighth year of his reign Nebuchadnezzar took 10,000 people of the elite population of Jerusalem into exile (2 Kings 24:14) and then approximately ten years later, following King Zedekiah's rebellion, he exiled another segment of the population centered around Jerusalem, leaving only "some of the poorest people of the land to be vinedressers and tillers of the soil" (2 Kings 25:11-12 NRSV).[13] What can reasonably be concluded from the biblical texts is that as a result of Babylonian aggression some of the population was murdered, some were deported, some fled, and some were left in the land. The fact that some remained while others were sent away created

---

[12]In 539 B.C.E. Persia conquered the Babylonians and inherited Israel as a result. Due to differing foreign policies on how to deal with subjugated people, some of the people of Judah returned to their land after 539. This is often referred to as the postexilic period. However, there is discussion about the term *postexilic* and its appropriateness as a description of the Persian period. For all intents and purposes Israel remained a captive people during this period, as they did under Greek and Roman rule in later eras. I will use the term *exile* even when referring to life in Persia (and subsequently) because I take the term to be a fair description of the continued life experience for Israel even after 539 B.C.E. even though the approach of their overlords may have changed. Jill Middlemas addresses the difficulty in terminology around *exile* and *postexile* (as well as the historical ambiguity of the experience) by suggesting that the term *exile* be dropped altogether and the term *Templeless Age* be adopted to properly describe the period between the destruction of the first temple and construction of the second. See Middlemas, *Templeless Age*, pp. 3-7.

[13]For a brief but helpful reflection on these varying numbers see Iain Provan et al., *A Biblical History of Israel* (Louisville, KY: Westminster John Knox, 2003), pp. 281-82.

interesting social and theological dynamics, which we will explore later. First, let us consider the fate of those who were sent from the land of Judah into exile in the kingdom of Babylon.[14]

A large point of agreement between the biblical text and contemporary scholarship is that it was primarily those from the educated and wealthy class who were sent to Babylon. In Babylon these people served the purposes of the burgeoning Babylonian state, which had a variety of needs that could be filled by educated people.[15] There are many indications that life in exile did not mean slavery in the same way that slavery is often understood in modern contexts. The book of Jeremiah demonstrates the ability of the exiles to build homes, develop business interests and marry (Jer 29:5-7). The books of Daniel (in Babylonia) and Esther (in the Persian capital of Susa), whether historical in all of their details or not, indicate that some of the exiles were able to attain significant positions in the governments of their captors. Nehemiah's position as royal cupbearer offers another example of such status. Extrabiblical evidence also gives credence to this perspective. For example, the archives of the Murashû family offer evidence from a local business, albeit from a slightly later period, that the firm had clients with Jewish names. These clients were landowners and were employed as officials and administrators of the state.[16] This shows that some Jews who stayed in their new land and did not return to their old home, even after Persia overtook Babylonia, experienced prosperity over a long period of time in their new home.

This example does not mean that prosperity was the common experience of all exiles. For some the experience of deportation would have been devastating. Even if their subjugators were reasonably benign, exile still represented the loss of political autonomy and familiar patterns of

---

[14]Jeremiah also makes reference to a group who took refuge in Egypt (Jer 41:11–44:30). What became of them is unknown, although it seems clear that some did return from Egypt to Judah, as the preservation of Jeremiah's oracle and description indicates. See Ackroyd, *Exile and Restoration*, p. 39n1.

[15]Jon L. Berquist, *Judaism in Persia's Shadow: A Social and Historical Approach* (Minneapolis: Fortress, 1995), pp. 15-17.

[16]For further explanation and notation see Provan et al., *Biblical History of Israel*, pp. 282-83. Also see P. R. Davies and John Rogerson, *The Old Testament World*, 2nd ed. (Louisville, KY: Westminster John Knox, 2005), p. 86.

life. The people were left to find new ways of practicing their customs and religious faith in a climate that was often less accommodating of what the local population would have determined to be strange practices.

Those left in the land were supervised by a garrison of troops and a Babylon-appointed leader named Gedaliah (2 Kings 25:22). The presence of Babylonian military and a non-Davidic leader were constant reminders to the people that life as they had known it was gone. While those who remained may have inherited some of the land left behind by the deportees, their lack of financial means (they are described as the "poor of the land") and education left them vulnerable to the Babylonians and those of other nations who may have used their power to take advantage of the Judahites' weakened situation.[17]

Sociological research indicates that dramatic displacement affects the displaced people's sense of identity and causes them to respond to their displacement in a variety of ways.[18] The reality of a military takeover that brought some real measure of violence, a removal of key citizens from the land, and a relocation of some of the population would have clearly shaped the communal response to displacement, both from those left in the land and those deported or fleeing from it. The evidence that this was the case for ancient Israel is clear in the work of the prophets. Their words display the trauma of exilic experience and the diversity of responses. The various perspectives on just how destructive the exile was again remind us of the basic fact that exile meant military defeat, loss of autonomy and domination by a foreign power. Such an experience leads people who are centered on a monotheistic understanding of the world (and who thus see themselves as uniquely chosen and blessed) to question how that reality can be understood in the midst of drastically different circumstances. For those left in the land, the presence of a

---

[17]While no foreign populations were deliberately introduced, there is evidence that some from other nations—the Edomites, Moabites and Ammonites—may have moved into the land and taken some of the land for their own purposes. See Davies and Rogerson, *Old Testament World*, p. 87. This is corroborated by Provan et al., *Biblical History of Israel*, p. 285.

[18]Daniel Smith cites the work of sociologist Brian Wilson, who offers seven different ways that religious people groups traditionally respond to displacement, in *The Religion of the Landless: The Social Context of the Babylonian Exile* (Bloomington, IN: Myer-Stone, 1989), pp. 51-52. Also see Middlemas, *Templeless Age*, p. 7.

puppet king and Babylonian soldiers was a constant reminder that they
were no longer an independent people. For those deported, their
presence in a foreign land never ceased to leave them aware of their
position as a conquered minority.

However, while it was true that not everyone in ancient Israel responded to exile in the same way, there was a prevailing response that
ultimately shaped the vision of the nation for its exilic existence. This
response can be identified as "reformulation."[19] It is one that shapes the
contours of the Hebrew Scriptures, as we see Israel offering a theological
interpretation of their new sociological circumstances so as to refor-
mulate their religion in a new context. Understanding the outworking of
this response will be tremendously useful, as it can provide theological
resources for the contemporary church as it responds to its own sociological circumstances.

The real emphasis of Old Testament exilic theology in the canonical
Scriptures is on those who were sent out of the land and into Babylon.[20]
It may even be significant to note the distinct sense that those who
were exiled from the homeland were somehow the "true" Israel and
those left behind were an apostate group who had abandoned their
"Israelite" status and, among other things, had intermarried with non-
Judeans.[21] This rivalry and the triumph of the returning exiles as the
ultimate shapers of canonical history gives the scriptural account its
exilic perspective. The religious nature of Israel drove the people to
seek a theological understanding for their captivity. The canonical materials contain these hopeful streams of thinking that call Israel to reformulation. The many voices of biblical exilic literature offer not only
a diagnosis of the people's situation but a prescription for reformu-

---

[19]Middlemas, *Templeless Age*, p. 7.

[20]Davies and Rogerson note the biblical authors' disinterest in the people who stayed in the land
by stating explicitly that "the majority who remained are of little or no interest or significance,"
Old Testament World, p. 88.

[21]Ibid., p. 88. Also see Jer 24:1-10; the prophet employs the image of two fig baskets, one filled
with good figs and one with bad ones. The good are clearly those in exile and the bad those left
in the land who are affiliated with Zedekiah and his policies. Ezekiel emphasizes that the deportees from Judea have suffered their punishment through their banishment from the land;
however, those left behind will still face further judgment for their iniquities (Ezek 33:21-31).

lation that can help inform our own exilic situation as the church in post-Christian society. For Israel, exile did not lead to an abandonment of the faith or utter despair. On the contrary exile was the impetus that inspired the most creative literature and daring theological articulations in the Old Testament.[22]

This demonstrates that while there are many ways that exiled groups will respond to captivity, and in Israel some may have thrown their lot in with their conquerors while others may have chosen a separatist approach, the core of Israel responded to its sociological exile with theological reform. The exilic period demonstrates the disorientation that new social realities bring, and how theological reflection on the nature of God as revealed through the sacred text and human experience can produce wisdom to respond effectively to these new realities. Thus an examination of biblical exilic literature offers us a way to consider exactly how Israel reoriented itself in its new state of exile. Out of this examination several key themes emerge.

God's presence on foreign soil. As already noted, prior to exile the three symbols of God's presence with Israel had been the land, the Davidic kingship and the Jerusalem temple. These three stood as signs of God's promises and covenant loyalty. Exile stripped Israel of all three foundational identity markers and left the people confused about where God was to be found in the midst of their new experience. The prophets spoke words of assurance that, despite outward appearances, God had not abandoned his people; he was still with them in their exile.

For example, the reality of God's presence is creatively presented in the mystical vision of Ezekiel 1. God is depicted on wheels and mobile as his glory departs the temple and flees the land because he can no longer be present in a place of such immense sin (Ezek 1:1-21). The key idea in this vision is that of a God who is not restricted to Jerusalem. He is on the move and is going into exile with his people. This being the case, life and faith can continue apart from the old institutions. A similar vision is presented in Ezekiel 8–10, where the temple of Jerusalem is clearly

---

[22]Walter Brueggemann, *Cadences of Home: Preaching Among Exiles* (Louisville, KY: John Knox, 1997), p. 3.

characterized as a place of heinous blasphemy and idolatry to the point that Yahweh can certainly not remain there. Ezekiel 10:15-22 depicts the glory of Yahweh leaving the temple and flying off to be with the exiles in Babylonia.[23] Yahweh's glory is not restricted to the temple; it is present wherever he chooses to reveal it, including Babylon.[24] This theology of the God who is present is essential to a people who find themselves stripped of old certainties, institutions and religious foundations.

In a slightly more oblique way we can see this theme in Jeremiah 29:4-7, where the exiles are instructed to work for the good of Babylon. While Jeremiah ultimately predicts deliverance from Babylon for the exiles (Jer 29:10), that blessing will come to Babylon as the exiles work for the good of their captors. This possibility of blessing is clearly tied to the sovereignty of Yahweh as the one who ultimately decides on whom to bestow favor. The idea here is that as God's people settle in and live faithfully, the Lord will give his blessing to their captor state through them. In other words, he will continue to be active in the affairs of his people and in the affairs of their host nation, despite the fact that the people are away from their land. This idea may have flown in the face of some in the community who would have rather seen God judge Babylon as opposed to bless them. Yet we see that God's commitment to blessing the obedience of his people is still intact, although now that blessing will also extend through them to their enemies. This affirms God's universal sovereignty and agency in the life of all nations but still gives Israel a special role to play as the instrument of God's blessing. Later, as we consider how exile also clarified the mission of Israel as a light to the nations, we will see how this principle is leveraged even further as God's ultimate desire is to see foreign nations become his worshipers. But that begins with Israel as an instrument of blessing to the Babylonians.

The explicit and implicit images of God as being in exile with his people are the foundation of hope for Israel. If Yahweh is truly present with them and willing to work among them as they work among their

---

[23]Walter Brueggemann, *Theology of the Old Testament: Testimony, Dispute, Advocacy* (Minneapolis: Fortress, 1997), p. 672.
[24]Ibid.

captors, then not only is there hope of survival, but the hope of deliverance also remains alive.

Holiness. Within the prophetic textual response to exile there is a call for the community to distinguish itself as a set-apart people through practices of holiness designed to bring a renewed sense of communal identity, specifically as a people separate from the practices of the larger culture. The heightened stress on renewing covenant practices of faithfulness can easily be understood as an attempt "to maintain a separate identity as an elect people in an alien culture, a culture in which assimilation seemed to offer more chance for success."[25] These practices were designated as acts of faithfulness to Yahweh, which in Babylon would have been "highly confessional" acts making Israel stand out from its environment.[26] Accordingly, the Holiness Code that takes its final shape during exile is both a response to exile and a witness to others.

There is general agreement that the Holiness Code was definitively shaped around the sixth century B.C.E., and it is usually considered to be a part of the Priestly stream within the Pentateuch. It is a "recognizable block of material in Leviticus 17–26 that shares an unswerving focus on the holiness of Yahweh and requirements for correct social relations within Israel."[27] This literature functions to help Israel establish its identity as a people in relationship with the holy God, Yahweh, and it gives concrete expression to what it means to live as Yahweh's holy people.[28] The code stipulates positive behaviors as well as ones that Israel must refrain from if it is to be identified as God's people and not bring his name into disrepute. These requirements are rooted in the relational nature of the deity and his people, which is clear through the repetition of the phrase "I am the LORD your God," which occurs twenty-two times in the code (e.g., Lev 20:7, 26; 21:8). The holiness of

---

[25]Klein, *Israel in Exile*, p. 6.

[26]Ibid., p. 126.

[27]Middlemas, *Templeless Age*, p. 126.

[28]For a brief overview of the scholarly discussion around the formation of the Holiness Code see Middlemas, *Templeless Age*, pp. 125-29. For an extended treatment see Jan Joosten, *People and Land in the Holiness Code: An Exegetical Study of the Ideational Framework of the Law in Leviticus 17-26* (New York: Brill, 1996).

their deity makes it imperative that his people also show themselves to be holy (Lev 19:2; 20:7).[29] This entailed things such as not profaning the name of Yahweh by participating in false worship to other gods (Lev 18:21), not lying to one another, not stealing from one another and not swearing falsely by Yahweh's name (Lev 19:11-12). Furthermore, an intrinsic part of this calling to be separate was a renewal of Sabbath keeping (Jer 17:19-27; Is 56:2-6; Ezek 44:24). This call to renewed holiness capitalizes on the blessing-curse scheme found in the Deuteronomic History (DtrH), which promises blessing for obedience to Yahweh's laws and curses for those who fail to obey, and reminds the people that the way to experience restoration and blessing is through renewed faithfulness in covenant practices.

For the exiles a commitment to holiness and separateness, demonstrated in acts of renewed covenant loyalty, would be a demonstration of their peculiarity in their world. It was also a subtle rejection of Babylonian norms, a way of saying that they were not of Babylon but residents of a different place. Daniel Smith-Christopher proposes the idea that "purity" in such a social context becomes the language of "nonconformity."[30] Indeed, this perspective was intrinsic to the prophetic response to Babylonian exile.[31]

The literature of exilic life for Israel reflects a return to purity as a way of securing a communal identity for Israel while it lived under the rule of foreign power. The call to holiness not only secured a distinct identity for the exilic community but also provided it with clear modes of behavior that functioned almost sacramentally, as a way for the community to consciously acknowledge God's presence among them and establish itself as a worshiping community.[32]

---

[29]Middlemas, *Templeless Age*, pp. 130-34.

[30]Smith-Christopher, *Biblical Theology of Exile*, p. 160. See also Brueggemann, *Cadences of Home*, pp. 6-7.

[31]The writings of Ezra and Nehemiah are particularly radical in this area. These texts employ their "purity ideology" to help reconfigure the Judean community through the redefinition of who is a Judean and the expulsion of those classed as aliens. For an exploration of this see Roger E. Olyan's article "Purity Ideology in Ezra–Nehemiah as a Tool to Reconstitute the Community," *Journal for the Study of Judaism* 35, no. 1 (2004): 1-16.

[32]Brueggemann explores this idea in *Cadences of Home*, pp. 8-9.

Mission. One of the most dynamic aspects of the turn to hope in exilic life was the renewal of Israel's sense of being a people of mission. Exile brought about a renewed sense that Israel had a role to play among the nations of the world in declaring the supremacy of Yahweh. This is most evident in Isaiah, where the prophet articulates a compelling call for the people of Yahweh to once again act as light to the nations (Is 42:5-7; 49:5-6). It is not strange that given their context as a captive people living among "the nations," Israel would reflect on its responsibility toward foreign people. The words of Isaiah recall the core teaching of Pentateuchal faith as found in Genesis 12:3, Exodus 19:6 and Deuteronomy 4:5-8, whereby Israel is founded as a people who will serve the good of the nations around them. This prompts a call for a renewed vision for Israel to see itself as not living in a vacuum but as a responsible steward of all the gifts that God has given it as his partner.[33] This calling audaciously reorients the sense of defeat that exile naturally brought with it and asserts that the conquerors are to be converted to the faith of the vanquished. In the ancient world, where the gods were often understood in a highly territorial way and the defeat of one nation by another was also assumed to be the defeat of one god by another, this was a highly counterideological thrust that offered mission as a radical response to exile. It denied that Yahweh had been defeated and promoted the counterreality that Israel's enemies needed to in fact become Yahweh worshipers.[34]

Central to this missional mindset are four passages found in Deutero-Isaiah (Is 42:1-9; 49:1-6; 50:4-10; 52:13–53:12). Traditionally referred to as the servant songs, they provide a daring theology of mission to Israel as Yahweh's unique servant.

The actual identity of the servant is a highly controversial matter in biblical scholarship, and a full exploration of all its dimensions is outside the scope of this study.[35] Yet there is good reason to believe that some of

---

[33]Brueggemann, *Old Testament Theology*, pp. 433-34.

[34]See Is 45:20-25; 56.

[35]For discussions on the issue of the identity of the servant see Klaus Westermann, *Isaiah 40–66* (London: SCM Press, 1969), pp. 92-93; and Christopher R. Seitz, "'You Are My Servant, You Are the Israel in Whom I Will Be Glorified': The Servant Songs and the Effect of Literary Context in

the poems refer directly to Israel itself as the servant in question. Rabbi Allen S. Mailer points out that Isaiah himself specifically refers to Jacob/ Israel as his servant a number of times in these chapters (Is 41:8; 44:1; 44:2; 44:21). These verses make it clear that Israel is God's chosen servant. "The national community is spoken of in terms of an individual, as is often the case in the Bible (Jer. 30:10)."[36]

In this sense Israel is the servant referred to in the poems, one who will act as a light to the nations, will be rejected and will suffer. If it is true that the servant actually is Israel, then it is clear that "she will suffer unjustly for the salvation of the world."[37] In a fully orbed theology of Israel's exile, "the overarching, historical purpose of her suffering is the world's conversion."[38]

This view of the servant's identity may not be accepted by all, but the theological thrust of the servant's work articulated by this perspective captures the significance of Isaiah's view that Israel's role as a nation in exile and its future hope resides in its missional identity as witnesses to Yahweh.

This vision aligns with the aforementioned instruction Jeremiah 29:7 to seek the welfare of Babylon. That passage can also be understood missionally. Israel's faithfulness to Yahweh will bring blessing to Babylon. This will testify to the fact that God is present with them and will act as a witness to their foreign rulers regarding the superiority of Israel's God.

Exile clarified the principle that Israel was not designed to be a segregated people in the sense that they were to remove themselves from interaction with foreigners. "(Israel) is rather intended for full partici-

---

Isaiah," *Calvin Theological Journal* 39 (2004): 117-34. Mark Gignilliat, "Who Is Isaiah's Servant? Narrative Identity and Theological Potentiality," *Scottish Journal of Theology*, 61, no. 2 (2008): 125-36, sums up the debate by stating, "The language used to describe the Servant is 'cryptic and veiled' with the intention of remaining historically diffuse" (p. 134). Middlemas, *Templeless Age*, pp. 100-102, also offers a concise overview of potential ways that the various poems may apply to one or more figures.

[36] Allen S. Mailer, "Isaiah's Suffering Servant: A New View," *Dialogue and Alliance* 20, no. 2 (2006): 9.

[37] David N. Freedman, "Son of Man, Can These Bones Live?" *Interpretation* XXIX (1975): 185.

[38] Ibid., p. 186. Joseph Blenkinsopp, "Second Isaiah—Prophet of Universalism," *JSOT* 41 (1988): 83-103, has commented that Israel begins to see herself as a "confessional community" who is now "open to converts" (86).

pation in the life of the dominant culture."[39] This does not imply that everything about foreign nations was positive, for Isaiah delights in the destruction of Babylon (Is 47), but Israel nonetheless had a role to play in the transformation of the nations. God had no intention of abandoning his mission to the world while Israel languished in exile. Through the exile God would use Israel redemptively, and the people were called to cooperate in the outworking of that ultimate purpose.

Conclusion. Although the events that were a part of Israel's exile were traumatic and had a permanent effect on the national life and psyche of the people, hope emerged through the theological response that was offered. The concepts that we have considered offered Israel a hopeful vision for its sojourn in exile. Similarly as the church in the West enters into a time of exile from the center to the margins, it too needs a theological vision to sustain it through the unique challenges that it now faces. The hope offered by the prophetic vision for Israel also offers guiding wisdom for us.

But this wisdom must be embodied. It must be demonstrable in the everyday lives of exilic people and be able to stand the trials that exilic life inevitably brings. Thus the prophetic vision was reiterated through a narrative device known as the diasporic advice tale. These stories creatively expressed hope in a practical way as their characters depicted faithful exilic living against the challenges of living on the margins of culture. They, along with the prophetic and liturgical material already considered, offered a vision of what life can be even in the midst of exile. It is worth considering a few of these stories, as they will further inform a contemporary theology of exilic hope.

STORIES OF EXILE: NARRATIVES OF WISDOM AND HOPE

As we have discovered, it is reasonable to assume that exile brought with it a tremendous amount of discontinuity for the people of Israel. It also presented them with the temptation to either integrate with Babylonian or Persian beliefs in order to get along or to separate completely from

---

[39]Brueggemann, *Cadences of Home*, p. 13.

them and thus remain aloof from the host culture. However, as the initial shock of drastically new surroundings began to wear off, Israel eventually responded to exile with creative theological reflection as its way of understanding God and its identity as his people. As we have already seen, the ability to imagine the activity of God as being equally potent away from the land of Israel, as well as a recasting of the missional nature of Israel, demonstrate how exile provoked creative engagement with theological ideas. New conceptions of faith were formed through reflection on God's apparent absence; ethical ideals were revived through stressing covenant loyalty; and Israel's role as servant to the nations was clarified.

Other nations were also subsumed by Assyria, Babylon and Persia (not to mention by the Greeks and Romans later on), and their defeat and capture ultimately led to the extinction of their respective cultures and religions. Yet Israel did not succumb to such a fate. As a people, it found its way through a protracted time of living in the shadow of powerful foreign enemies without completely losing its distinct identity, both culturally and religiously. Certainly the experience of defeat, exile and the years of captivity provoked significant questions. Where is God? Is God really powerful? Does God really love his people? Is God really faithful? How do we survive?

These questions inspired creative theological reflection that was not simply intellectual or theoretical but rather sought to answer the kinds of real-world questions that the exile produced. It also rendered some of the most eloquent and risky literature of the biblical canon: the diasporic advice tale. This literature provided a narrative response to exile that helped Israel see how its identity as God's people could be embodied in real exilic situations. This form of exilic literature was a clear expression of Israel's hope for its future.

The diasporic advice tale is a form of literature that offers a story in which the protagonist can be understood as representing the exiled nation—in this case, Israel—as a whole. Furthermore, the protagonist's actions offer advice for how the nation should behave while in captivity. As we specifically consider the stories of Esther, Daniel and

Jonah, we will see how exilic themes, ideologies and theologies are woven into their stories so as to offer narratives of hope that depict exiled men and women who are not overcome by their exilic experience. In fact, in distinct ways, each of them faces exile in a way that advances the purposes of God and facilitates the safety of the protagonist and his or her people. These stories provide us with a rich resource for discerning an appropriate theological response to the experience of exile and help to inform our consideration of how the motif of exile can positively shape the life of the post-Christian church in our own day.[40]

In the context of ancient exilic (or diasporic) existence, narratives that depicted the lives of exiles were a form of didactic literature. In Israel's case these narratives usually featured Jewish men or women who were able to thrive in their displaced context and even rise to places of significant influence. These characters appear in diasporic novellas, which illustrate how clever, pious heroes are able to overcome much more powerful members of the dominant ethnic group and gain favor from the ruling power. Diasporic advice tales are presented in a number of places in Scripture and offer wisdom for the Israelite community to draw on for diasporic living.[41] Many of these tales emanate from the so-called postexilic period but inform the lives of a people who are squarely in an exilic or diasporic state.

Such stories are typical of displaced peoples. Often it is the narratives of a people that most vividly depict the people's understanding of life as it really is and express their beliefs about the best way forward.[42] This kind of narrative remains alive and well today among displaced groups

---

[40]As an example of how these characters can bring core exilic texts and theological ideas into conversation with contemporary needs, see Smith-Christopher, *Biblical Theology of Exile*, especially chaps. 5–7.

[41]Some examples of biblical stories that potentially qualify as diasporic advice include Esther, Daniel, Jonah, Ruth, Mordecai, Nehemiah and Joseph.

[42]Stories like the diasporic advice tales found in the Hebrew Bible can be found in many (if not all) marginal cultures. For instance, the black spirituals from the African American slave experience function similarly, as does a genre known as the "clever fox" stories that come from Japanese American detainment camps, or "black Jesus" stories from South Africa. See Smith, *Religion of the Landless*, p. 163.

in the contemporary world as they offer cultural analysis and contest the oppression of living on the margins of society.[43]

For our purposes we will examine three diasporic advice tales from Old Testament literature—Esther, Daniel and Jonah—and we will consider how they demonstrate (or embody) the theological themes that we have already seen emerge from the prophetic literature. These highly creative narratives helped Israel formulate both theological and anthropological ideas that created not a new God but a new understanding of its relationship with God.[44] For contemporary Christians, diasporic advice tales can provide new understandings about who we are and who God is in our current experience as the church in the Western world.

---

[43]Roger Bromley, *Narratives for a New Belonging: Diasporic Cultural Fictions* (Edinburgh: Edinburgh University Press, 2000), p. 3.

[44]Andre LaCocque, *Esther Regina: A Bakhtinian Reading* (Evanston, IL: Northwestern University Press, 2008), p. 10.

3

Esther as Advice for Exiles

The book of Esther provides one of the most engaging and controversial stories found in the Bible. It offers readers both high drama and comedic farce as it unfolds the story of a Hebrew orphan who rises to become queen of Persia and the savior of her people. While Esther is set in the Persian period, when King Ahasuerus (Xerxes I) was ruler (486–465 B.C.E.), it was certainly written later than this period, as the opening phrase suggests: "This is what happened during the time of Xerxes." The majority of scholars agree that a precise date for the book is hard to determine.[1] It is generally assumed, however, that the final Hebrew form of Esther is of late Persian or early Hellenistic origin.[2] From a purely literary perspective it seems obvious that Esther, which is foundational to the Jewish celebration of Purim, was written to demonstrate the potential of exilic life for those still experiencing this kind of existence.

Esther is an orphaned Jewish girl raised by her cousin Mordecai. Esther is identified early on as a beautiful young woman, and when the king of Persia is looking for a new wife, Esther ends up in a beauty contest

---

[1]For a concise but thorough discussion see Michael V. Fox, *Character and Ideology in the Book of Esther* (Columbia: University of South Carolina Press, 1991), pp. 39-41. For an argument for an earlier date (first half of the fifth century B.C.E.) based on an analysis of the Hebrew grammar of the book, see Hillel I. Millgram, *Four Biblical Heroines and the Case for Female Authorship: An Analysis of the Women of Ruth, Esther and Genesis 38* (Jefferson, NC: McFarland, 2008), pp. 100-102.

[2]Fox, *Character and Ideology*, pp. 39-41. See also Carol M. Bechtel, *Esther* (Louisville, KY: John Knox, 2002), p. 3. Bechtel reflects the breadth of opinion as well as the "agreement" among scholars that Esther is to be dated somewhere between 400 B.C.E. and 200 B.C.E.

whose winner will be named queen. As the contest transpires, Esther is the contestant who most pleases the king with her beauty and various other charms and as a result is crowned the new queen of Persia. Throughout the process, at the urging of Mordecai, she conceals her Jewish identity. Shortly after her appointment as queen, a royal official named Haman talks the king into issuing an edict that will have the entire Jewish population of Persia exterminated. Hearing of the plot, Mordecai adjures Esther to use her influence as queen to intervene on behalf of her people. Despite great personal risk and through a series of remarkable coincidences and plot reversals, Esther manages to demonstrate to the king that Haman is a man of questionable character, and thus she is able to secure deliverance for her people. Her cousin Mordecai is elevated to vice-regent of Persia, Haman is put to death, and many Persians convert to Judaism as a result of Esther's actions.

Esther is a narrative born out of Israel's theological reflection on its exile. Esther's role as a marginalized person in the powerful empire of Persia offers an example of how God is present on foreign soil, how holiness can be lived out, and how mission can take place.

THE MESSAGE OF ESTHER

God's "hidden" presence on foreign soil. As we have already noted, in exile the people of God ponder the presence of God on foreign soil. This is a crucial issue for Israel as it seeks to reconstitute itself in a foreign place. Could the people count on their God to help? In his anger, had he abandoned them for good? The answer of the exilic prophets Isaiah, Jeremiah and Ezekiel was yes to the first question and no to the second. Yet as exile wore on, the same questions likely recurred. If God had not abandoned them, why was it taking so long for a return to autonomy? Were their days as a people ultimately numbered? It is questions like this, questions that even the church in a post-Christendom Western culture asks, that a narrative such as Esther addresses.[3]

---

[3]For exploration of these and similar issues, see Linda M. Day, *Esther* (Nashville: Abingdon, 2005), pp. 1-3, and Andre LaCocque, *Esther Regina: A Bakhtinian Reading* (Evanston, IL: Northwestern University Press, 2008), pp. 35-38.

Esther is well known as the only book in the Bible that does not mention the name of God. This omission has brought about more than its share of speculation. Some scholars have asserted that Esther is a "secular" book in which God plays no role.[4] While it is true that the absence of God's name is a feature unique to Esther, we will see that it in no way eradicates the presence of God in the story.

The nonappearance of God's name has been explained by numerous theories, including the idea that it was an intentional deletion to avoid its profanation during the highly festive celebration of Purim. It has been asserted that the festival, known for its heavy drinking, was no time to pronounce the sacred name.[5] Other commentators see the book as accentuating the human element of the story. The author wants to stress the role of human beings in shaping the course of history and their need to take individual responsibility.[6] Yet attempts to explain God's "hiddenness" in the story rarely deny that the book has a religious tone.[7] At the very least, as Michael Fox offers, there is the possibility that the author is seeking to convey "uncertainty about God's role in history."[8]

The presence of God in the book of Esther can be detected in several ways. There are various allusions to it in a number of places, most notably Esther 4:14, where Mordecai asserts that deliverance for the Jews will come from "another place," if not from Esther. While it is debatable whether he is referring to a divine initiative, such a position is highly tenable based on the already-established prophetic writings that assert that God can surely be counted on, whether in Israel, Babylon or Persia.

Furthermore, we see the divine presence in Esther's own plea for her people to set aside three days and nights for fasting on her behalf

---

[4]See Fox, *Character and Ideology*, p. 235, for a synopsis.

[5]Lewis B. Paton, *The Book of Esther* (Edinburgh: ICC, 1908), p. 95. Fox offers an exploration of this theory in *Character and Ideology*, p. 239.

[6]Beth Berg, "After the Exile: God and History in the Books of the Chronicles and Esther," in *The Divine Helmsman*, ed. J. L. Crenshaw and S. Sandmel (New York: KTAV, 1980), pp. 107-27.

[7]Fox, *Character and Ideology*, pp. 237-47, explores various theories concisely but informatively.

[8]Ibid., p. 247. This perspective reflects Walter Brueggemann's overall view of Old Testament theology. Brueggemann says: "The rhetoric of the Old Testament is characteristically *ambiguous and open*. . . . So much is left unsaid that the reader is left uncertain" (Walter Brueggemann, *Theology of the Old Testament: Testimony, Dispute, Advocacy* [Minneapolis: Fortress, 1997], p. 110 [emphasis original]).

as she prepares to visit her husband, the king, and make her case for the salvation of the Jewish people (Esther 4:16). While the nature of the fast is not explicitly religious in the text, there is ample evidence to demonstrate that fasting in the later Jewish tradition was a religious act.[9] Indeed, the tenor of the request is infused with humility. Esther recognizes that her hope of convincing the king to overturn Haman's plot is not in her hands alone; she needs the support of her people, and of her God.

One may also discern the presence of God in the numerous "coincidences" that occur throughout the story. For instance, in chapter 6 the king's insomnia leads to his discovery of Mordecai's unrewarded loyalty. The whole series of events that lead to Esther's being chosen as queen is full of "coincidences." Haman's entrance into the royal court just as Ahasuerus is trying to think of a way to reward Mordecai (Esther 6:4) and the king's return from the garden at the precise moment that Haman literally throws himself on Esther's mercy (Esther 7:8) both reflect "coincidental" timing. While the reason for the writer's reluctance to attribute one or any of these "coincidences" directly to God remains a mystery, as David Clines notes, taken together these chance occurrences have a cumulative effect. They demonstrate the guiding hand of God.[10]

Reversals that occur within the plot must also be considered as evidence of God's divine direction in Esther. We see this in Mordecai's elevation to vice-regent while Haman takes his place on the gallows that he had built especially for Mordecai, and most explicitly in Esther 9:1 where it says that "the tables were turned and the Jews got the upper hand."

Ultimately it is the rootedness of Esther within the Hebrew exilic tradition that leaves the reader with the impression that God, while veiled, is intimately involved in the outcome of the narrative. As a work designed to offer advice to Jewish exiles, it reflects the prophetic assumption that God is at work in the nation even if that influence is not always

---

[9]See Sidnie Ann White, "Esther: A Feminine Model for Jewish Diaspora," in *Gender and Difference in Ancient Israel,* ed. Peggy L. Day (Minneapolis: Fortress, 1989), p. 162, referring to the work of Wilhelm Vischer, *Esther* (Munich: C. Kaiser, 1937), p. 15.

[10]David J. A. Clines, *The Esther Scroll: The Story of the Story* (Sheffield: JSOT, 1984), p. 153.

immediately apparent. In this sense Esther seems to reflect the community's latent doubt about God's presence by presenting a tale of God's subversive activity in coming to the aid of his people in ways that are only discernable in retrospect. Indeed, his deliverance is at least in part a cooperative effort between himself and the actions of his people.

The assertion of God's presence with Israel in its exile, as we have seen, reaches back to the exilic prophets themselves. This is a decisive theological perspective for the community. What comes into play at this point in the community's life is a return to the concept of Israel as a people rather than a place.[11] Such a perspective takes them back to Abram and to God's constituting a people for himself long before they were established in a land. According to biblical history, it was five hundred years after God's promise to Abram that his line finally took possession of the land that was promised. Nonetheless, God's blessing on the patriarchs is evident in occasional theophanies (Gen 15; 28:10-17) and ongoing prosperity even when they find themselves in exile, like Joseph did in Egypt (Gen 39:2). Joseph's presence in a foreign kingdom is a key parallel to Esther, as Joseph brought prosperity to the foreign kingdom as well as status and deliverance for his people. In the same way Esther does this for the Jews in Persia. This link reminds us of the central truth that God's presence with his people is tied to covenant more than to land or temple.[12]

This most ancient of theological paradigms needed to be reappropriated in exilic life. The author of Esther's veiled reference to deliverance is rooted in a theological perspective that understands that God will not break his covenant with his people. Covenant transcends land. It is rooted in relationship, and thus Mordecai is assured that deliverance will come because Israel is a people in relationship with the sovereign God.[13]

While it is undeniable that the author goes to great literary lengths to

---

[11]Tim Laniak, "Esther's *Volkcentrism* and the Reframing of Post-Exilic Judaism," in *The Book of Esther in Modern Research*, ed. Sidnie White Crawford and Leonard J. Greenspoon (London: T & T Clark, 2003), p. 82. Laniak further states regarding Israel: "God is available to them anywhere first, then at a designated somewhere (cf. 1 Kgs 8:27)" (p. 82).

[12]Ibid., p. 81.

[13]Ibid., pp. 79-82.

veil the presence of God and thus acknowledges the reality of that experience within the diasporic community, there is ample evidence to point
to the fact that despite there being no mention of Yahweh and no explicit
reference to Jewish religious practice in the entire text, Esther brings
assurance to exiles that God is nonetheless present, for in the events of
Esther divine providence is indeed at work.[14]

For contemporary exiles the veiled presence of God in the book of
Esther continues to address the latent doubt that we also may feel about
where God is. We witness the marginalization of the church and Christian
belief, and the powerful rise of forces that often run so contrary to them.
We watch as people neglect, disregard and even revile the person of Jesus
and doctrines of the Christian faith. We wonder why God does not show
himself more powerfully, more clearly. We experience the infighting and
fractiousness of the church itself and ponder why God lets it go on. Why
does he not move more evidently in ways that strengthen the church and
allow its witness to shine more brightly? Exile leads us to doubt, though
it is often unexpressed, about the presence of God. It also causes us to
experience a sense of God's absence at certain times. It is to these questions and experiences that the book of Esther speaks an eloquent word
of assurance—though it is not always clear where God is, he is here, in
exile with us.

Embodied holiness. As oblique as the presence of God is in Esther, the
integration of the heroine within Persian society is quite explicit. The
ease with which she functions in Persian culture and her apparent moral
ambiguity have at times been a point of contention for readers of the
book. There is certainly room for these charges against Esther and her
overall moral comportment. Esther seems to settle well into her role of
being married to a Gentile; she moves effectively within a heathen environment; she conceals her Jewish identity and seems to possess im-
pressive erotic capacities. Later additions to the book of Esther were

---

[14]Ibid., p. 89. Laniak further reminds us that "muted allusion to the presence of YHWH in time
and space is characteristic of the wisdom tradition." That is, the nonmention of God's name is
a literary device that functions in a way that acknowledges the sense of God's absence in exile
but calls for readers to look for and expect it nonetheless.

composed, adding prayers and explicitly stating that Esther hated being married to a Gentile and being forced to prepare his food. These were added, it seems, to somehow rehabilitate Esther's image.[15]

Esther is an example of one who was enmeshed in Persian culture, perhaps to some overly so. Yet this is not disconnected from Jeremiah's words to prepare for an extended exile by settling into life under foreign rule (Jer 29:4-7). Esther epitomizes Jewish ability to thrive in the service of a foreign king. Her story is one of coming to terms with living in a foreign land under extraordinary circumstances. The story of Esther mirrors Israel's. She is an orphan, separated from her parents and home, as is Israel, with no control over her fate, which was also Israel's story. Yet she finds a way to engage her circumstances and overcome them for the good of her people.

The particular exilic issue that Esther speaks to is that of living with limited power.[16] While Esther and Mordecai rise to certain places of power, for the majority of the story they are not the ones who control the situation. Their "success" in the story is always the result of their ability to behave wisely in the circumstances that they face. Esther's wise behavior is characterized by her ability to compromise in just the right way so as to allow her cause to advance. This attempt at "critical compromise" is contrasted with less subtle approaches that backfire and lead to detrimental results.[17] For instance, Queen Vashti, in her short appearance at the beginning of chapter 1, dramatically refuses, when summoned by her husband the king, to appear at his party. While Vashti's courage in standing up to the king's desire to show her off may be admirable and has endeared her to centuries of feminists, it results in her being banished from the royal court, and an edict is declared that seeks to repress any woman who would dare try to defy her husband in a similar way (Esther 1:19-

---

[15]Ibid., p. 83. See also White, "Esther: A Feminine Model," pp. 161-62. Terry Muck writes in his general editor's preface to Karen Jobes's commentary on Esther that Esther's behavior would not pass any test of modern ethical theory; see Jobes, *Esther* (Grand Rapids: Zondervan, 1999), p. 13.

[16]Bechtel, *Esther*, p. 11.

[17]Ibid., p. 12.

22). In contrast, Esther's more flexible approach is depicted as having much more positive consequences.[18]

Esther acts as a model for cultural engagement in situations of limited power. As one with a minimal amount of official power, she is able to find ways to work within her culture and advance the cause of her people. This is the way that exiles must learn to work if they are going to have any hope of transforming the host culture.

Esther's model is also helpful as she demonstrates that her engagement with culture is marked by a proportionality that is distinct from what is characteristic of the people around her. Esther is a book in which key characters are depicted as acting in highly disproportionate ways. King Xerxes throws a six-month drinking party during which he proudly displays his wealth and the splendor of his kingdom (Esther 1:3-8). However, Haman easily out-distances Xerxes in disproportion. When a single man (Mordecai) refuses to bow to him, he calls for the extermination of a whole people (the Jews; Esther 3:5-6). When he wants Mordecai to be hanged, he builds a gallows that is the equivalent of a modern six-story building (Esther 5:14).[19] Esther, on the other hand, represents a distinct contrast to this excess in the way she conducts her life in the Persian court. When given the opportunity to take whatever she wants for her one night with the king, she requests nothing except what Hegai the eunuch advises (Esther 2:13, 15). When hearing of the plot to have the king killed, she quietly acts to save his life and make sure that Mordecai gets the credit (Esther 2:22). As she prepares to approach the king for her momentous uninvited interview, she calls for a three-day fast, which is in contrast to the book's other lavish banquets yet fully appropriate to the significance of the occasion (Esther 4:16). When invited by the king to make a request for herself, up to half of the kingdom, Esther simply asks that the king and Haman attend a banquet she has prepared for them (Esther 5:7-9). When the right time comes for her to unmask Haman's deceit toward the king, Esther's speech demonstrates a modesty

---

[18]Ibid., pp. 11-14, explores how the theme of working effectively from a subordinate state versus taking stringent stands is depicted in a variety of characters in the book of Esther.
[19]Ibid., p. 9.

that contrasts the excess of Haman's demands (Esther 7:1-6). This modesty and sense of proportion is one of the marks of Esther's wisdom as she works within the constraints of Persian culture.[20] She is a model of perpetual cultural engagement: embedded in the culture, employing cultural norms, functioning as a full member of her society, but with a humility and sense of proportion that makes her distinct from those around her.

Furthemore, Esther's womanhood cannot be overlooked as a part of what makes her an exilic model. She is particularly effective as an exilic model because as a woman she is able to illuminate the power relationship at play between a mighty monarch like the Persian king and a subjugated partner like Israel. Like Esther, the young girl chosen to serve the king's need for a trophy queen, the Jews in Diaspora are also in a weak position as a subordinate population.

For these reasons Esther is able to serve as a vivid example to the diasporic population. She demonstrates an ability to adapt to life in Persia and thrive despite all the odds against her. In this regard Esther models an embodied purity that demonstrates the importance of holiness for exilic life. While she is not a "tidy" character whose behavior is so one-dimensional that no ambiguity remains, Esther cannot be judged apart from her context.[21]

It would seem that the key to a proper understanding of Esther's morality (and thus any demonstration of purity) lies in her relationship to and actions on behalf of her community. If seen in isolation her behavior could be understood as selfish, vain or even immoral. But when understood as part of a tale that describes deliverance for the Jews, these actions take on a much more complex, even heroic, hue.

Following Orlando Costas's study we can identify a number of ways in which Esther exemplified exilic purity. First, we see her loyalty to her people over her own personal safety. She acts on their behalf by going to

---

[20] See ibid., pp. 7-11, for a full discussion of this point.

[21] Charles Harvey, *Finding Morality in the Diaspora?: Moral Ambiguity and Transformed Morality in the Books of Esther* (Berlin: Walter de Gruyter, 2003), p. 208. See also Gordon J. Wenham, "The Gap Between Law and Ethics in the Bible," *Journal of Jewish Studies* 48, no. 1 (1997): 17. See also White, "Esther: A Feminine Model," pp. 161-62.

see the king even though the cost may well be her own life (Esther 4:16). Remembering her heritage, she determines that the salvation of her people should take precedence over her own well-being.[22]

Furthermore, we can fairly surmise that she demonstrates loyalty to her God by calling her people and her court to a fast, a deeply religious practice, before she attempts to appear before the king in what might have ended up an act of political if not personal suicide (Esther 4:16). Her piety is one of action and not just words.[23] As the king unexpectedly extends his scepter to Esther, in an act of mercy (Esther 5:2), she courageously moves forward in her resolve to save her fellow Jews from execution. Her plot to expose Haman and his diabolical scheme demonstrates Esther's faith, again not in words but in deeds. She acts cleverly and effectively on her people's behalf. Costas notes that "Esther represents a 'word of action' rather than an 'action of the word.'"[24]

What we see in Esther is a character whose actions must be understood in the communal context. She acts not according to what is "right" by the law, for to do so may ultimately endanger the welfare of many. Instead she acts in a way that subverts the power structures of her Persian conquerors and in so doing represents an exilic piety of action that points toward the delivering hand of God. Esther navigates the many potential pitfalls of her situation by knowing how to play by the rules in a hostile society. Hers are the virtues of courage, shrewdness, loyalty, discernment and honor.[25]

This kind of wisdom challenges those of us who find ourselves on the margins today to find ways to radically engage the world that we live in as well as to redefine the categories of holiness that may traditionally govern the constituency to which we belong. Esther's proactive morality, rooted in a self-sacrificial orientation to the welfare of her people above everything else, can be informative to that endeavor. Her holiness is defined by a positive ethic of engagement with Persian culture, and our

---

[22]Orlando Costas, "The Subversiveness of Faith: Esther as a Paradigm for a Liberating Theology," *Ecumenical Review* 40 (1988): 71.

[23]Ibid., p. 72.

[24]Ibid., p. 78.

[25]Laniak, "Esther's *Volkcentrism*," p. 83.

definition of holiness needs to also be increasingly marked by how we offer a positive influence on our culture as we engage it from the margins. This should be our focus, rather than a vision that defines holiness by how effectively we avoid certain behaviors traditionally considered taboo by the modern church.

Mission. Can a book that never uses the name of God reflect the missional intention of God? Can the exile of Israel result in other nations coming to know the God of Israel? The missional effect of Esther's actions seems to find its expression in the eighth chapter, when Mordecai is elevated to vice-regent and we are told that many people of "other nationalities" become Jews (Esther 8:17). This is a dramatic expression of the overall impact of Esther's mission. Out of her position of weakness God brings deliverance, and that deliverance works to serve as a light to many. The fact that the people who "converted" do so as a result of "fear" of the Jews can be understood as a reflection of the expected response to a display of God's power (Deut 2:25; 11:25).[26]

This also speaks to God's decision to use unlikely people to participate in his mission to the world.[27] Esther is an orphaned, exiled female. She is a most unlikely leader. Her only qualification is that she has won a beauty contest. Yet she joins a long line of unlikely heroes in the history of Israel. Her participation in God's program speaks eloquently about how God will work through one who is of seeming low esteem to make his name known.

This is a message of deep encouragement to the Western church as it learns to work from the margins of culture. From such locales God can do his best work. He is able to use marginalization and weakness for his missional purposes, and the church in the post-Christendom age needs to embrace this very Esther-like perspective at its core as it seeks to be the people of God in a foreign culture.

SUMMARY

The book of Esther also calls for an understanding of exile that reframes

---

[26]Ibid., p. 89.
[27]Ibid., p. 87.

Jewish hopes and aspirations. Exile was a time when the people of Israel longed for a return to Zion and for a restoration of their autonomy. Such a return would display the power of Yahweh to the nations. Esther calls for a different way for Israel to understand the concept of restoration. As do other diasporic advice tales, it beckons not for a return to nationhood predicated on place alone but to nationhood rooted in community. This type of national identity includes a vision for ongoing mission under the rule of a foreign governor. Esther ends not with everyone living happily ever after back home in Jerusalem but with everyone living happily ever after in Susa. Esther's risks are not for the sake of her people's return to an autonomous existence "back home." They are for a safe existence in Persia. In this way, Esther contributes to the mission of reforming Judaism within new contexts. Redemption will come from the Jewish people acting faithfully on behalf of their community and their God. A recasting of the nation's self-understanding along these lines was absolutely necessary for it to thrive as a people in exile.

The book of Esther provided the ancient Jewish people with a theological narrative of hope, because it assured them that God was with them and that even though they were a marginalized people they could still live holy lives and serve God's purposes. They could penetrate the power structures of society, as Mordecai's enduring role in the Persian government indicates, and they could serve the welfare of the Jewish community, as Esther did. The creative reflections posited by the book recast Israel's understanding of themselves as a people and created fresh possibilities for lives in captivity. It may be that the approach offered by Esther can continue to serve in a similar way even to contemporary communities that experience themselves living in a culture that is "foreign" to them, and thus that the wisdom of Esther's story can speak to the church as we explore our own exilic identity.

4

Daniel as Advice for Exiles

The similarities between Esther and Daniel are striking and well documented.[1] Both stories take place in the royal court of a foreign king, and both display the protagonist faithfully serving the interests of the foreign empire and the Jewish people alike. In both cases the narrative indicates that Jews can thrive in a foreign context. The protagonist's success is based in part on their attractive physical appearance (Esther 2:7-17; Dan 1:4). Both Daniel and Esther include scenes in which great banquets occur, the heroes and/or heroine find themselves in great danger, the king's sleep is disturbed, and the heroes/heroine's change in fortune extends beyond themselves and touches the lives of others. Daniel, like Esther, also offers advice to exiled Jews as to how they can live successfully under foreign rule.

As we have considered in our examination of Esther, narratives in the form of advice tales became important vehicles for engaging the imagination of Israel and helping to cast a fresh vision for its self-understanding as a people who must learn the art of living with dual loyalties—to Yahweh and to a foreign king—in their new circumstances.

THE MESSAGE OF DANIEL

Daniel is set during the Babylonian exile but most likely came into its final

---

[1]Added to this is the story of Joseph in the book of Genesis. See John J. Collins, *Daniel* (Minneapolis: Fortress, 1993), p. 39. See also Sandra Beth Berg, *The Book of Esther: Motifs, Themes and Structures* (Missoula, MT: Scholars Press, 1979), pp. 143-45.

form in the second century B.C.E. However, the source material for the
first six chapters of the book dates much earlier, likely from the Persian
period.[2] Many tales that offer wisdom for living in an exilic context can
be attributed to this period, which suggests a "common literary type
which was apparently quite popular in the Ancient Near East at this
time."[3] The similarities between advice tales as a genre suggest stock characters, settings and scene types that were popular among diasporic Jews.[4]
These were the kind of narratives that offered practical wisdom for those
who desired to be faithful to their identity as Jews in a context that was
not conducive to that kind of orientation. Since these texts contain similar
characteristics, it is not surprising to find that some of the same categories
of theological reflection already evident in Esther can be seen in Daniel
as well. The five tales of Daniel 1–6 offer "an anthology of various situations that the faithful may encounter as a people living under foreign
domination."[5] Regardless of whether those over the faithful are benev-
olent like Darius or the guards in Daniel 1 or more autocratic like
Belshazzar, the people of Israel must learn to live out their faith just as
modern-day Christians must in our own set of trying circumstances.

God's presence on foreign soil. Unlike Esther, Daniel is a highly theo-
centric book. God is not only mentioned, but also all that happens is
ascribed to God. He is the one in control of all of history, including the
events of exile (Dan 1:2). God is the one who enables Daniel and his
companions to excel (Dan 1:17), and who delivers them from death (Dan
3:17; 6:22). The foreign rulers even perceive the hand of God at work in
the circumstances of which they are a part (Dan 3:28; 6:26). This narrative portrayal is the antithesis of God's hiddenness in Esther. For the
reader of Daniel there can be no doubt that God will remain with his
people apart from the land and temple.

---

[2]W. Lee Humphreys, "A Life-Style for Diaspora: A Study of the Tales of Esther and Daniel," *Journal of Biblical Literature* 92 (1973): 218; John J. Collins, "The Court-Tales in Daniel and the Development of Apocalyptic," *Journal of Biblical Literature* 94, no. 2 (1975): 229; John Goldingay,
Daniel, Word Biblical Commentary, vol. 30 (Dallas: Word, 1989), p. 326.
[3]Humphreys, "Life-Style for Diaspora," p. 217.
[4]Berg, *Book of Esther,* p. 145. She and others note the Tale of Ahiqar as a story similar to those of
Joseph, Esther, Mordecai and Daniel.
[5]C. L. Seow, *Daniel,* Westminster Bible Companion (Louisville, KY: John Knox, 2003), p. 10.

While Esther emphasizes the actions of the human protagonist, Daniel and his friends do not bring about their success or release from trouble by any action of their own. Rather they are the beneficiaries of direct divine initiative.[6] It is accurate to say that "the God of Daniel is always there where we least expect him: in a stone, a crematory oven, on a whitewashed wall, or in a pit of ferocious beasts."[7]

God's presence in Babylon is made explicit by the way to which he is referred in the book of Daniel. He is not only sovereign but is also depicted as "King of heaven" (Dan 4:37), "Lord of heaven" (Dan 5:23), "God of heaven" (Dan 2:18, 19) and the "Most High God" (Dan 4:2). As one commentator points out, "The special name of Yahweh all but disappears in favor of terms that make explicit that he is not merely a peculiarly Jewish god, but the God in/of heaven."[8] This is the shared theme of the stories in Daniel 1–6: that the God of the Jews is the one true God to whom all people owe their allegiance. This was an important exilic message evident in the words of Isaiah, who assured his Babylon-based audience that their God was superior to any god worshiped by their foreign hosts.[9]

Yet, however transcendent he may be, God is not aloof. He is willing to involve himself in human affairs on a regular basis. He not only administrates the events of history but also aids his servants in interpreting dreams and comes to the aid of those placed in furnaces and lions' dens. God's presence in Daniel is both transcendent and immanent. On this theological basis the book lays a foundation for the possibility that one can be a good Jew in dispersion.[10]

The book of Daniel reiterates a key theme also found in Esther, that of deliverance. Part of the message of Daniel is that God can be counted on to bring deliverance to his people when they find themselves having to take a stand against the powers that rule the culture. This message has

---

[6]Collins, "Court Tales in Daniel," p. 225.

[7]Andre LaCocque, *The Book of Daniel* (Atlanta: John Knox, 1979), p. 108.

[8]Goldingay, *Daniel*, pp. 329-30.

[9]See, for example, Is 40:18-20; 44:25. See Tim Laniak, "Esther's *Volkcentrism* and the Reframing of Post-Exilic Judaism," in *The Book of Esther in Modern Research*, ed. Sidnie White Crawford and Leonard J. Greenspoon (London: T & T Clark, 2003), p. 88; Collins, "Court Tales in Daniel," p. 223.

[10]Goldingay, *Daniel*, p. 333.

currency for Western Christians too, as it also speaks assurance to us that
on occasions when it is necessary to take a stand against the ways of the
empire, God is present in a way that can see us through the situation.
This is a foundational theological perspective for exilic life at all times
and one that Daniel offers to us even today.

Embodied holiness. Daniel is forced into the service of the Babylonian
king (Dan 1:3), identifying him with the exiles of Judah. Even if Daniel
were to be given a privileged position in the royal court, he would not be
there because he desires to be but because he has been placed there by
Babylonian power. Nonetheless, Daniel embodies Jeremiah's call for
Israel to settle and work for the benefit of their new home. Daniel is a
Jew who is fully integrated into Babylonian society and who successfully
portrays the potential for exilic life and influence through his service to
the various kings with whom he comes in contact. He and his companions impressively demonstrate the possibility of dual loyalties. They
serve both king and country yet without compromising their ultimate
commitment of covenant purity and faithfulness to God.

This is explicitly demonstrated by Daniel's three friends when they are
faced with death as a result of their refusal to follow Nebuchadnezzar's
edict that all people must bow to his image when the signal to do so was
sounded. As the three face the prospect of being burned to death in a
Babylonian crematorium if they do not comply with the royal dictum,
they express their allegiance to Yahweh by flatly stating,

> If the God we serve is able to deliver us, then he will deliver us from the
> blazing furnace and from Your Majesty's hand. But even if he does not, we
> want you to know, Your Majesty, that we will not serve your gods or worship
> the image of gold you have set up. (Dan 3:17-18)

Their commitment is not dependent on any definite expectation of deliverance or divine reward; it is simply a refusal to bow to any God other
than Yahweh.[11] Their primary reason for standing firm is not their con-

---

[11]LaCocque, *Daniel*, pp. 63-64. There is debate around the proper translation of and interpretation
of Daniel 3:17-18, although the way that I am approaching it here, as well as an overview of the
discussion, is well articulated by LaCocque and also Ernest Lucas, *Daniel* (Downers Grove, IL:
InterVarsity Press, 2002), pp. 90-91.

fidence that God will deliver them but their determination to obey the first two commandments of the Decalogue. They will not honor any God but the God of Israel, and they will not worship any idol. Their stand is one of religious commitment, whether or not it is prudent.[12]

In this scenario we see how collaboration with the state has its limits. Daniel and his three friends will serve the purposes of Babylon as far as they are able, but they demonstrate to the reader that fidelity to God's law is more important than keeping the law of the land even if it means risking one's life.

Here in Daniel there seems to be an acknowledgment that God is somehow withdrawn and that there is a possibility he will not deliver. Of course, he does deliver the three young men, but their acknowledgment that he may not amounts to recognition of what every Jew of the post-Babylonian exilic period knew: that God, for whatever reason, does not always deliver the faithful in the way that they may want.[13] This does not, however, negate the need for Jews to remain faithful to the law of Yahweh.

The complexity of practicing dual loyalty between God and king is best demonstrated in chapter 2, when Daniel and his three colleagues offer to interpret the king's dream.[14] Here the four young men participate in a Babylonian category of wisdom, dream interpretation, in order to demonstrate the superiority of their God over the human wisdom of the Babylonians. When the wise men of Babylon are unable to interpret King Nebuchadnezzar's troubling dream, Daniel volunteers to give the interpretation (Dan 2:16). This places him squarely in the domain of Babylonian convention, although he turns the convention inside out. Dreams certainly found favor as prophetic oracles within Hebrew tradition (e.g., 1 Sam 28:6, 15; Gen 28:12; 31:10-13; 37:5-20), so Daniel volunteers to act as the king's dream interpreter and thereby seeks to beat the Babylonian wise men at their own game. He is willing to serve a Gentile

---

[12]Lucas, *Daniel*, pp. 90-91.

[13]Collins, *Daniel*, p. 188.

[14]This is not the only place where Daniel is called on to interpret dreams or unusual phenomena; see also Daniel 4-5.

king by adapting Hebrew traditions into a Gentile context in order to secure his own and his friends' survival.

He does this by engaging fully in the Babylonian court but insisting on the inferiority of Babylonian techniques compared with reliance on the one true God.[15] When it comes to interpreting the king's dream, the Babylonian wise men are depicted as inept and unable to satisfy the king's request because they only have themselves and their own human resources on which to rely. It is striking that the gods of Babylon are absent from the story. The this-worldly wisdom of the Babylonian seers is juxtaposed with the supernatural wisdom of Daniel as it is supplied by Yahweh.[16]

In contrast to the absence of any reference to the Babylonian gods, three times Daniel states that it is Israel's God who reveals mysteries (Dan 2:20-23, 27-28, 29-30), and each time he recognizes that the one true God is the source of his own wisdom.[17] This is where Daniel's loyalty to the king and his ability to work successfully within Babylonian categories work in harmony with his faithfulness to the ways of Yahweh. He is able to work diplomatically with the king and buy himself some time to interpret the dream, as opposed to the court wise men, whose request for time is interpreted by the king as a sign that they are devoid of any power to determine the content or meaning of his dream. Yet Daniel remains faithful to God because his allegiance to God necessitates that he give the credit for his interpretation to God. A story like this has no place in the traditional ancient Near East (ANE) court tale, since in the ANE court tales wise men succeed on their own.[18] Yet Daniel, while fully integrated in the royal court of Babylon and fulfilling the role of "wise man" within that court, depends on his God to enable him to serve the king effectively.

Subsequently Daniel remains willing to work within a Babylonian

---

[15]Here Daniel is in the same stream of contempt for Babylonian "wisdom" and its sages as Second Isaiah is.

[16]Goldingay, *Daniel*, p. 54. LaCocque, *Daniel*, p. 33, also understands this scenario as "the difference between wisdom of divine origin and wisdom of human origin."

[17]Lucas, *Daniel*, p. 78.

[18]Ibid. Also Goldingay, *Daniel*, pp. 54-55, explores the contrast between divine and human wisdom as a key theme in this story.

framework and takes charge over the country's "wise men" (Dan 2:48) and serves as chief dream interpreter (Dan 4:6). In doing this Daniel maintains a positive attitude toward the king and other court officials in Babylon. He is depicted as a collaborator with the state but on Hebrew terms. His rise to prominence does not mean abandoning his religious commitments. Daniel is integrated into Babylonian life, and his example serves the exilic community, as the patterns of behavior and the priorities the story advocates would have been broadly applicable.[19]

Their exilic community's interpretation extends into modern exilic situations as well. Daniel's example continues to model how the church can thoroughly engage Western culture, living lives that participate in various arenas of societal life that we discern appropriate. Like Daniel, who obeyed the law of God and clearly confessed allegiance to Yahweh, our calling is to demonstrate a distinctly Christian character and unashamedly confess our attachment to Jesus. Daniel teaches us that God will honor the life lived in this way and will use it, from the margins, to continue his purposes in the land.

This does not always mean that living this way will be easy. In the book of Daniel there is nothing subtle about Jewish holiness. It is not only clearly embodied by the main characters but also is often the very source of their troubles. The need to refrain from engaging in many of the practices of their host culture is clear and is depicted in Daniel through three separate acts of piety: dietary observance, prayer and allegiance to their God at all cost.

Daniel 1 depicts Daniel and his three friends making arrangements with their Babylonian supervisor to be allowed to eat a vegetarian (and therefore kosher) diet as opposed to the food provided for them by royal decree. The result is that they appear better nourished than their Gentile colleagues and thereby surpass them as candidates for leadership in Babylon. The point of the story is clear. Jews who rise at court do so because of their wisdom, given to them by God. God gives wisdom to his servants who faithfully obey his laws.[20]

---

[19]Collins, *Daniel*, p. 51.
[20]Collins, "Court Tales in Daniel," p. 227.

Observance of worship expressed through prayer is a further demonstration of a distinctive lifestyle in the Diaspora. Daniel's prayer
habits reflect his faithfulness to worship and trust in God (Dan 6:10).
Indeed it is his commitment to such piety that his opponents use as a
way to entrap him so that they can dispose of him (Dan 6:5). As in
Esther, where Haman's premise for exterminating the Jews is that they
keep themselves apart and practice unusual ways (Esther 3:8), we see in
Daniel how the conscientious practice of Jewish religion will be used as
a mechanism for persecution. Once again, however, the book's prevailing message is that God delivers those who are faithful in the practice
of their religious obligations.

The observance of these practices reflects a general ethic that is per-
vasive throughout the book of Daniel, namely, intense loyalty to God.[21]
This loyalty is all-consuming as characters willingly risk everything in
taking their stand for their God. Shadrach, Meshach and Abednego are
thrown into a (devastatingly) hot furnace (only to survive by God's
hand), and Daniel is placed in a den of lions (only to experience God's
deliverance)—because they are unwilling to renounce their commitment to Yahweh. While their piety leads them into conflict and to
face the prospect of death, the message of their example is clear: exiled
Jews can stand for their distinct identity as people of the highest God
and expect to experience his faithful presence in the midst of the challenges they face.

Daniel Smith-Christopher suggests that purity is an act of diasporic
nonconformity to subjugating powers.[22] It is a quiet but bold way of
critiquing the norms of the prevailing culture and also presenting an
alternative way of being to those in authority. No better example of such
practice can be found in the book of Daniel than in the actions of the
title character and his friends. Their commitment to purity nonviolently
protests the conventions of Babylon in ways that ultimately turn out to

---

[21]For a full exploration of this theme see John Barton, "Theological Ethics in Daniel," in *The Book
of Daniel: Composition and Reception*, vol. 2, ed. John Collins and Peter W. Flint (Leiden: Brill,
2001), pp. 661-70.

[22]See chap. 6 in Daniel Smith-Christopher, *A Biblical Theology of Exile* (Minneapolis: Fortress,
2002).

benefit the state. The perpetrators of this subversive behavior outperform other state administrators and lead the king to become a worshiper of Yahweh, and in turn he leads the people along the same path. This piety provides hope to those living in exile that as they practice a nonconformist piety they too can anticipate that God will intervene in the circumstances of their lives in a manner similar to that experienced by Daniel and his friends. Furthermore, Daniel's career, which lasts and prospers through the reign of three kings and various empires, is a powerful reminder to the readers of the book that faithful practice of covenant piety can lead to a lowly exile outlasting the empire and its leaders.[23]

The message of Daniel reminds us that embodied holiness, that is, the faithful practice of the teachings of the Christian faith, is a positive force in society and will bring a blessing to the world around us as we conscientiously put our faith into practice. The consistent practice of our faith will bring benefits to our world. Often this will be very subtle and won't draw any special attention. At other times it may be more dramatic as our actions offer an overt critique of the accepted behavior of our particular context. While integration with culture is necessary, conformity to it in all aspects is not. Daniel's challenge is for the believer to take a stand for what is right according to God's intentions for this world with trust that such a stand will ultimately be seen as beneficial to those around us.

Mission. It is impossible to read Daniel without noticing the striking royal edicts that acknowledge the superiority of the Jewish God over all others (Dan 2:47; 3:29; 6:26). These occur each time Daniel and/or his friends have suffered a near-death experience and are ultimately vindicated. There is in Daniel an overarching theme of the superiority of Yahweh over all other deities. The actions of Daniel and his compatriots lead to an acknowledgment by non-Jews that the Jewish God is Lord indeed. This motif expresses the exilic hope that suffering will be redeemed and that Israel's faithfulness will be held up as an act of witness to the nations. The exilic community should remain faithful in the face

---

[23]Seow, *Daniel*, p. 96.

of tremendous pressure and genuine suffering yet trusts that it will be redeemed from its plight by the hand of God. This redemption will bring about an acknowledgment of Yahweh's ultimacy. Daniel speaks of the preeminence of the Hebrew God and points to the fact that, no matter what, God's plan cannot be thwarted. While the book as a whole speaks of an eschatological age in which God's purposes will be fully realized, the first six chapters remind us that God still demonstrates his power in this age.[24]

This revelation of divine sovereignty in Daniel depicts a theme that is not found as clearly elsewhere in the Old Testament, namely, that of the kingdom of God.[25] Notwithstanding Daniel's high office, the book is concerned to show how God's reign can become a reality through the faithful witness of a diasporic community whose trust is not in mechanisms of political power but in the power of Yahweh. Again, such a witness can demonstrate the reign of God apart from the land of Israel: "Believers under pressure can stand by their convictions sure that the powers that be will ultimately acknowledge where true power lies and who its witnesses are."[26]

Furthermore, one cannot help but recognize the negative consequences for those who oppose Daniel and his friends. Similar to Mordecai, who is raised up to significant leadership in the Persian kingdom, so too is Daniel raised to leadership above the other wise men subsequent to his successful interpretation of Nebuchadnezzar's dream (Dan 2:48). Also, similar to Haman, who is put to death for his actions against the Jews in Persia, so after Shadrach, Meshach and Abednego are spared in the furnace a decree is proclaimed that anyone who says anything against their God should be chopped up into little pieces and their homes turned into rubble (Dan 3:29). Similarly, after Daniel is removed from the lions' den, those who falsely accused him (and their families) are thrown into the den and meet their demise (Dan 6:24). These events serve as signals that those who oppose Yahweh and his servants risk

---

[24]See LaCocque, *Daniel*, p. 121; and Goldingay, *Daniel*, p. 136.
[25]Goldingay, *Daniel*, p. 330.
[26]Ibid.

facing judgment. This confirms Hebrew texts such as Deuteronomy 19:16-21; Proverbs 19:5, 9; 21:28; and Esther 7:10, which teach that adversaries should be executed in the place of those that they wrongly accuse. The implementation of these decrees speaks to the infiltration and triumph of Hebrew ideals in a foreign context, thus bearing witness to the superiority of the ways of Yahweh.[27]

Daniel also speaks to the transience of empires and the redemptive potential of the community of God's people. Empires crumble like old statues (Dan 2:35), and wise people know that taking a stand for God's ideals, which do not give way, will serve as a witness to those who are not able to see as clearly. Such faith-driven, integrative, pious, missional wisdom embodies Jesus' words to be "as shrewd as snakes and as innocent as doves" (Mt 10:16). It is the wisdom of exile.

Such wisdom supplies contemporary communities of faith with hope that they have both a role to play in the current context and a future to look forward to. Currently the church can flavor the culture through a life of good deeds and verbal witness, even if it comes from a place of far less power and influence than it once did. Despite our marginalization, our witness will be received by some and when executed properly will ensure that the church continues to play a meaningful role in the life of our society for many years to come.

SUMMARY

The book of Daniel presents a practical theology of exilic living to its audience by making its hero an exemplar to them. Daniel's "success" as a Jewish person in a foreign empire reminds Israel that it too can succeed as a nation through faithful obedience and piety because God is still with it and still in control. Faithfulness to the ways of its God will not only enable Israel to thrive in exile but also will offer a witness to foreign nations that points to the superiority of Yahweh above all other gods, secular powers or political systems. A perspective such as this not only sustained the nation of Israel through its multifaceted, prolonged time

---

[27]Ibid., pp. 134-35; see also LaCocque, *Daniel*, pp. 119-20.

of exile but remains as much-needed wisdom for the Western church today if it is to "succeed" in its own contemporary "exile."

Applying this wisdom to our specific circumstances is not always clear or easy. Often the decision as to whether to take a particular stand is hard to make, not just because of potential consequences but also because the factors involved are numerous and complex. However, Daniel calls us to live with a certain kind of orientation to exilic life, one of commitment to obedience despite the cost. While knowing exactly what to do in each circumstance can be difficult at times, deciding that we will ultimately choose to live in obedience to God is an orientation with which we are called to live in exile. It is out of this orientation that God will make us a blessing to our world and bring deliverance as necessary.

5

Jonah as Advice for Exiles?

Jonah is one of the Bible's most unusual books, the subject of immense scholarly debate regarding its exact nature and proper interpretation. The dating of the book within the diasporic era, sometime well after the fall of Jerusalem, is one of the few issues that garners a consensus among scholars.[1] One of the major points of discussion among those who study the book has been its genre.[2] The possible options include history, legend, allegory, midrash, parable, satire and advice tale. Clearly there is a sense in which this most enigmatic of biblical books can fit into any of these categories and none of them at the same time.[3] However, the genre that

---

[1]See Daniel Smith-Christopher, *A Biblical Theology of Exile* (Minneapolis: Fortress, 2002), p. 130, and Andre LaCocque and Pierre-Emmanual LaCocque, *Jonah: A Psycho-Religious Approach to the Prophet* (Columbia: University of South Carolina Press, 1990), p. 20. For further discussion see R. B. Salters, *Jonah and Lamentations* (Sheffield: Sheffield Academic Press, 1994), pp. 23-26, who sees 350 B.C.E. as the earliest possible date. Ehud Ben Zvi, *Signs of Jonah: Reading and Rereading in Ancient Yehud* (London: Sheffield Academic Press, 2003), takes the view that the Persian Yehud is the likely time of composition. Katherine J. Dell, "Reinventing the Wheel: The Shaping of the Book of Jonah," in *After the Exile: Essays in Honour of Rex Mason*, ed. John Barton and David J. Reimer (Macon: Mercer University Press, 1996), p. 86n7, offers a brief, insightful rationale for a postexilic date. Miller Burrows, "The Literary Category of the Book of Jonah," in *Translating and Understanding the Old Testament: Essays in Honor of Herbert Gordon May*, ed. Harry Thomas Frank and William L. Reed (Nashville: Abingdon, 1970), p. 104, cites the Persian period as the most probable time for the composition of book. Despite the variance in exact opinion represented here, the consensus view of a post–587 date is enough to warrant the view that will be taken in this study of the book and its meaning.

[2]For an overview of the primary contours of this discussion see LaCocque and LaCocque, *Jonah: A Psycho-Religious Approach*, pp. 7-66, and Burrows, "Literary Category of Jonah." For a briefer treatment see Salters, *Jonah and Lamentations*, pp. 41-50.

[3]Thomas Bolin, *Freedom Beyond Forgiveness: The Book of Jonah Re-Examined* (Sheffield: Sheffield Academic Press, 1997), pp. 46-53, concludes his analysis of Jonah's genre by stating that the question is "insoluble."

may best encompass all these possibilities and provide the most fruitful approach to appropriating the book's message for our day is that of the diasporic advice tale. While the setting of Jonah is less clear than that of the other stories we have considered, like those stories Jonah has a didactic character and involves an individual whose story can both represent and inform the nation. Jonah's presence in a foreign land and the fact that his actions result in a positive outcome for the people of that land is the key theme that commends it as a variation on a common type of advice tale.[4] Like the other two narratives we have considered, Jonah casts a fresh vision for exilic possibilities for the nation of Israel.

THE MESSAGE OF JONAH

The story of Jonah centers on the prophet Jonah the son of Amittai, who is known also from a brief statement found in 2 Kings 14:25, where he is described as a prophet who predicts the return of prosperity and the extension of territory for the northern kingdom of Israel during the reign of Jeroboam II (786–746 B.C.E.). The positive, nationalistic tone of his prophecy should not be missed, nor should the fact that Nineveh was the capital of Assyria, which conquered the northern kingdom in 722. The book of Jonah records God's call for the prophet to preach a message of repentance to the Assyrian city of Nineveh, which represents the worst of God's enemies. Jonah refuses the mission and flees to Tarshish, as far away from Nineveh as possible. While at sea Jonah is swallowed by a great fish and spends three days in the beast's belly, where he finally repents of his disobedience and, after being spit out by the fish, carries out his mission to the city of Nineveh. Nineveh responds positively to the message Jonah brings, and the city is spared from God's judgment, whereupon the prophet makes his way out of the city and begins to sulk because of the mercy God has shown to the evil Ninevites. A final conversation between God and the prophet, in which the prophet expresses his frustration at God for his care for the Ninevites, concludes the book.

---

[4]Sandra Beth Berg, *The Book of Esther: Motifs, Themes and Structures* (Missoula, MT: Scholars Press, 1979), p. 148. This position acknowledges that while Jonah fits within the broad category of "advice tale" it is also a unique story and its genre is not easy to pinpoint.

The same themes we have seen in Esther and Daniel can be seen in Jonah as well. Just like Esther and Daniel, the book of Jonah embodies key theological perspectives for exilic realities both ancient and contemporary.

God's presence on foreign soil. One of the most striking features in the story of Jonah is God's concern for the people of Nineveh. As a city within the Assyrian empire, Nineveh would have been perceived by Jewish readers as the worst of the worst in terms of an ungodly enemy nation. The general concept of God caring for nations other than Israel and being present among them is in line with many canonical perspectives, but this work goes even further in presenting a perspective on exilic events and how to live in light of them.

Employing irony as a narrative device, the author juxtaposes the obedience of the people of Nineveh with the stubbornness of his own people. Jonah, who as a prophet of Israel in some way characterizes the nation as a whole, is reluctant to serve as a witness to enemies and see God's grace extended to them, so he flees God's call. Furthermore, Jonah shows great disappointment in Nineveh's positive response to his message. This reflects a character much different from that of his God. In contrast, Nineveh, who as conquerors characterizes the "nations," responds immediately with a thorough repentance when confronted with God's word through the prophet. The portrayal of Nineveh's people responding faithfully to God's word is ironic when compared to how Israel is sometimes depicted in biblical literature. For instance, Nineveh's response can be contrasted with that of King Jehoiakim in Jeremiah 36. Jehoiakim flagrantly refuses to repent after a lengthy written exhortation by Jeremiah, whereas Nineveh repents after just five short words by the foreign prophet. Also, the Ninevites' repentance depicts the kind of comprehensive response to which the exilic prophets called Israel, including penance, fasting, prayer and avoidance of sin.[5] This contrast pointedly reminds Jonah's audience that it does not have a corner on God's care and that God is active in the life of nations other than Israel.

More specifically, Jonah 4:2 presents one of the central confessions of

---

[5]LaCocque and LaCocque, *Jonah: A Psycho-Religious Approach*, p. 22. The LaCocques see numerous links between Jonah and several other texts in the Hebrew Bible.

Israelite liturgy (Ex 34:6) within a universalistic framework. God's gracious mercy and compassion, known to Israel as core attributes of Yahweh, are now explicitly demonstrated toward a foreign nation, and to make the point even finer, toward the Assyrians. This turns the doctrinal assumptions of Israelite faith—that Yahweh's grace and compassion were particularly directed toward Israel—around by casting a vision of their God as one who shares himself with all people.[6]

As an example of creative exilic theological conversation, Jonah could be considered a critique of the message of Ezra and Nehemiah, which stress a more isolationist approach toward foreign nations, or to those who limited the vision of Isaiah, which foresees the nations coming to Jerusalem to worship and their people even becoming Levites and priests (Is 66:21). For the book of Jonah, as in Esther and Daniel, Yahweh can be (and is) worshiped on foreign soil, much to the chagrin of those who do not share such a vision. The book of Jonah radically challenges the dogma that Israel is worth more than the other nations, teaching instead that God cares for its enemies. Accordingly, Israel's restoration will include participation with other nations rather than separation from them.[7]

Of course such a message also challenges the parochial ideas that sometimes infiltrate a church nurtured in centuries of Christendom-like culture. We too can develop a mentality that is sometimes overt but more often unspoken that believes God's presence is restricted to the church, or the Christian home, or at least to places that we deem to be not "too unclean." In exile Israel was dramatically reminded of a core truth about God that it had forgotten: that God has a heart for and is present with all people, even people like the Assyrians.

Embodied holiness. The primary feature of Jonah's teaching about Israelite holiness is found in the prophet's repentance. It is in Jonah's repentance while in the belly of the great fish that his willingness to bend to Yahweh's will is demonstrated, and thus he offers a lesson to Israel that speaks to its own need to repent and be restored as God's holy people. However, in keeping with the overall tone of the book, Jonah's repen-

---

[6]Ibid., p. 22.
[7]Ibid., pp. 41-43, 126-27.

tance is characterized in a satirical tone that demonstrates the author's intent to make Jonah look ridiculous.[8] His actions are incongruous with someone attuned to the ways of Yahweh. Thus Jonah offers Israel a mirror through which it is invited to reflect on its own ungodliness as a people with a view to prompting its own reprentance.

A key theological perspective reflected in the call for Jonah to preach to Nineveh is the potential transformation of one's enemies through repentance.[9] Clearly what God has in mind—and Jonah knows it—is to change the Assyrians' hearts so that God will not send judgment on them. Jonah would rather maintain Nineveh as an enemy than see them transformed into followers of Yahweh and thereby escape divine judgment.

This perspective leads Jonah to flee God's call and choose a destination as far from Nineveh as possible: the city of Tarshish.[10] Jonah's flight from God's call epitomizes his lack of willingness to participate in the salvation of other nations, even as his apparent willingness to sacrifice himself in the sea for the safety of the other sailors rather than go to Nineveh demonstrates the intensity of his lack of desire to engage in the mission to which God has called him. Nonetheless, God is committed to acquiring Jonah's participation in his plan for Nineveh, and the storm that he sends is not designed as retribution but rather is an opportunity for reorientation. Both the storm and the fish are indications of God's beneficence as they act as agents of the divine will, designed to move Jonah back into the center of that will.[11] In particular the great fish acts as a place of transformation that allows Jonah to act as a didactic model for Israel.

---

[8]Raymond R. Person, *In Conversation with Jonah: Conversation Analysis, Literary Criticism, and the Book of Jonah* (Sheffield: JSOT, 1996), p. 153.

[9]Smith-Christopher, *Biblical Theology*, p. 132.

[10]Although certainly not an invented place, the exact location of Tarshish is impossible to pinpoint. However, it is fair to understand it in this context as the geographical opposite of Nineveh. In keeping with the thick irony in the Jonah story Tarshish is mentioned in Is 66:19 as a place where the inhabitants have not heard of God's name. Yet God promises that he will send some who survive the exile to proclaim his name to the citizens of those places. Thus Jonah is just as foolish to think he can escape God's missional purposes by fleeing there. See Jack M. Sasson, *Jonah*, The Anchor Bible: A New Translation with Introduction, Commentary and Interpretation (New York: Doubleday, 1990), p. 79.

[11]Peter Ackroyd, *Israel Under Babylon and Persia* (Oxford: Oxford University Press, 1970), p. 338.

Yvonne Sherwood, drawing from ancient rabbis' interpretations of Jonah, points out how Jonah can be understood as one who becomes a teacher/rabbi to his people through his watery incarceration. Interacting with the ancient midrash *Pirke de Rabbi Eliezer*, Sherwood casts the whale's belly as a synagogue where Jonah is schooled and also schools his fellow Israelites in the ways of Yahweh.[12]

From the fish's gut we can see how Jonah's response reflects Israel's response to exile, that is, prayer (Jon 2:1-9).[13] Jonah prays to God in a way that reflects the prayer tradition of Israelite exile as found in the book of Lamentations and the exilic psalms.

In his prayer Jonah reflects on the way God has treated him as he languishes in aquatic incarceration. His words in Jonah 2:3-4, "*You* hurled me into the deep. . . . *Your* waves and breakers swept over me. I said, 'I have been banished from *your* sight,'" represent his clear sense that God has brought this torment on him and that he is now experiencing the horrifying reality of the divine absence. This discourse with God regarding Jonah's sense of displacement and his lack of comfort with it reflects a connection with Israel's prayer tradition and a desire on Jonah's part to be restored to God. Jonah's prayer includes a report on past events and his thanksgiving to God for deliverance. It also can be understood as an act of repentance, as it represents Jonah's turning to God and away from his disobedience and rejection of God's mission. It is an embrace of God's good character and thus a change of heart within the wayward prophet. While it may never become a total transformation, the

---

[12]Yvonne Sherwood, *A Biblical Text and Its Afterlife: The Survival of Jonah in Western Culture* (Cambridge: Cambridge University Press, 2000), pp. 109-12. Sherwood bases these reflections on a midrash from the ninth century C.E. known as *Pirke de Rabbi Eliezer: The Chapters of R. Eliezer the Great*, trans. G. Friedlander (New York: Sepher Herman, 1981). Also see LaCocque and LaCocque, *Jonah: A Psycho-Religious Approach*, p. 72.

[13]Sasson carefully demonstrates how the poem of Jonah connects with other prayer traditions in the Old Testament. However, he notes that these traditions "float" and that these categories can be seen at many points in Israel's history. See also LaCocque and LaCocque, *Jonah: A Psycho-Religious Approach*, p. 98, and Douglas Stuart, *Hosea–Jonah*, Word Biblical Commentary (Waco, TX: Word, 1987), pp. 467-78. That being said, Jonah's prayer continues the ironic tone of the book as it depicts Jonah praying in a way that is appropriate for him (or Israel) to pray, yet his subsequent attitude fails to reflect a genuine repentance and thus calls into question the sincerity of his prayer itself. In this way he continues as a kind of antihero for Israel.

journey away from God's calling has come to an end, and the movement back toward God is beginning. In Jonah 2:4 the prophet states that despite feeling banished from God's sight, "I will look again toward your holy temple."

Likewise in Jonah 2:7 he prays,

When my life was ebbing away,
    I remembered you, LORD,
And my prayer rose to you,
    to your holy temple.

Furthermore, in Jonah 2:9, he says, "But I, with shouts of grateful praise, will sacrifice to you."

Clearly this is a declaration of thanksgiving. This prayer can be understood as a *tôdâ,* which is a form of thanksgiving that also carries with it elements of confession and remorse.[14] Its placement at this point in the book indicates that it is an expression of piety that signals Jonah's turning back to Yahweh and begins the process of reconciliation between God and his prophet.

Once again here we see that the spiritual life of exiles is marked by a steadfast refusal to abandon their God despite their sense of abandonment by him. Jonah's turning to God in prayer and repentance demonstrates a traditional form of exilic piety and expresses his own hope of restoration. While Jonah's tale ultimately reflects an imperfect repentance, and his story is more of a satire than an ideal, his prayer epitomizes the kind of response that is appropriate to exile.

The holiness expressed by Jonah through his repentance is a reminder to the Western church that we too may have become complacent about God's mission, as a result of many years of living in a culture in which most at least knew the basic tenets of the gospel and could converse at least in a rudimentary way about Christian faith. Taken further, the fact that we used to live in a highly evangelized culture dulled our missional motivation and made large sectors of the church not only ineffective in

---

[14]See Mark J. Boda, "Words and Meanings: YDH in Hebrew Research," *Westminster Theological Journal* 57, no. 2 (1995): 296, for an exploration of the *todah* form. Also see Sasson, *Jonah,* p. 199.

reaching out to their neighbors but unconcerned about doing so. The church could be accused of arrogance about its sense of "having the right answer" to life and about looking down on those who did not agree or who refused to live obediently. Both the church's complacency and its arrogance are areas where the antidote of repentance needs to be applied. This could help to engender a sense of humility that reflects genuine holiness much more effectively than previous attitudes of superiority did.

Mission. Jonah's call to mission is simple and clear and may be understood to represent Israel's commission to a similar vocation as prophet to the nations.[15] Nineveh, as we have already seen, can be understood as representative of other nations. The fact that it was the capital city of Israel's former captors and one of the vilest, most feared nations should not be overlooked, even if the regime had long since met its demise.[16]

Since Jonah is more than the story of a reluctant individual prophet, and since his story is designed to have consequences for Israel as a people, the thrust of Jonah's message is to clarify Israel's own missional purposes. Not only does the text clearly present the universal presence of Yahweh, but it also reminds the nation, through its identification with Jonah, that it has a central role to play in God's salvific concern for all people—even hated enemies. The closing question of the book, "Should I not have concern for the great city Nineveh?" (Jon 4:11), is a rhetorical device that both discloses God's heart for the nations and, in its context, implies the role that Israel plays in serving his purposes.

Thus Jonah's anger at God's relenting from destroying Nineveh is a foil that points out, albeit sarcastically, what Israel should already know, namely that God is "gracious and compassionate . . . slow to anger and abounding in love, a God who relents from sending calamity" (Jon 4:2; cf. Ex 34:6). This also represents an important stream of exilic theology found in texts such as Jeremiah 36:3 and Ezekiel 18:23, in which the for-

---

[15]For insight into the missional nature of Israel see Christopher Wright, *The Mission of God: Unlocking the Bible's Grand Narrative* (Downers Grove, IL: IVP Academic, 2006), especially chaps. 6–8, which offer a close study of the topic as it pertains to preexilic Israel. Also Michael W. Goheen, *A Light to the Nations: The Missional Church and the Biblical Story* (Grand Rapids: Baker Academic, 2011), chaps. 2 and 3.
[16]See Nahum 3 for another perspective on the evil of the city of Nineveh.

giving nature of God toward those who repent is emphasized. Furthermore, it reiterates the ideas made clear in Isaiah regarding the place of foreigners in the Israelite community (Is 56:6-8; 66:20-21). Jonah reflects the theological development in exilic Israel in a way that was intended to cause Israel to think more clearly about its role in the salvation of humankind.[17]

The message to those in Israel who could not countenance the idea of Nineveh receiving God's favor is clear, as it condemns those who stand opposed to such theological possibilities. Put in positive terms the story of Jonah calls for recognition of the fact that God is engaged even with cultures that appear to us as ungodly and even oppressive. The book of Jonah is a direct assault on the ideology of those within Israel who think that separation from "the nations" is the way to go. The story of Jonah teaches that restoration from exile will occur only *with* the nations, not without them.[18]

Ultimately Jonah plays the role of both the erroneous, disobedient prophet *and* struggling Israel, wrestling to find its new place in its exilic situation. Therefore God's offer to Israel through Jonah is a call to reconnect with its missional identity. Jonah's example presents a radical theological reorientation of Israelite identity in its new exilic condition. For Israel, to embody a "Jonah" message in the world means that the Israelite community must recognize that it is a tool of God's transformative justice and mission. But just as the Israelite people are penitent about their own sin, so are the "nations" to be penitent about their sin. "Such language is a radical change from the notions that guided pre-exilic bravado toward the nations, including even prophetic rhetoric of punishment. It is a change, and one that is particularly intelligible in a diasporic context."[19]

As a didactic story, Jonah connected ancient Israel with key theological themes that would guide and sustain it in its exilic life. It is also

[17]Smith-Christopher, *Biblical Theology*, p. 130.
[18]Andre LaCocque and Pierre-Emmanual LaCocque, *The Jonah Complex* (Atlanta: John Knox, 1981), p. 72 (italics original).
[19]Smith-Christopher, *Biblical Theology*, p. 135.

informative to the Western church in that it speaks about how restoration does not necessarily mean going back to the way things were. The former days have come to a close, and whatever the future holds will be different from the way things worked in the past. Exile inherently brings irreversible change, and thus the way forward is to accept the loss of former ways and to participate in the unfolding agenda that God has for making things new in a completely different context.

Summary. Jonah is not a typical hero, but then again neither is Esther. Like Esther, Jonah is a flawed character and yet one chosen to undertake a mission set by God. Some have referred to Jonah as an antihero,[20] or even as a "pitiable and ludicrous caricature of a prophet."[21] While it is not difficult to understand how these impressions have arisen, the primary issue is that the book of Jonah depicts for his people the potential of exilic life.

As Jonah 4:11 makes plain, through Jonah's story readers are invited to question their own theology and even that of other exilic writers and thinkers in light of Jonah's experience. Thus Jonah fits well as a diasporic advice tale whose message aims to teach its readers how to make sense of and live in the light of their current experience as an exilic people.[22] This includes cultivating an appreciation for the universal nature of God's salvation and of Israel's role as "missionary" to the nations. Its cooperation is demanded even as this requires repentance and a restored obedience to its calling to be a vessel through which God can work for the good of others. Jonah also reminds us of how in a time of exile that call to mission means working from the margins. He epitomizes one who engages in the mission of God without worldly power. This was Israel's new reality, as it is increasingly the reality of the church in a post-Christian society.

CONCLUSION

For Israel the exile initially brought forth a response of incredulity and deep sadness that slowly graduated into a sense of understanding that it

---

[20]Dell, "Reinventing the Wheel," p. 89.
[21]Burrows, "The Literary Category of Jonah," p. 86.
[22]Salters, *Jonah and Lamentations*, p. 48.

was indeed responsible for its own fate. However, these somber reactions gave way to a hope that found expression in a variety of forms, embodied in the lively stories of Esther, Daniel and Jonah. These tales taught Israel that God was still present and active in its national life, that holiness would help to establish it among foreign nations, and that as his people it still had a significant role to play in his mission.

Can these theological responses to exile speak to the church today? For some this is a rhetorical question. To quote Daniel Smith-Christopher, the potential of exile as an organizing motif for ecclesiological identity represents the most exciting "re-strategizing option for contemporary Christian existence."[23] The response to ancient exile presented by the prophets as well as diasporic advice tales offers highly provocative insights and survival strategies for the life of the church today. The embodied theology of Esther, Daniel and Jonah presents the church with stories that can help to inform its engagement with a culture that is clearly opposed to the ideas of the gospel. While the materialistic consumerism, agnosticism and increasing secularism in which we find ourselves in our post-Christian context are different from the issues faced by exilic Israel, its challenges still present a template for how we can respond as the church to our situation.

It may well be that the power once held by the church in the West was not only temporary but ultimately detrimental to a vibrant gospel witness. The church may find its strongest voice when in conscious exile. It is from this position that the presence of God is discovered most meaningfully, where subversive strategies of integration such as those demonstrated by Esther and Daniel are developed and, as in Jonah, the demise of our once-comfortable circumstances can cause God's people to reconsider its once-privileged place and reconnect with its missional nature. As the Old Testament demonstrates, in exile dramatic new conceptions of faith can be realized. Accordingly we should seek to embrace an exilic paradigm for modern church ministry and apply the wisdom of the ancients to guide and energize our collective life.

---

[23]Smith-Christopher, *Biblical Theology*, p. 191.

For Israel the experience of exile served to guide the community past Persian control and into Greek and Roman rule. This period, usually referred to as the Second Temple period, shaped the work of the New Testament writers, who continued to employ exilic motifs in their reflection on the incarnation, life, crucifixion and resurrection of Jesus. These works lay the foundation for how the motif of exile informed the early church and can also inform the exilic identity of the contemporary church, as we will see in our next section.

6

Jesus and Exile
in the Early Church

The coming and going of empires may have changed Israel's particular circumstances over time, but these changes did not alter the nation's overall experience of displacement, Diaspora and exile. As the centuries passed Israel remained a subjugated people living under the rule of the prevailing superpower of the age. It is fair to say that the Jewish culture into which Christianity was born retained a strong sense that being in exile was a part of its identity. This self-understanding provided a working foundation for the exilic perspective found in the New Testament, particularly if one accepts the idea that the first Christians understood themselves as Jews—a new and distinctive brand of Jews, perhaps, but Jews nonetheless.[1]

N. T. Wright hypothesizes about the worldview that many first-century Jews would have held. Using what he refers to as four foundational worldview questions, Wright submits that a majority of Jews would have understood themselves in the following ways:

1. Who are we? We are Israel the chosen people of the creator god.

[1]The scholarly discussion on this point in voluminous. For some introductory comments that support the perspective offered here, see Gabriele Boccaccini, *Middle Judaism: Jewish Thought 300 BCE to 200 CE* (Minneapolis: Fortress, 1991), pp. 15-18, and Frederick Murphy, *Early Judaism: The Exile to the Time of Jesus* (Peabody, MA: Hendrickson, 2002), specifically chaps. 9 and 11. Also see Paula Frederickson and her discussion of the term *conversion* in "Mandatory Retirement: Ideas in Study of Christian Origins Whose Time Has Come to Go," *Studies in Religion* 35, no. 2 (2006): 236-39.

2. Where are we? We are in the holy Land, focused on the Temple; but, paradoxically, we are still in exile.

3. What is wrong? We have the wrong rulers: pagans on the one hand, compromised Jews on the other, or half-way between, Herod and his family. We are all involved in a less-than-ideal situation.

4. What is the solution? Our god must act again to give us the true sort of rule, that is, his own kingship exercised through properly appointed officials (a true priesthood; possibly a true king); and in the mean time Israel must be faithful to his covenant charter.[2]

This perspective reflects the ongoing role that an exilic consciousness played in the Jewish mindset in the period between approximately 400 B.C.E. and the start of the Common Era (C.E.). This period, often known in Jewish history as the Second Temple period due to the reconstruction of the Jerusalem temple during the Persian period, was one in which the concept of exile continued to play a role in the identity of many Jews.

While a full study of this assertion is beyond the scope of this book, it will suffice for us to briefly review some indications that the idea of being in exile shaped the thinking of Israel as a people during this significant period of history.

EXILE IN THE SECOND TEMPLE PERIOD

Knowledge of this period and its literature has often been neglected in Protestant circles, but in very practical terms it is foundational to a proper understanding of early Christianity. While some literature in the Second Temple period treats the exile in neutral terms, referring to it only as a past event (e.g., Jdt 4:3; 5:18), the majority of passages that make reference to the exile do so in far from neutral ways. Indeed, Peter Ackroyd, in his seminal study *Exile and Restoration,* makes a clear case for the importance of the *idea* of exile in the writings of the Hebrew Bible and for how exile became the predominant point of view for Hebrew authors of the postexilic period as well.[3] Michael Knibb follows Ackroyd

---

[2]N. T. Wright, *The New Testament and the People of God* (Minneapolis: Fortress, 1989), p. 243.
[3]Peter Ackroyd, *Exile and Restoration* (London: SCM Press, 1968), pp. 237-47. I use the term

in exploring this thesis.[4] Starting in the canonical book of Jeremiah and the prophet's assertion that the exile would last seventy years (Jer 25:11-14; 29:10-14), Knibb investigates the way in which these passages became paradigmatic for the Israelite understanding of exile. Of special note is not the predicted length of time but the widespread use of these passages in other Old Testament literature (allusions are found in Zech 1:12; 2 Chron 36:21; Ezra 1:1) and subsequent writings (1 Esdr 1:57-58 and Josephus, *Antiquities of the Jews* 11:1,1), indicating that Jeremiah's theological perspective of an exile that would last for an extended period of time was also shared by other writers. While some clearly understood exile as a specific historical period that lasted only a few decades and had a particular beginning and ending, a second view understood the exile as an ongoing condition that includes the present time and extends to the final judgment.[5] It was the latter that shaped the experience and literature of the period most profoundly.

Highly representative of the exilic view in intertestamental literature is the vision of animals in 1 Enoch 85–90 (late second to early first century B.C.E). Because Enoch was believed to have been caught up into the celestial realms (Gen 5:24), he functioned as the perfect informant on cosmic matters. Various writers used him as a mediator for esoteric knowledge and thus legitimated certain Jewish views on celestial things, including divine decrees that related to Israel.[6] The vision of animals traces key historical epochs in Israel's history from Adam and Eve until the Maccabean revolt in 160 B.C.E. by employing animal imagery to depict Israel and its various enemies.[7] The story is not a simple retelling

---

postexilic here because it is the term employed by Ackroyd (and many other scholars) to describe this period.

[4]Michael A. Knibb, "The Exile in the Literature of the Intertestamental Period," *Heythrop Journal* 17 (1976): 253-79.

[5]James Vanderkam, "Exile in Jewish Apocalyptic Literature," in *Exile: Old Testament, Jewish and Christian Perspectives,* ed. James Scott (Leiden: Brill, 1997), p. 91. Vanderkam helpfully catalogues the various ways that exile was employed in Jewish apocalyptic literature of the Second Temple period.

[6]Larry R. Helyer, *Exploring Jewish Literature of the Second Temple Period* (Downers Grove, IL: InterVarsity Press, 2002), p. 77.

[7]Knibb briefly explores the commonality of such analogies in the Old Testament literature; see "Exile in the Literature of the Intertestamental Period," p. 256.

of the biblical account but rather a carefully crafted literary work that ultimately goes beyond the writer's time period to paint a picture of a coming judgment and the time of redemption in the age to come.

In the particular use of this analogy in 1 Enoch, the writer chooses a familiar biblical image, that of a flock of sheep, to symbolize the people of Israel. The flock is owned by the lord of the sheep (God) but in the second half of the vision is ruled poorly by seventy shepherds. Israel's enemies are represented by a variety of animals and birds, all of which are depicted as predators. There are periods of both harmony and disharmony in the relationship between the owner of the sheep and his flock. The author states that though various prophets made appeals to the flock for greater levels of obedience, their voices were ignored. Thus at a decisive moment, depicted in 1 Enoch 89:56, the lord of the sheep abandons their house and leaves them to the lions and other violent creatures. The text specifically says, "I saw how he left that house of theirs and that tower of theirs and cast all of them into the hands of lions— (even) into the hands of all the wild beasts—so that they may tear them into pieces and eat them."[8]

At this point seventy shepherds enter and rule the flock for successive periods of time, often in less than faithful ways. Conditions worsen as groups of ravenous birds and dogs set on the flock and leave only a few survivors and bare bones (1 En. 90:2-4). Shortly after this, an apparent turning point occurs. Enoch reports that some lambs were born to "white sheep" from within the flock, and as they open their eyes they call out to the other sheep (1 En. 90:6). This group, which appears to represent a reform movement, meets with little success, as the majority of the sheep pay scant attention to the cries, their eyes remaining "extremely blind" (1 En. 90:8). Shortly thereafter, God acts in judgment:

> Then those seventy shepherds were judged and found guilty; and they were
> cast into that fiery abyss. In the meantime I saw another abyss like it, full of
> fire, was opened wide in the middle of the ground; and they brought those

[8]James Charlesworth, trans., *The Old Testament Pseudepigrapha*, vol. 2 (New York: Doubleday, 1985). All quotations from 1 Enoch are from Charlesworth's translation unless otherwise specified.

blinded sheep all of which were judged, found guilty and cast into this fiery abyss. (1 En. 90:25-26)

After this a glorious new age begins:

> I went on seeing until the Lord of the sheep brought a new house, greater and loftier than the first one, and set it up in the first location which had been covered up—all its pillars were new, the columns new, and the ornaments new as well and greater than those of the first (that) is the old (house) which was gone. All the sheep were within it. (1 En. 90:29)

What seems to be clear from the vision of the animals is that the conditions of exile persist even after the "return." The people are only depicted as secure and at home after the decisive judgment of God. While the word *exile* is not explicitly used in this highly symbolic narrative, the language of dispersion is used and continues to be used even after the historical exile comes to an end in the story (see, e.g., 1 En. 89:75). For the author, exile was an ongoing condition whose end would only come with the final judgment.[9]

First Enoch further demonstrates this perspective in a section known as the Apocalypse of Weeks (1 En. 91:12-19; 93), which, like the vision of animals, divides biblical history into units of time, here weeks. The sixth week includes the historical exile, while the seventh depicts the time in which the author lives. The eighth week begins a series of final judgments (1 En. 91:12-19), which lead to the culmination of history and to Israel's release from exile. In no place prior to this is return from exile ever mentioned. Thus the clear implication is that the author did not see his own situation of exile—extending from the fall of Jerusalem up until his own day in the early to mid-second century B.C.E.—as having come to an end. Indeed, exile is not destined to end until the coming of a final judgment.[10]

First Enoch is certainly not the only work of religious literature to reflect this perspective. Similar ideas about the ongoing nature of exile

---

[9]Vanderkam, "Exile in Jewish Apocalyptic Literature," p. 100. Also see Knibb, "Exile in the Literature of the Intertestamental Period," p. 256.

[10]Vanderkam, "Exile in Jewish Apocalyptic Literature," p. 96.

are seen in works such as Tobit, *Jubilees*, Baruch and the *Testaments of the Twelve Patriarchs*. This is hardly an exhaustive list of intertestamental books that offer this viewpoint of exile to its readers; many others that reiterate this vision of life for Second Temple Jews could be cited.[11]

This discussion is not to assume that our contemporary experience of exile is the same as that of Second Temple Jews in either its theological or its sociological contours. It is simply to help us understand that an exilic identity has helped to fuel the existence of God's people throughout many epochs of their history. In every case, certain theological themes emerged that shaped and sustained them. While it would be incorrect to assume that Second Temple Jews all agreed on what those themes were, a certain commonality of practice and outlook emerged and reflected key theological distinctives within the Jewish community.[12] This vision continued the Old Testament practice of reformulating the faith for new contexts and aided the Jewish community in its understanding of itself as a people.

Israel continued to adapt its beliefs and practices to the realities of living "in exile." The theological developments that emerged reflect its ongoing attempt to establish its distinct identity and understand the person and work of its God in the context of its exilic experience. Five key developments are worth noting here.

First, Jews of the Second Temple period responded to "exile" by formalizing a canon of sacred Scripture, a group of documents understood as authoritative guides for Israel's life as a distinct people. These documents became the nation's story and plumb line for distinctive Jewish identity. Second, the synagogue developed as a place of community life and worship. This was in response to the practical reality that the people were dispersed throughout the world and that access to Jerusalem was limited for many, but it was also in response to the theological devel-

---

[11]For an overview see Knibb, "The Exile in the Literature of the Intertestamental Period." Also see Craig Evans, "Aspects of Exile and Restoration in the Proclamation of Jesus," in *Exile: Old Testament, Jewish and Christian Perspectives*, pp. 299-328.

[12]How uniform this theology was is a disputed point within scholarly dialogue. A case for what he calls "normal" or "common" Judaism in this period is made by E. P. Sanders in *Judaism: Practice and Belief* (London: SCM Press, 1992), especially pp. 47-76.

opment that God could be worshiped on foreign soil as much as on the soil of the land of Israel itself. Exile had aided in developing a theology that no longer saw the same need for a single, central temple as a place for national worship. Third, a particular type of sacred literature, the apocalyptic genre, emerged. Ultimately the emphasis in apocalyptic literature is on God's victory over the forces of evil in both their historical and cosmic manifestation. The experience of exile provided an impetus to this genre of literature, as exile caused the Jewish community to consider that perhaps its only way out of its circumstances was through the dramatic and decisive intervention of God at the end of history. Fourth, the hope for a messiah or messiahs took root as people began to put their hope in the idea of an "anointed" leader who would come from God as a deliverer to the people of Israel. Fifth, in keeping with the development of apocalyptic themes, speculations about resurrection and the afterlife began to take root in the thought of the day. While Greek (and before that Persian) culture and religious ideas had some influence on the theological development of Judaism in the Second Temple period, the idea of resurrection took on unique contours for the Jews. This, along with the increase in apocalyptic literature, was a direct response to living in exile for such an extended period. Hope of restoration increasingly was transferred from this world to the life to come. These themes all emerged in the thinking of Second Temple Jews and had a shaping effect on the thinking and religious practice of many of the people of that time.

These theological developments were central to Judaism's struggle for identity throughout the Second Temple period. While disparate in many respects, they reflect a striving for an identity that would anchor the people to their past and help them function as God's people under Persian (and then Roman) rule. These ideas reflect the core conviction that Israel was bound by a theological and religious identity. Thus Scripture was central to the work of forming a distinctly Jewish identity. New and evolving trends helped inform the community as it struggled with its identity and shaped the direction it would take in the years to come. The emergence of apocalypticism, belief in life after death, and resurrection all placed the return from exile beyond the present age. These were understandable responses to exile given that the exile showed no signs of ending and that having autonomy restored seemed a remote hope.

What is most important to note from this overview of the Second Temple period is how Israel continued to develop theological and social approaches to living in exile. The faith of the nation continued to be a sustaining center for the people, and it demanded reinterpretation in changing circumstances. While the categories did change, the people of the Second Temple period attempted to understand their God and his working in their circumstances in the same way that their ancestors had done in earlier days of exile. In this way they continued the work and the model of living as God's people in exile.

As exile continued under Roman rule, a new movement emerged within Judaism that encompassed, in distinct ways, all of these emerging streams within Second Temple theological thought. This new movement would eventually be called Christianity.

Indeed, it would seem that Jesus' own self-conscious Jewish identity, which was at the heart of his ministry, would lead to an understanding that exile was one of the motifs that guided his work. Furthermore, in the embryonic stages of its development, the church also continued to understand itself as an exilic people, as its early documents indicate. Gaining an understanding of how the early church's identity and ministry were shaped by the idea of exile will aid the church today in its response to the context in which it finds itself.

EXILE AND THE MINISTRY OF JESUS

Exile played a distinct role in the ministry of Jesus. He is foremost a model of exile insofar as he is depicted as one who is away from his true home (Jn 1:1-14; Phil 2:3-8). Furthermore, we can identify ways in which Jesus' ministry contains exilic overtones. Two scholars who have given much thought to this are N. T. Wright and Craig Evans.[13] Their writing offers a lucid argument that Jesus, as he is depicted in the Gospels, saw

---

[13]Wright deals with this theme extensively throughout his *The New Testament and the People of God*, and in *Jesus and the Victory of God* (Minneapolis: Fortress, 1996). This is also the focus of Evans's "Aspects of Exile."

himself as entering into an exilic situation and acting as the beginning of the end of his nation's exile, although not necessarily in the way that most of his fellow Jews would have expected.

Evans offers six categories from Jesus' teaching and activity that reveal that exilic theology played an important role in his ministry.[14] The single most important of these is his appointment of the twelve. Evans notes, "It is probable that Jesus' appointment of the twelve was intended to symbolize the reconstitution of the twelve tribes of Israel."[15] This view is echoed by E. P. Sanders, who also sees the twelve as a symbol of "restoration."[16] Thus the implication of appointing twelve disciples is that they will act as heads of the scattered-but-soon-to-be-gathered tribes of Israel. This view is strengthened by Jesus' own teaching that the twelve will sit on thrones and judge the twelve tribes of Israel (Mt 19:28; Lk 22:30). The disciples are depicted here as having been chosen to provide just leadership to the nation. This coheres with a motif of restoration from exile being implicit in Jesus' choice of the twelve.[17]

Evans concludes his study by noting that the emphasis Jesus places on the books of Daniel, Zechariah and Second Isaiah (all three of which reflect periods of exilic life in Israel's history) strongly suggests that "Jesus identified himself and his mission with an oppressed Israel in need of redemption and that he himself was the agent of redemption."[18] Jesus understood that his message and ministry were connected to Israel's exile and were influenced by a vision that he had come to represent the beginning of the end of Israel's exile.

Particularly in *Jesus and the Victory of God,* N. T. Wright asserts that Israel at the dawn of the first century C.E. understood itself to be in exile. Wright looks particularly at Jesus' proclamation of the kingdom of God in his teaching and various aspects of Jesus' ministry that define his work as a response to exile and a harbinger of restoration. While Wright dis-

---

[14]For a complete overview of these categories see Evans, "Aspects of Exile," pp. 316-28.

[15]Ibid., p. 318.

[16]E. P. Sanders, *Jesus and Judaism* (London: SCM Press, 1985), p. 98.

[17]Evans, "Aspects of Exile," p. 318. Wright agrees with this perspective and offers it in his own project; see *Jesus and the Victory of God*, pp. 430-31.

[18]Evans, "Aspects of Exile," p. 328.

cusses these in great detail, he summarizes how Jesus' ministry enacted
them when he writes:

> Healing, forgiveness, renewal, the twelve, the new family and its new defining
> characteristics, open commensality, the promise of blessing for the Gentiles,
> feasts replacing fasts, the destruction and rebuilding of the Temple: all de-
> clared, in the powerful language of symbol, that Israel's exile was over, and
> that Jesus was himself in some way responsible for this new state of affairs,
> and that all that the Temple had stood for was now available through Jesus
> and his movement.[19]

These were the foundations of Jesus' proclamation of the kingdom of God.
For Jesus exile would be overcome by the breaking in of God's kingdom,
and Jesus understood his ministry as the beginning of this transition.

While it is true that Jesus is never portrayed as using the term *exile*
by any of the Gospel writers, this does not mean that the motif is an
illegitimate one to apply to him. Scot McKnight contends that
"kingdom language is 'end of exile' language; 'end of exile' is the negative to the positive 'kingdom.'"[20]

It may be stated that Jesus' role as Messiah ultimately secures the
promise of a return from exile for Israel, even if that return is not complete in this life.[21] Because the early church was a marginalized people
not yet in complete possession of the promised inheritance, the theme
of exile in Jesus' life and ministry resonated with them as a motif that
helped to define their identity living in the light of both Jesus' death and

---

[19]Wright, *Jesus and the Victory of God*, p. 436.

[20]Scot McKnight, *A New Vision for Israel: The Teachings of Jesus in National Context* (Grand Rapids:
Eerdmans, 1999), p. 83n51.

[21]Wright, *Jesus and the Victory of God*, pp. 218-19. Some scholars see Wright's emphasis on exile
as an overemphasis. For a constructive but critical engagement see Klyne R. Snodgrass, "Reading and Over-Reading the Parables in *Jesus and the Victory of God*," in *Jesus and the Restoration
of Israel: A Critical Assessment of N. T. Wright's* Jesus and the Victory of God, ed. Carey Newman
(Downers Grove, IL: InterVarsity Press, 1999), pp. 61-76. For another perspective, sympathetic
to Wright's but original in its approach, see Douglas S. McComiskey, "Exile and the Purpose of
Jesus' Parables," *Journal of the Evangelical Theological Society* 51, no. 1 (2008): 59-85. Also Brant
Pitre, *Jesus, the Tribulation, and the End of Exile: Restoration Eschatology and the Origin of the
Atonement* (Tübingen: Mohr Siebeck, 2005), engages Wright's perspective, often critically. Ultimately this idea is only an adjunct to the work of this study, since the relevance of the exilic motif
for the contemporary church, while it may be helped by Wright's work, does not hinge on his
particular theological position.

his resurrection. As the contemporary church also faces the reality of marginalization but also the hope of eschatological restoration, the theme of exile can once again offer it a way to understand itself as it seeks to engage the world from the fringes of its context and continue its journey as God's people in a place that is not fully home.

EXILE IN THE EPISTLES

The motif of exile continues both explicitly and implicitly in the New Testament beyond the ministry of Jesus. The first church understood that the spiritual consequences of exile had ended and that the people were now citizens of a new kingdom ultimately not located in a particular earthly place. This meant that while they may not have experienced exile from "the land" they were still experiencing a distinct sense of displacement. For many early believers, their place in society changed as a result of their embrace of Christianity. Some were marginalized; others who were already marginalized found their lot in life worsened; persecution ensued for others. As a result, exile continued to be a fruitful motif for the church's self-identification.

James. James and 1 Peter both explicitly utilize the motif of exile as a way to address their audiences. In James 1:1, the author writes to the "twelve tribes in the Dispersion" (NRSV). While there is debate over exactly how this phrase should be understood, it leaves little doubt that in the early church believers were still operating out of a view that they were living away from home.[22]

At first glance the phrase "twelve tribes in the Dispersion" appears to be a reference to Jewish people who are still living away from the land of Israel. However, this phrase had begun to take on a new meaning in certain theological streams of the Second Temple period, and it came to designate the true people of God in the last days, whether Jew or Gentile, as early Christians came to understand that God's eschatological people

---

[22]For concise but representative discussions see Pheme Perkins, *First and Second Peter, James and Jude* (Louisville, KY: John Knox, 1995), pp. 85-86. Also see Douglas J. Moo, *The Letter of James* (Grand Rapids: Eerdmans, 2000), pp. 23-24.

included people from all nations.[23] The point is clear, regardless of to
whom the term is applied—that the authors of these epistles saw their
audiences as continuing to live in a state of exile.

For James it is likely that the term is used to describe Jews living
outside the confines of Israel. This is possible because of the highly
Jewish character and probable early date of the epistle.[24] His reference
to his audience as belonging to the twelve tribes of Israel (Jas 1:1) hints
that the nation is experiencing a restoration, albeit ultimately an eschatological one, in line with what we have already considered regarding the
ministry of Jesus and his choosing of the twelve as a sign of his reconsti-
tuting of the new Israel.[25] James's use of the descriptor, which in its
context likely has high ethnic (Jewish) connotations, recognizes that all
those who were once exiled from their homeland are still not at home
even as they continue their journey as those who are now followers of
Christ and members of the church.[26] However, the point that the author
continues to see exile as an appropriate picture for his audience should
not be lost, even in light of the fact that they are recipients of Christ's
liberating work.

1 Peter. The epistle of 1 Peter, which we will explore in depth in the
next chapter, is clearly addressed to "exiles" (1 Pet 1:1). On the surface,
this seems to cohere with James's vision of the church in its first-century
setting. However, Peter's audience is likely a collection of both Gentiles
and Jews, as 1 Peter 1:4, 18; 2:9-10, 25; 3:6; 4:3-4 show.[27] Despite the fact
that Peter is known as the apostle with the mission to the Jews (Gal 2:6-
10), it seems that he has a mixed church. Furthermore, it seems that what
he has in view here is that those who have aligned themselves with the
person and mission of Jesus are now a part of the true people of God and
are thus properly understood as exiles among the nations. This is a re-

---

[23]Moo, pp. 23-24.
[24]Ibid., p. 50. See also Andrew Chester and Ralph P. Martin, *New Testament Theology: The
Theology of the Letters of James, Peter and Jude* (Cambridge: Cambridge University Press, 1994),
pp. 11-15.
[25]Wright, *Jesus and the Victory of God*, p. 330.
[26]Richard Bauckham, *James* (London: Routledge, 1999), pp. 25-28.
[27]Peter Davids, *The First Epistle of Peter* (Grand Rapids: Eerdmans, 1990), p. 8.

minder of the now-but-not-yet quality of their deliverance as a result of
Jesus' work. On the one hand they are participants in the deliverance that
Jesus provided from exile through his death and resurrection and are
thus included in the people of God. Yet, on the other, they are now a part
of a people who sojourn in a world ultimately not their home while
awaiting a final deliverance to come in the eschaton. In this epistle the
author transfers some of the titles of Israel to the church: "chosen people,"
"royal priesthood" and "holy nation" (1 Pet 2:9). This places the church
solidly in the plot line of Scripture; in fact, 1 Peter 2:4-9 contains a clear
allusion to Exodus 19:6, in which Israel is declared to be "a kingdom of
priests and a holy nation." Thus the church is aligned with and of the
same nature as Israel in that it has a special bond with God, who has
acted to rescue it and has entered into covenant with it just as he did with
Israel.[28] It is thus not surprising that the author of 1 Peter would also
transfer to the church the perspective that had defined Israel as a people
for so long—that of exiles.

Beyond the reference in 1 Peter 1:1, Peter calls his audience "foreigners"
in 1 Peter 1:17 and "foreigners and exiles" in 1 Peter 2:11. As Joel Green
states, "In varying ways each of these descriptions points to an essential
characteristic of Peter's audience: they are not at home."[29] This does not
mean that they are physically away from their home soil; instead it means
that as members of God's people they now participate in the socio-
theological reality of the exile. As followers of Jesus, they are not fully at
home in this world and are indeed living away from their ultimate eschatological home (cf. 1 Pet 1:4-5; 4:13; 5:4). This use of exilic terminology
demonstrates how the early church continued to see itself as living in exile.

Hebrews. The author of the letter to the Hebrews reflects the reality of
the early church's experience as an eschatological community when he
acknowledges that while God has subjected all things to his angels, "at
the present we do not see everything subject to them [or him]" (Heb 2:8).
Furthermore, he reminds his readers that, although Joshua led Israel into
the Promised Land, this was not the ultimate place of rest for God's

---

[28]Joel Green, *1 Peter* (Grand Rapids: Eerdmans, 2007), pp. 55, 62.
[29]Ibid., p. 195.

people. A Sabbath rest still awaits the people of God, including those
under God's new covenant (Heb 4:8-9). F. F. Bruce comments that the
recipients of the letter were obviously not currently experiencing this
rest. However, it does belong to them as a heritage, and "by faith they
may live in the good of it here and now."[30] This was the experience of the
early (and contemporary) church; many of the promises that were part
of Jesus' delivering work carried a future hope of ultimate fulfillment
mingled with a current glimpse of what that future may look and feel like.
The church would be where the liberty of release from exile could be
anticipated through Christ's work as savior in embryonic form by life
together as a believing community. However, functionally, the church
continued to live as a people away from home.

Other epistles. The view that the church was a people in exile is apparent (if not explicitly at least implicitly) within other New Testament
epistles through their emphasis on the church living counter to the
culture in which it is immersed. An emphasis in many of the epistles is
to help the church or churches that receive the letter to forge a distinctly
different Christian identity against their context within the Roman
Empire (Col 3:1-17; Eph 4:17–5:20). To fit in with the Roman Empire
meant participating in the imperial cult and other forms of civic worship
that from a Christian or Jewish perspective would be nothing less than
idolatry.[31] Green notes how Christians living in the Roman Empire
could easily have felt like exiles, and maintaining a separate Christian
identity was of paramount concern to church leaders. Just as Israel
needed its religious literature to help define itself as a distinct people in
exile, the literature of the church helped it forge an identity within a
sociologically foreign context, as Green makes clear.[32]

Clearly the epistles of the New Testament are concerned with the
question of how to cultivate and maintain a distinctive Christian
identity separate from the ethos of the Roman Empire. In this way
they are a continuation of exilic theology, which saw itself against a

---

[30]F. F. Bruce, *The Epistle to the Hebrews*, rev. ed. (Grand Rapids: Eerdmans, 1990), p. 110.
[31]Green, *1 Peter*, p. 194.
[32]Ibid., p. 197.

larger and more powerful empire and thus had to figure out ways to express itself in this context. Thus, for example, in the view of Brian Walsh and Sylvia Keesmaat, Colossians is designed to lead Christians to faithful living as exiles against the backdrop of an invasive Roman Empire. Colossians is one example of how the New Testament reflects a call to Jesus' followers to see themselves as not at home in the empire but as exiles.[33]

Such a perspective can be discerned throughout the New Testament documents, in which the writers help the church to understand its distinct identity and the implications of that identity. In general terms the New Testament authors, not unlike the authors of the Old Testament and Second Temple literature, do the work necessary for a people in exile by helping them understand themselves as God's people in conditions that are tolerant at best and hostile at worst. In sum, the church is called to reenact the life and ministry of Jesus and participate in the inbreaking of God's kingdom. Indeed, the remedy to exile, the kingdom of God, is an emerging, ongoing experience. It reflects the eschatological reality of being both now and not yet. For while the end of exile has begun and is surely coming, exile continues to be the lived experience of the church even after Jesus has departed.

Summary

Does this ancient teaching still have meaning for us today? Do the ways in which Second Temple Jews and early Christians share in the motif of exile have any implications for our experience as Christians in the twenty-first century? Furthermore, how does this shared identity connect with us in the Western church today? There are at least three links. First, all share a sense of social or political marginalization: of being dominated by powers that compete with the just reign of the one true God. In each of these three contexts, while unique in their details, there is a shared sense that in each era the people of God have found themselves on the margins in a society that largely does not share their worldview

---

[33]Brian J. Walsh and Sylvia Keesmaat, *Colossians Remixed: Subverting the Empire* (Downers Grove, IL: InterVarsity Press, 2004), p. 95.

or core theological beliefs. Second, all share a sense of eschatological hope, acknowledging that the return from exile will not quickly be completed in this present life. And, finally, all have a lively (sometimes, perhaps in the case of Second Temple Jews and early Christians, even competing) sense of themselves as the true people of God, those through whom God is even now working out his purpose in the world.

This is why the New Testament deals with the practice and self-identification of the church. As a body it is not at home but must continue to determine how to live as a minority people under the shadow of a more powerful ruling empire/hegemony. This is an ongoing experience for the church and one that resonates with Western Christians in the twenty-first century.

As we have already briefly considered, a significant voice that informs this experience and will play a central role in the rest of this book is the epistle of 1 Peter. First Peter is offered as a template for contemporary exilic thinking primarily because it is a self-consciously exilic letter. The author is clearly interested in helping his audience engage its culture as those who live on the margins of it. As we will see, 1 Peter reflects an exilic theology that fits well with themes that emerge from the exilic theology of the Old Testament and Second Temple literature, but it also applies themes such as holiness, mission and eschatology to the experience of its first-century audience. We will also begin to see how 1 Peter is a suggestive guide for contemporary application in today's post-Christian society, too, because the author demonstrates how exilic theology can continue to be utilized in new contexts.

7

The Exilic Wisdom
of 1 Peter

The old adage that those who do not learn from history are doomed to repeat it was not lost on the author of 1 Peter. He is not shy about employing ancient wisdom for the challenges of his contemporary context. The author is clearly concerned with helping the churches to which he is writing to live as "exiles and aliens" as faithfully as possible, and to do this he draws from wisdom that correlates directly to the exilic theology of his ancestors. The theological insight and its practical application that served Israel through its Babylonian and Persian captivities, as well as the developing perspectives from later Second Temple Judaism, became the basis for the exilic strategy Peter delivers to his first-century readers. First Peter offers several perspectives that will help its readers navigate the challenges they face as God's people in their particular contexts. A close look at these themes will also yield some highly suggestive insights and offer guiding wisdom to those seeking to build God's kingdom from the margins of twenty-first-century Western culture as well.

CREATIVE THEOLOGICAL REFLECTION

First Peter follows in the tradition of the Old Testament and Second Temple authors who were thoroughly engaged in the task of interpreting the faith for their particular epoch. This work of interpretation was a necessary task in every instance, as the changing context demanded a new understanding of how the faith should be practiced and in some cases also what it now meant. The issue of interpreting their faith was a significant one for the Jewish members of 1 Peter's audience since they were now interpreting the Old Testament and their new religious experience through a christological lens. For Peter, who consciously understood his audience as in exile, reinterpreting former ways of understanding was part of what would sustain the community in its exilic life.

It is telling that there are eleven specific Old Testament references in 1 Peter and several other potential allusions to Old Testament texts. This is a significant number in comparison with other New Testament epistles of similar length.[1] This demonstrates the author's interest in working with the traditions out of which the church was born. Thus 1 Peter presents us with a template for the ongoing work of creative theological reflection, which the current church in exile must engage in if it is to properly practice and understand the faith with which it has been entrusted. It must remain moored to the traditions of its birth but not be afraid to reinterpret them in light of the new contexts in which we find ourselves. This activity must always be done with a certain amount of care, but it is an activity that defines exilic existence for God's people and, for that reason, is necessary. We can see several places in 1 Peter where its author is clearly engaging in fresh thinking about the faith of his church. The following examples are not meant to be prescriptive for contemporary circumstances, as we have our own issues that need to be addressed; rather, these are illustrative of how 1 Peter engages his culture theologically.

The church and Israel. In 1 Peter 1:10-12 Peter makes it clear that Scripture must be read christologically when he writes that the prophets were ultimately pointing to Christ and the time of the church when they wrote about the sufferings of Christ long ago. Having established this perspective, Peter then demonstrates how such a reading informs the identity of the church, namely, that the church is directly in the plot line of Scripture and that the Holy Spirit guided the prophets and the for-

---

[1]For instance, in Ephesians there are four, in Philippians one, in Colossians and 1 John one. Of the shorter epistles only Galatians surpasses 1 Peter with fourteen.

mation of the church. This is confirmed in 1 Peter 2:4-10 when Peter identifies Jesus ("the living Stone") as specially chosen by God as the foundation of the church who "also, like living stones" (1 Pet 2:5) are "being built into a spiritual house." In this sense 1 Peter sees the church as the people through whom God has chosen to specially work in this particular time. The church is the "spiritual house" in the line of Israel of old. Peter's vision of the biblical story thus consists of three movements: Israel, Jesus, church. The church is now the place/people in which God's work is being done most specifically as it continues the legacy of Israel and Christ.

In 1 Peter 2:9 Peter employs language that is intentionally reminiscent of Exodus 19, where God reestablishes Israel as his particular people. There God declares to Israel, "Out of all nations you will be my treasured possession. . . . You will be for me a kingdom of priests and a holy nation" (Ex 19:5-6). In 1 Peter 2:9 the writer declares the church to be "a chosen people . . . a holy nation, God's special possession." The church is of the same nature as Israel; it receives God's affection and demonstrates his purposes in the same way that Israel did/does. Furthermore, the paradoxical description of his audience as chosen and exiled (1 Pet 1:1) offers a strong linkage between the church, Israel and Jesus, for this seeming dichotomy of being chosen and yet exiled recurs in the stories of all three. As Joel Green notes: "This is the story of Israel. This is the story of Jesus. And, we now discover, this is the ongoing story of God's people."[2] Peter's theological construction of the church as a continuation of Israel is not unique to this author; it was an integral part of the theological reflection that was taking place throughout the early church (Eph 2:21-22; 1 Cor 3:16; Jn 20:21-23). However, just because it is not original to 1 Peter does not lessen the importance of our recognizing that Peter is making a bold theological move that caused a great deal of controversy in the early church (see Acts 10–11; 15). Yet this radical act of theological innovation gave the church an identity legitimately rooted in God's ongoing story of

---

[2]Joel Green, "Living as Exiles: The Church in the Diaspora in 1 Peter," in *Holiness and Ecclesiology in the New Testament*, ed. Kent E. Brower and Andy Johnson (Grand Rapids: Eerdmans, 2007), p. 317.

activity in the world. Furthermore, it implied to its audience that by looking back to its ancestry the church could move forward in its participation in the ongoing work of God in the world. A significant part of that story was of exile, and the church's experience of exile gave it a common bond with its spiritual ancestors. This link was something it could draw on for its own journey through exilic circumstances.

Establishing a separate ecclesiastical identity. As we have seen in previous chapters, the authors of the Old Testament worked with characters and events in Israel's past, infusing them with meaning by placing them against the backdrop of a foreign empire and demonstrating the protagonists' heroism and piety by juxtaposing them with the mores of the pagan culture in which they found themselves. Their success as Jews in a foreign land was intended to have an identity-shaping effect on the recipients of their story. Peter follows suit by seeking to establish the identity of his church on distinctly non-Roman terms and by casting a vision for his audience of faithfulness to Christ as always more important than following the behavior of cultural hosts.

The worldview of the Roman Empire dominated first-century culture. It was propagated by Rome's armies and inculcated through its religion. The basic contours of Roman ideology offered that the Roman Empire was the peak of civilization and offered salvation to the world, with Caesar as the actual savior of the world. Caesar had been appointed ruler by the gods and thus deserved to be worshiped at least as a son of a god if not a god. This vision was the glue that held the empire together. Giving honor to Caesar was part of the thread that began by honoring the gods, then the emperor, then the elite, eventually to the lowest echelons of society.[3]

Against this view Peter's audience is encouraged not to identify themselves with Rome but with Christ, and even further back with Israel. They are not citizens of Rome but citizens of the kingdom who are called to present themselves as an alternative society. In fact they are exiles and foreigners in the world (1 Pet 2:11) and so have a very different approach

---

[3]Ibid., p. 285.

to life in the empire. Their identity is shaped by rejecting the ways of the empire, which at one time were the ways they adopted for themselves (1 Pet 4:3-4), and embracing being in Christ (1 Pet 4:1-2). This is in no way intended to segregate Christians from the world any more than Daniel or Esther segregated themselves from the empires of their day, or how Jonah reminds us that segregation is not God's ideal at all. Instead it is to draw firm boundaries between what it means to live centered in Christ versus affiliated with Rome.

Furthermore, Peter seeks to nurture in his audience a view that faithful living according to God's principles will lead to "success." He posits that if they live good lives before pagans, the pagans will ultimately recognize their good deeds and glorify God (1 Pet 2:12), unbelieving husbands will come to faith (1 Pet 3:1-2), and those who speak maliciously against their good behavior will be ashamed of their slander (1 Pet 3:16). This is exilic advice affirming that as the church establishes its identity and faithfully lives out God's intentions it will ultimately win out over pagan practices. This bold assertion offers a creative revisioning of ancient theological perspectives for Peter's contemporary audience and echoes the wisdom of Daniel and Esther, who acted faithfully and were rewarded for their behavior.

Marriage. Another concrete area of life with which Peter engages is the marriage relationship. Here Peter works subversively with a foundational institution of Roman society in order to demonstrate how the Christian gospel affects traditional understandings and demands a fresh interpretation within the context in which his church found itself.

Peter's instruction on marriage is set in the context of his section on the household code and the epistle's overall call for submission in human relationships. For Peter, self-subordination is an act of obedience to God, holiness and witness. It is also a "free" expression offered volitionally in response to Christ (1 Pet 2:16-17). Thus a wife's submission to her husband, while certainly culturally conditioned, is a proper act of Christian belief in the human relationship of marriage (the phrase "in the same way" [1 Pet 3:1] serves as a transitional clause). However, from here Peter gently subverts the traditional view of marriage in a number of ways.

First, in the Roman world the husband's religion was the household religion, and a wife was to adopt that religion if it was different from that of the home from which she came.[4] Contrary to this, Peter certainly does not encourage wives to follow their husbands' religions; it is clearly implied that wives will remain and live as Christians before their unbelieving husbands. This is a clear encouragement to independence, with the further encouragement that through their free act of submission they may even be able to win their husbands to Christianity. This makes their submission a highly subversive act that has the potential for a wife to lead a husband in religious choice rather than the other way around.[5] To put an even finer point on it, Peter, once again using the transitional clause "in the same way," calls husbands to treat their wives with consideration and respect and as coheirs in the "gracious gift of life" (1 Pet 3:7). In the first-century context such honor was typically unidirectional, flowing from those with lower status to those with higher status. Given this reality, the call for a husband to honor his wife would have struck a countercultural chord. Such behavior on the part of a husband toward his wife would have questioned the status systems that were assumed and defended in first-century Greco-Roman culture.[6] Even further, the author states that for husbands to neglect this kind of behavior is to run the risk of their prayers being hindered (1 Pet 3:7). This reflects the overall theology of 1 Peter that the "weak" are those chosen by God. Therefore Christian husbands should be mindful of such an eventuality and treat their wives in the same way that God treats the church.

This is a further example of how Peter seeks to reflect creatively on how the theology of the gospel can function in the Roman society in which his church resides as exiles. Peter's reflections offer us insight into

---

[4]For an overview of first-century views on women and wives see David L. Balch, *Let Wives Be Submissive: The Domestic Code in 1 Peter* (Chico, CA: Scholars Press, 1981), pp. 95-109, and Jeannine K. Brown, "Silent Wives, Verbal Believers: Ethical and Hermeneutical Considerations in 1 Peter 3:1-6 and Its Context," *Word and World* 24, no. 4 (2004): 399-401.

[5]Both Brown, "Silent Wives," p. 400, and Balch, *Let Wives Be Submissive*, p. 109, surmise that it is quite likely that believing wives may have been facing coercion and even persecution from their unbelieving husbands. Brown writes, "The reassurance not to be alarmed by such intimidation, coupled with the missional thrust of the wives' submission, would have provided a subversive element to the otherwise traditional contours to this part of the household code"; "Silent Wives," p. 400.

[6]Brown, "Silent Wives," pp. 400-401.

how the church constantly must be doing this kind of work and employing a progressive hermeneutic that allows the tenets of the gospel to find fresh ways of expression. This means that we approach Scripture not as a series of facts that only need to be applied correctly, with as little flexibility as possible so as not to violate the "true meaning" of the text. Rather, we must see that the text of Scripture can be read differently in different contexts, and that the spirit of the text has human transformation and not just information as an ultimate goal.

In our current context this means that, while traditional understandings of Scripture remain vital to the ongoing life of the church, they cannot remain static. Reading and rereading Scripture with the contemporary context as a conversation partner in the interpretive enterprise is part of our heritage as an exilic people. Creative theological reflection will seek to remain faithfully rooted in historic trajectories of interpretation but will not be bound to specific applications or misapplications of those ideas. The writer of 1 Peter, like ancient Israel before him, embraced the idea that former understandings needed to be reframed in light of evolving circumstances. This is a mark of exilic wisdom for God's people in any era.

HOLINESS

Just as holiness became a central response for Israel to its exile, in the same way it plays a central role in Peter's letter. As with ancient Israel, holiness is an identity issue for the first-century churches to which Peter writes. Their lives are to be distinct from the broader culture and will define them as those who are attached to Christ.

Holiness in 1 Peter is a call for the church to live out its salvation identity. That is, as those who now are in Christ and are designated as God's chosen people (1 Pet 2:9), the epitome of their human vocation is to be holy as God is holy (1 Pet 1:15-16). This occurs as Peter's audience no longer conforms "to the evil desires you had when you lived in ignorance" (1 Pet 1:14). This is the same call issued to Israel and represents the fundamental calling of God's people in all times to represent him in the world by portraying his otherness to those around them. While this call to holiness includes individual dimensions, its real potency is manifest in its communal expression.[7]

As Joel Green observes, the primary text that Peter seems to have in mind is Leviticus 19, which is a thorough exposition of communal holiness that encompasses a vast array of relational and life settings. One can see in the call to holiness in Leviticus 19 a correlation to Peter's call to be holy in "all you do" (1 Pet 1:15). The chapter in Leviticus covers topics such as family life (Lev 19:3, 32), religious loyalty (Lev 19:3, 4, 8, 12, 26-31), care for the poor (Lev 19:9-10), worker's rights (Lev 19:13), social compassion (Lev 19:14), integrity in justice (Lev 19:15), neighborliness (Lev 19:16-18), sexual integrity (Lev 19:20-22, 29), racial equality (Lev 19:33-34) and business ethics (Lev 19:35-36).[8] God's purpose in the world is not the creation of holy individuals so much as a holy community, a people whose very existence in the world is a testimony to his rule. First Peter implies that this is the foundation for how the church will demonstrate the distinctiveness of its God to its surrounding culture.

Tied directly to this premise is Peter's understanding of the church as a creation of the Holy Spirit and its ongoing life as remaining dependent on the Spirit's work. This is especially true in terms of its development as a holy community. In 1 Peter 1:2 he is clear that the church is formed through the "sanctifying work of the Spirit." Furthermore, the church is formed by the preaching of the gospel, which is empowered by the Holy Spirit (1 Pet 1:12). When Christians are insulted for the name of Christ, he writes, the "Spirit of glory and of God" rests on them (1 Pet 4:14). Thus the Spirit is the agent of church formation, and as its members yield to the Spirit his work in them continues.[9]

Holiness as engagement. The foundational call to be holy as God is holy is all-inclusive. Peter adds the words "in all you do" (1 Pet 1:15) to indicate that the holiness he has in mind is a holiness of engagement with all aspects of life. Peter does not counsel withdrawal from the world, as if holiness cannot stand the pressures of secular life. First Peter positions

---

[7]Green, "Living as Exiles," pp. 322-24.
[8]Joel Green, *1 Peter* (Grand Rapids: Eerdmans, 2007), p. 44.
[9]Green, "Living as Exiles," pp. 320-21.

its overarching call to holiness in 1 Peter 1:15 on the practicality of on-going life choices such as submission to every human authority (1 Pet 2:13), slaves submitting to masters (1 Pet 2:18), wives submitting to husbands (1 Pet 3:1), husbands honoring their wives (1 Pet 3:7), not repaying evil with evil or insult with insult but rather repaying evil with blessing (1 Pet 3:9), offering hospitality to one another (1 Pet 4:9) and elders shepherding the flock (1 Pet 5:2). Each of these ideals assumes that the church will remain engaged with the mainstream of its culture. First Peter's vision is that holiness is to be worked out in the realities of this world.

Holiness as missional. Peter's vision of holiness has an explicitly missional quality to it. In 1 Peter 2:12 the audience is instructed to "live such good lives among the pagans that, though they accuse you of doing wrong, they may see your good deeds and glorify God on the day he visits us." Later he instructs wives to submit to their husbands so that unbelieving husbands will be won over through the quality of their wife's life (1 Pet 3:2). Thus for Peter the call to holiness is an essential part of the church's witness to the gospel and its evangelistic potency in its cultural setting.

Holiness as relational. The relational aspect of Christian holiness is a consistent theme throughout the New Testament and is emphasized in 1 Peter as much as anywhere else. At its core, 1 Peter emphasizes love as the center of relational life (1 Pet 1:22; 3:8; 4:8). Furthermore, 1 Peter 4:7-11 stresses specific behaviors such as hospitality and serving others as reflections of holiness. Each of these is intrinsically linked to relationships within the body of Christ. Also, submission to others is a central aspect of the relational holiness that Peter espouses. As we have seen, Peter provides specific applications of this principle to particular relationships, but ultimately his audience is instructed to submit "to everyone" (1 Pet 2:17). For Peter, holiness is established and demonstrated in human relationships.

Further to this, the key concept that Peter espouses is that holiness is an embodiment of the community's life in Christ and as God's unique people. In this sense holiness is not offered in a way that negatively condemns what is not in keeping with God's intentions; rather, Peter's vision of holiness is positive in that it is offered as an act of identification with Jesus and faithfulness in following his ways (1 Pet 2:21). For Peter, the church is not against the world in that it does not express holiness by reciprocating the world's animosity toward it, and neither does the church demonstrate holiness by condemning the ways of the world with self-righteous living and rhetoric. Instead the church is to be different because it is in relationship with a God who is different, and it is simply trying to stay in step with his ways in the world.

For 1 Peter's audience this was a subversive posture, one that acknowledged the people's lack of power yet offered them a vision that empowered them to see that even their quiet lives of holy living could make a difference. In the post-Christendom church this kind of vision can provide a unique challenge. For many of us, living as those without power is a new experience to which we have not become fully accustomed yet. We are used to having an opinion that represents the majority and a voice that curries influence with those in power. This has changed radically, and learning to function in a way that relinquishes old assumptions about power and influence is difficult. However, this is increasingly the church's reality in the West, and the call to subversive holiness offered by 1 Peter thus becomes increasingly relevant for us.

MISSION

Just as Israel needed to see that despite its exile God was still calling the people to be his witnesses, the recipients of 1 Peter are also invited to see that their social marginalization in no way negates their calling to fulfill the commission Jesus gave to the church to be his witnesses. First Peter offers a template for exilic living as it exhibits a thoroughly missional perspective to its audience in terms of how they are to function as the church in their particular cultural circumstances.

Mission and the identity of the church. In 1 Peter 2:4-10, Peter applies Israel's identity to the church, and with that comes Israel's vocation to mediate the presence and purpose of God. In 1 Peter 2:9 Peter is concerned with the priestly function of the church and equates its chosenness with its vocation as a people chosen to proclaim the praises of God to the dark world out of which they have been called. This vision of the church functioning in a priestly way implies that just as the priests of the sacrificial system acted as mediators who helped the people come to God, so now the church functions in a similar way on behalf of the people outside the church. This vision, as we have seen in earlier sections, is in keeping with the scriptural and exilic identity of God's people. They have been established by God to be a blessing to all nations (Gen 12:3), and their core identity is as a community of peace for the world to see.

First Peter does not present a vision for great social change. Instead, in keeping with the Old Testament writers, it envisions an alternative community that offers a witness to the world through its collective life.[10] First Peter's modest yet powerful approach is epitomized in 1 Peter 2:12 when Peter writes, "Live such good lives among the pagans that, though they accuse you of doing wrong, they may see your good deeds and glorify God on the day he visits us." For Peter the church is not called to overthrow the culture and its norms but instead to subvert them. The church functions as a witness by lives that reflect integrity and righteousness, so that even if it draws derision from some, eventually the people's lives will have an effect that brings even their critics to see God through their actions. This is a work of subversion that does not seek to conquer culture but rather to live differently within it.[11]

Mission through relationships. The missional identity of the church as described in 1 Peter is played out primarily in the context of social relationships characterized by mutual submission. Again, as we have already considered, this specifically includes submission to "every human authority" (1 Pet 2:13), slaves to masters (1 Pet 2:18) and wives to husbands (1 Pet 3:1), but it is also manifest in the tone of other instructions Peter offers to his audience. They are to "show proper respect to everyone"

---

[10]See Torrey Seland, "Resident Aliens in Mission: Missional Practices in the Emerging Church of 1 Peter," *Bulletin for Biblical Research* 19, no. 4 (2009): 588-89. In his study of 1 Peter as an epistle that can be characterized as "missional," Seland concludes that Peter's vision is for "a church representing God and his gospel in daily life, thus participating in the works of God in this world" (p. 589).

[11]Scot McKnight, in his study of Jewish mission in the Second Temple period, suggests that 1 Peter's approach to cultural subversion continues established patterns of cultural engagement. He notes that, "Gentiles converted to Judaism through a variety of means, especially through the good deeds of Jews"; McKnight, *A Light Among the Gentiles: Jewish Missionary Activity in the Second Temple Period* (Minneapolis: Fortress, 1991), p. 117. McKnight's comments demonstrate that missional identity was rooted in a commitment to live faithfully as God's distinct people.

(1 Pet 2:17), implying that while respect for Caesar and other authorities is expected, it is also expected that a Christian believer will show respect in reverse order as well (i.e., one with authority will respect one without). Husbands are to treat wives as coheirs of God's grace (1 Pet 3:7). Relationships are to be characterized by love, humility, compassion (1 Pet 3:8) and mutual service (1 Pet 4:10). In his instructions to church elders, Peter appeals to them on the basis of his place as "a fellow elder" rather than as an apostle (1 Pet 5:1), indicating an egalitarian view of congregational life. These behaviors are designed to embody a quality of relational life that reflects the distinctive character of the church. This continues to reflect the overall philosophy of the epistle—that by living holy lives people will be influenced for Christ (1 Pet 2:12).

This emphasis on submission and its missional potency is grounded in the submissiveness of Jesus, who acted in submission and suffered as a result but whose actions result in salvation for the world (1 Pet 2:20-25). The church's submission therefore resembles that of Christ's and holds the same redemptive potential that his did.

Mission through proclamation. While the primary evangelistic strategy offered by Peter involves nonverbal action, in 1 Peter 3:15 he counsels the use of words. His readers are to give

> an answer to everyone who asks you to give the reason for the hope that you have. But do this with gentleness and respect, keeping a clear conscience, so that those who speak maliciously against your good behavior in Christ may be ashamed of their slander. (1 Pet 3:15-16)

Here Peter continues to encourage a subversive, missional engagement that employs testimony, rooted in personal piety and offered in the (fairly submissive) form of answering an inquirer's questions with gentleness and respect. Nonetheless, it further demonstrates the seriousness with which Peter takes mission for his church of exiles. Despite their position as a marginalized minority, they are still called to declare their faith when given the opportunity.

Again, this kind of evangelistic "strategy" may require a reorientation in perspective for some of us. It may not seem to be nearly aggressive enough by those nurtured in the times of pseudo-Christendom, when door-to-door evangelism and large evangelistic crusades were quite common. Doing ministry from the margins rather than from the center requires a shift in our understanding as to how mission can be carried out most effectively. First Peter speaks from just this perspective and offers us guidance for a new post-Christian context.

ESCHATOLOGY

The eschatological orientation of 1 Peter is evident from the opening section, in which Peter encourages his readers by reminding them that they have been born into an "inheritance that can never perish . . . [and] is kept in heaven for you" (1 Pet 1:4). Later in chapter 1, Peter instructs his audience to keep their minds and hope fixed on the grace that will come to them "when Jesus Christ is revealed at his coming" (1 Pet 1:13). In 1 Peter 4:3-5 Peter reminds his audience that those who live counter to the gospel will have to give an account for their actions to the one "who is ready to judge the living and the dead." In 1 Peter 4:7 he reminds his audience that the end is near. He also calls them to endure suffering as a way of identifying with Christ so that "you may be overjoyed when his glory is revealed" (1 Pet 4:13). In 1 Peter 5:4 the churches are encouraged by Peter's assurance that they will receive a "crown of glory" when the "Chief Shepherd appears." Finally, as the epistle closes, Peter offers words that speak explicitly of the eternal quality of his audience's participation with Christ and point to the hope of a coming eschatological restoration: "And the God of all grace, who called you to his eternal glory in Christ, after you have suffered a little while, will himself restore you and make you strong, firm and steadfast" (1 Pet 5:10).

New Testament writers use a number of metaphors to express the mystery of eschatological hope, and Peter uses both spatial (heaven) and temporal (end of time) metaphors in this epistle. Along with the idea of "heaven" as a distinct dwelling place, the concept of a "new earth" signals hope for the redemption (or renovation) of the existing creation. Both of these are valid New Testament concepts and capture the classic New Testament tension between now and not yet. In the "now," Peter's audience is experiencing the reality of being God's people, who are called to live as citizens of the heavenly kingdom, experiencing a taste of it in their life together. However, living in the now also means that they face the distress of trials, the reality of marginalization, and the challenge of engaging in mission. But there is a "not yet" that is to come when Christ returns and provides his church with an eternal inheritance, a full salvation and ultimate vindication from the scorn of the world. Now is a time of perseverance, but when the church receives its eternal reward, everything that first appeared hard and harsh will then appear light. Peter seeks to engender this perspective in his churches. For Peter, this idea should not be understood as just plodding along until Christ sets us free from the dreariness of this world. Rather, it is offered as a backdrop against which to live in this world. Thus eschatological hope encourages the pursuit of holiness, mission and continued contextualization of the faith, because they are things that help to keep us in tune with the God of eternity and give meaning to our current "not yet" existence.

This perspective was a theological continuation of Second Temple ideology that, as we have seen, also emphasized a future hope for release from exile. It also legitimizes the motif for today in the sense that it reminds us that the ultimate end of exile is always eschatological, and until then we live in a time where we are never fully at home. However, for the suffering church in Peter's day, it is not hard to understand how his emphasis on living with an eschatological vision would have been especially relevant to his readers, acting as an encouragement to help them persevere in the midst of their exilic experience.

CONCLUSION

If it is true that the Christian church of the first century continued to see itself as in exile, then it is appropriate for the contemporary church, in places where it finds itself increasingly marginalized, to share in this perspective. Certainly the way in which the people of Israel for centuries theologized and adapted their faith to their circumstances while living under the influence of foreign conquerors is informative for any people who are in a position that, while sociologically distinct, is not theologically dissimilar. In the context of a North American culture dominated by consumerism, materialism, affluence and a growing agnosticism, the church needs models and resources to inform its existence as a marginalized people. The example and resources of ancient Israel and the early church provide these very things for us. Just as Israel survived life under a regime that was unfriendly to its faith, so too do we have to find ways to survive in a culture whose perspectives and practices are not congruent with those of fidelity to the gospel of the kingdom. Learning from and adopting some of Israel's approaches may in fact provide the contemporary church with resources that will aid in its own exilic existence.

Rather than succumbing to the challenges of our own exile, we can choose to take another approach altogether and seek the road of a church renaissance, attempting to bring renewal. This effort may in fact be aided by our current cultural reality of living on the social margins, just like Second Temple Jews and first-century Christians did. Being moved to the margins by more powerful forces has a way of shaking people's perspective on what they are doing and why. It causes a reevaluation of belief and practice that potentially can bring about appropriate changes. Accordingly, we may draw on the insights of Old and New Testament literature in order to understand the nature of theological hope and in order to formulate strategies of resistance, even while we acknowledge the difference in theological perspectives occasioned by the Messiah's having delivered creation from divine judgment and having inaugurated the reign of God. Perhaps many of the struggles and the perspectives that developed in the time of our ancestors in the faith can still serve as foundational principles for us to follow. Furthermore, their wrestling with issues of interpretation, their willingness to respond to their circumstances with new ways of understanding and practicing their faith, and their contextualization of ancient Judaism in new environs could provide us with the liberty and courage that we need to do the same in our exilic context in North America and parts of Western Europe.

Exile as a lens for understanding the situation of Israel, Second Temple Jews and the early church is not only an appropriate way of perceiving the historic situation, but it is also a potent resource for helping us to understand our own. The implications of this perspective are the concern of the rest of this study.

Part Two

The Practices of Exile

8

Leading the Church in Exile

GENERATING HOPE

On the night before his assassination, while giving a speech to a group in Memphis, Tennessee, Dr. Martin Luther King Jr. talked about the future with an eerie sense of foresight. He talked of the challenges that lay ahead for the civil rights movement but also of his surety that the movement would prevail. That night King spoke these words:

> Like anybody, I would like to live a long life. Longevity has its place. But I am not concerned about that now. I just want to do God's will. And he allowed me to go up the mountain. And I've looked over. And I've seen the Promised Land. I may not get there with you. But I want you to know tonight, that we, as a people, will get to the Promised Land![1]

This speech, while striking in its almost premonition-like foretelling of the events of the next day, was characteristic of King's leadership. It sought to inspire hope in the midst of the challenges that his people were facing as a marginalized minority in the United States of the late 1960s.

Napoleon Bonaparte is reported to have said, "A leader is a dealer in hope." In a time of exile one of the primary functions of ministry leadership is to engender hope. The kind of hope necessary for the church in exile is not a feeling of optimism or an assurance that things will get

---

[1]Martin Luther King Jr., "I've Been to the Mountaintop" (speech, Memphis, TN, April 3, 1968). For a copy of King's speech see www.americanrhetoric.com/speeches/mlkivebeentothemoun taintop.htm.

better but rather a generative hope that sustains faith, inspires new initiatives and allows faith to be expressed in ways that facilitate the ongoing
mission of God in the midst of exile. As we have seen, the exilic hope of
our ancestors in the faith was predicated on the idea that hope is culti-
vated as we embrace our exile as an opportunity for renewal. Just as exile
did not sideline God's missional intentions through Israel or the early
church, neither will our exilic circumstances thwart God's missional intentions today. The changed cultural situation in which the church finds
itself is an opportunity for translating the faith in new, inventive ways.
Inspiring this kind of vision within congregational life today is one of the
great challenges that we face, but cultivating vision and hope is a necessary task of exilic leadership. Facing this challenge requires many
things. The following suggestions consider what it means to try to lead
the contemporary church in a hopeful vision.

CULTIVATING PROPHETIC IMAGINATION

The term *prophetic imagination* as employed here describes the need for
spiritual leadership to infuse the community of faith with the kinds of
resources that empower it to see its God as in control when everything
around seems to say otherwise.[2] This faith-sustaining imagination
forms the basis for construing ways in which faith may be expressed in
exile. As an example of this kind of work, Walter Brueggemann points
to the prophet Isaiah in Babylon and his uttering of God's words to the
people of Israel in Isaiah 43:8-12. Here the prophet speaks on behalf of
the Lord and reminds Israel that it is still his "witnesses" (Is 43:10). Offering them a juridical metaphor, Isaiah tells Israel that it is now called
to testify on Yahweh's behalf in a court of law where all the nations and
their gods have been summoned to appear (Is 43:9). In this courtroom
the nations are entreated to bear witness on behalf of their respective
gods in a contest to determine which god is most trustworthy. The people

---

[2]The following exploration of Walter Brueggemann's use of prophetic imagination is based on a
talk given by Brueggemann at the Association of Theological Field Educators conference in
Atlanta, Georgia, January 25, 2009. The thoughts presented here are a mingling of Brueggemann's
and my own.

of Israel are called to stand as witnesses to their God and declare him the true God among all the gods of the nations. This prophetic challenge to Israel comes in the midst of its Babylonian captivity and against the notion that Israel's God must not be as great as Babylon's god (or Assyria's, for that matter) since he has not been able to provide victory for his people. Instead, in Isaiah 43 is God's declaration that he predicted Israel's exile. His faithfulness is proved by the fact that he warned Israel about the potential for exile and has now allowed exile to occur, yet he will be present in exile and will redeem it from exile. Isaiah delivers the prophetic word that reminds the people of these things and calls them to stand as Yahweh's witnesses in the face of theologically charged exilic circumstances. By all accounts the preaching of Isaiah is risky, foolish behavior. Such audacity takes faith inspired by an imagination fueled by the assurance that things are not what they seem; the current situation is not fully described in terms of its outward circumstances alone.

For people in our congregations it is not out of the question that hopelessness can take root as a result of the marginalized position in which the church finds itself. The ways of Western materialism, pluralism, political correctness and agnosticism seem to have won the day. Is there any real alternative? Can the Christian faith be taken seriously now that it has lost its cultural footing as the defining narrative? Isaiah challenges his audience with the idea that there is an alternative vision that offers hope for a different configuration of things. The work of exilic leadership in both ancient and post-Christendom times is to cast that vision of hope.

The same kind of prophetic imagination continues later in exilic history. In Nehemiah 1, approximately one hundred years after the words found in Isaiah 43, Nehemiah receives a report about the discouraging circumstances back in Jerusalem.[3] Those who have returned under the Persian repatriation policy have found the city in utter disrepair (Neh 1:4). Nehemiah's sadness is detected by the Persian king, Artaxerxes, for whom Nehemiah works as royal cupbearer. When asked what is wrong,

---

[3]This is not to infer that Nehemiah is directly indebted to Isaiah but rather to offer that Nehemiah carries on the tradition of prophetic imagination. The contrast between the two is that while Isaiah inspires hope with his message, Nehemiah inspires hope with his actions.

Nehemiah overcomes his fear to speak and tells the king about the conditions in Jerusalem (Neh 2:1-3). The king then asks what he can do for Nehemiah. Nehemiah first prays to Yahweh and then asks the king to allow him to go back to Jerusalem and rebuild the city's walls. The king grants his request and also provides military protection and materials for the construction project (Neh 2:4-8). Thus the walls of Jerusalem are rebuilt with Persian government funding, and through the work of Nehemiah the people of Israel receive fresh encouragement for their continued exilic journey.

Nehemiah is both a child of and a purveyor of prophetic imagination, in the sense that he continues in the exilic tradition of leading his people in a way that encourages their faith by imagining a better future and also initiates faith-sustaining action. Both Isaiah and Nehemiah spoke and acted in audacious ways that demonstrated their faith that Israel still had a role to play among the nations. While both men believed that exile would end and restoration would occur, in the meantime they offered a vision, through word and deed, that engendered hope in their people by stretching them to imagine who God was and what he could do.

In the contemporary setting, church leadership must continue this tradition by offering a similar kind of imaginative vision to the church, one that refuses to be overcome by the circumstances around us that often speak of decline, demise and death. A prophetic imagination will offer a vision of something different, an alternative future.

Imagination is an indispensable tool for exilic leadership, because it is our imagination that enables us to see beyond the ways that have shaped our experience and become so entrenched in our thinking. Imagination enables us to see a different vision of things and creates the possibility that something other than the status quo is possible. This is not the childlike imagination of unattainable dreams or wishful thinking; rather, it is the kind of vision that offers new possibilities for understanding who we are as the church and what we can be in the midst of our current circumstances. It is a way of leading people into a new and deeper trust in God. Alan J. Roxburgh and Fred Romanuk, in their book *The Missional Leader*, write about the importance of imagination to the mission of the church: "A missional church is a community of God's people who live into the imagination that they are, by their very nature, God's missionary people living as a demonstration of what God plans to do in and for all of creation in Jesus Christ."[4] Cultivating this kind of imaginative vision can be done in the following ways.

Define reality. Just like Isaiah in Babylon, leaders must present an alternative view of things. In practice this will mean casting exile in terms that stress how exile is a time to reconsider Christian identity and practice. One of the key leadership practices involved in accomplishing this is helping the church to understand the times in which it lives. Leadership guru Max De Pree states that the first job of a leader is to "define reality."[5] In order to see both the reality and potential of exile, Christians must be helped to grasp exactly what has and is happening in Western culture that contributes to the church's exile. Doing this means outlining the significant shifts that are taking place in our culture, the philosophical realities of postmodernism, and the way that these affect how the church is perceived and how it does ministry today. Unless the church is educated so that it can fully comprehend the reality of its situation, people will not sense the urgency for change or the need to embrace the motif of exile as a time for renaissance. Leaders must understand their times and help their people understand them as well.

This can be almost like evangelistic work. That is, it is the work of trying to convert people from one way of seeing things to another, in this case converting the church from a Christendom orientation to a post-Christendom orientation. In some cases this will seem like an impossible task, as such a conversion will call for a radical shift in people's lives. In my own work with local churches when I teach, even in a rudimentary way, on the realities of Western culture, I have found that there is a truly conversion-like experience that takes place in some people's lives. Suddenly they begin to understand what is going on around them and why their church is struggling in ways that it did not in the past. It is my ex-

---

[4]Alan J. Roxburgh and Fred Romanuk, *The Missional Leader: Equipping Your Church to Reach a Changing World* (San Francisco: Jossey-Bass, 2006), p. xv.
[5]Max De Pree, *Leadership Is an Art* (New York: Currency, 2004), p. 11.

perience that there are many people living in Western culture, even people who are well educated and astute in many other areas, who do not understand the dramatic shifts that are taking place, let alone the ramifications of them. Like the proverbial frog in the kettle that adapts to its environment as the water it is in slowly comes to a boil, thus rendering the frog unable to extract itself until it is too late, many Christians in the West today live in a culture they do not understand.

Many who live largely within a Christian bubble can proceed thinking that things really are not that bad. If the church is struggling, it probably is because the church needs a new pastor, or needs to deal with its sin, or needs a new facility and so on. Defining reality can be the beginning point of helping these people see that the situation requires much more than some minor adjustments. Helping people to grasp the overarching contours of secular Western society and their implications on daily life is akin to a doctor offering a diagnosis and explaining the nature and ramifications of the disease to a patient. Diagnosis is not a cure and it may not even offer a cure, but it does allow the patient to understand what he or she is up against. Ultimately, defining reality is an act of empowerment, because it orients people in a way that allows them to proceed with the facts as they currently stand. Without this act of truth telling, a legitimate hope can never emerge.

This act of orientation is at the core of leading with prophetic imagination, because it sets the stage for moving people forward as it helps them see that cultural circumstances are fluid and that the future has not been decisively cast. By embracing this new cultural reality and learning how to work effectively within it, the church may indeed still have a voice to offer. This can be the beginning of hope for many.

This leads us to recall that exile is a time for a people to consider where they have come from and to discuss what traditions and practices from the past no longer function effectively as ways of doing ministry or articulating faith in a new contextual reality. Again, as I work with various groups who are trying to figure out how to adapt to the realities of their context, I have found that once they begin to more clearly understand the culture in which they now find themselves, a new openness to change and the potential that change can bring is formed in them.

In this way leaders cultivate a prophetic imagination in the life of their congregations by teaching on the evolution and current state of the post-Christian culture we now reside in. Until we define our reality, a rooted, genuine hope will not emerge. But once this act of defining reality begins to occur, the possibility of engendering a vision for the future can also emerge.

Crucial to this is a theological vision that recognizes that God is ultimately in control. This may seem quite basic, which is the very reason that it must be given our attention. The simple truth that God is ultimately in control can be so obvious that we miss it. It is like being so determined to get to our destination that we forget to check the gas gauge in our car, only to find that while on route we are almost out of gas. In our haste to get to where we want to be, the most essential element of our journey can easily be overlooked. Isaiah made the sovereignty of God and his supremacy over the gods of Babylon the central marks of his preaching. This may have been theologically obvious, but it was not experientially obvious to his audience. The opulence of the city of Babylon, renowned throughout the ancient world for its beauty, would have certainly offered some evidence of the superiority of Marduk to Yahweh, especially in light of the fact that Jerusalem was now a shadow of its former self. The same is true for those of us in the Western church today. Much around us offers evidence that Jesus has lost in the war of gods. The gods of consumerism, hedonism and agnosticism seem to have a lot more momentum these days. While most in the church may want to believe that their God is ultimately in control, everything around them calls that claim into question. It is the job of the Christian leader and preacher to kindle people's imaginations with a compelling vision of the sovereignty of God over the gods of our culture. It is only from here that we can invite the church to reimagine its role in the community and once again perceive how it can live into its identity as the people of God.

A key component of this is the act of helping the church to reflect on what it can become in this context. Congregational conversation is central to this, and convening conversations that allow for a meaningful engagement of current realities and future possibilities is the catalyst to

generating imaginative possibilities for church mission. This may include giving people the opportunity to voice their laments concerning
the state of things as they now stand. There is a degree of despair in the
church today around the reality of its decline and relative ineffectiveness.
This is evidenced in the number of people who are leaving the traditional
church and looking for more fulfilling ways to experience their faith.[6]
These realities must be named in order for them to be properly addressed,
and leadership cannot be scared to confront them as a part of leading
the church into a hopeful vision.

However, the overall need is for a positive emphasis. What we focus
on becomes our reality, and a hopeful vision will only emerge out of a
positive conversation. Leaders must put effort into leading these kinds
of congregational discourses.[7] Central to this is the use of questions
like: "What is your dream for our church?" "What opportunities for ministry do you see in our community?" "Where do you see God at work
and how can we live into what he is doing more fully?" Questions generate the kind of conversations necessary for cultivating a hopeful vision
in a congregation trying to navigate exile and do ministry from the
margins. Leaders who choose to give attention to the most positive and
generative resources in a church will be most effective in helping to
maintain hope and cultivate a compelling vision for the future.[8]

Leaders must emphasize new ways of thinking that help the church to
imagine what it can do to respond to exilic realities, energizing the spirit
of the church with a vision for what it can be in its current and future
circumstances.[9] This is as vital a work for God's people today as it was
for Israel in the sixth century B.C.E., for it not only inspires today's exiles
but also empowers those who will lead the church in its exilic life for
generations to come. Just as Isaiah's sharing of God's imaginings for his

---

[6]See Julia Duin's exploration of this in her book *Quitting Church: Why the Faithful Are Fleeing*
(Grand Rapids: Baker, 2008).

[7]Mark L. Branson, "Gratitude as Access to Meaning," in *The Three Tasks of Leadership: Worldly
Wisdom for Pastoral Leaders* (Grand Rapids: Eerdmans, 2009), pp. 152-53.

[8]Ibid., pp. 151-57. For a wonderful study on congregational conversation using a method known
as appreciative inquiry, see Mark Lau Branson, *Memories, Hope and Conversations: Appreciative
Inquiry and Congregational Change* (Herndon: Alban Institute, 2004).

[9]Some of the particulars of what this might look like will be explored in the material below.

people was crucial, so too are the hopeful visions cast today vital to the generations that will follow.

Lead in creative missional activities. Prophetic imagination, as we have seen, ranges beyond inspirational images and stimulating discussion. Exilic leadership also takes action in ways that reflect the prophetic imagination at work. Just as Nehemiah's imagination of what could be done in Jerusalem led him to take the risk of asking for Persian blessing on the project, so too does exilic leadership in today's church call for risky ventures of faith that demonstrate that fruitful ministry is still possible. The task of church leadership in a post-Christian context is to faithfully imagine what forms and practices the church needs to adopt in order to properly be the church in exile. This is a work of the imagination, as it demands the ability to discern new patterns of faithfulness, but it is also a work of the blood, sweat and tears necessary for implementation of these visions. There may have been some in ancient Israel who could not envision that Jerusalem would ever be rebuilt or that worship in the temple would occur again in their lifetimes. Yet through Nehemiah—and those who came around him—it happened. These events would have been faith inspiring, as in fact the books of Nehemiah and Ezra demonstrate they were. They reminded the ancient people that God was still alive, that he was with them and that they had a future.

In a similar way, initiatives inspired by prophetic imagination that come to fruition today will provide vitality to the church and benefit to communities. They will speak eloquently about God's continued existence and interest in his work in places where the church seems to be waning. In some cases they will be ministries of revitalization that undertake the difficult task of reengineering established congregations so as to lead them into new ways of doing ministry that fit the changed context. In other cases spiritual entrepreneurs will rise up and imagine how the church can be different from what it has been and how new ecclesial initiatives can respond to the realities of a postmodern, post-Christian world where the church can no longer function as chaplain to the state. The new cultural identity of the church in the Western world is that of missionary.

The future hope of the church begins with theological reflection on this contextual reality, since it will require, as we have already considered, a "conversion" of the church.[10] This means that local churches will need to undergo a conversion-like experience that brings a complete change in self-perception—from one that sees the church itself as the primary focus of attention to one that sees the community (or world) as the focus. Furthermore, it will call for local churches to learn how to "read" their context and, like crosscultural missionaries, determine how they can engage that context in evangelistically effective ways.[11]

A practical outworking of this new orientation will be in the new missional forms the church can potentially take as missionary to its particular context. Can a church be a group of people who incarnate as a coffee shop or meet in movie theaters? Can a church be a group of people who meet in a house with no intention of ever finding a "real church" building? Can a church be a network of house churches? Can a church meet in the boardroom of a Wall Street law firm on a Tuesday afternoon? Does a church need a building, bylaws, denominational affiliation? Can a church be a group of people who meet weekly for supper, Bible study and prayer, and then go serve the poor in a neighborhood shelter?

Traditionally few questioned foreign missionaries who went to unreached lands and figured out how to make connections with the people there in ways that fit the culture. Many of us delighted in hearing the stories of these missionaries as they reported on what seemed to us to be unusual ways of reaching out and forming people into the church. We understood that, in a land where Christ was not known and the church had little presence, creative missional innovations were necessary. Increasingly our Western context has become that mission field, and the same strategies that served our foreign missionaries in previous generations are now how the Western church must approach its role in its cultural context.

---

[10]This is Darrell Guder's language; see *The Continuing Conversion of the Church* (Grand Rapids: Eerdmans, 2000), esp. chap. 7.

[11]For an exploration of this concept see Scott Frederickson, "The Missional Congregation in Context," in *The Missional Church in Context: Helping Congregations Develop Contextualized Ministry*, ed. Craig Van Gelder (Grand Rapids: Eerdmans, 2007), pp. 44-64.

The answer to the questions above about what constitutes a church will affect some areas of the church in significant ways. In some sectors of the church, congregations define themselves by their buildings. They spend large amounts of money to manage them and to restore them as they get old. The building is not only a source of ecclesiastical pride but also the only place for real ministry to take place. In many of these cases, congregations have lost all influence in their communities and are barely managing to hang on in terms of members, yet the building is maintained at all costs. Exile will kill these churches. They will die within a generation (or less), and the buildings will be sold, probably at a bargain price.

While some may see this as a tragic loss, the truth is that exile can inspire innovation if a congregation is willing to enter into the experience of a new birth by abandoning old ideas and maybe even structures that no longer give life and embarking on new ventures of faith that incarnate Christ's ministry in new ways and places.

Established churches can encourage new entrepreneurial leaders by empowering their voices in these discussions and then supporting them with financial and spiritual resources, enabling them to embark on innovative—even experimental—ministry projects. This is being done in Centre Street Church in Calgary, Alberta, Canada. Centre Street is one of Canada's largest churches; its weekend services draw thousands each week. However, well aware that the cultural context that it finds itself in has changed drastically, and of the need for a variety of approaches, it is using its influence and resources to extend its ministry in nontraditional ways by establishing new congregations across the Calgary region. Each site has its own pastoral staff and programs but is connected to the main site organizationally and relationally. These new congregations establish their own identities but are supported administratively and financially by the main site. These initiatives include a house church network and a developing array of small missional initiatives driven by various causes or common interests. In most cases people who are involved with the house churches will never enter the doors of the main site and neither will some who are involved in the missional initiatives being launched.

While Centre Street continues to function as a traditional megachurch in many ways, it is also captured by a vision for the future that includes empowering new ways of being the church in a post-Christian context.

Another such example is Crossings Community church/the Roxy Coffee shop in Acton, Ontario, just outside Toronto, Canada. As part of the Christian and Missionary Alliance in Canada, Crossings is a church plant/coffee shop dedicated to engaging with its community relationally in ways that are untraditional for most churches. Throughout the week, the church's storefront building functions as a place of business, the Roxy Coffee shop. It is designed to be a place of hospitality and connection for people in the community. Day in and day out people come to the Roxy for a delicious cup of fair-trade coffee, one of the Roxy's famous cinnamon buns and some warm conversation. In the back of the building is a small auditorium that hosts art shows and small concerts. The building can be (and is) rented for small social or business gatherings. Throughout the week the church runs a number of programs both at and away from the building, and on Sunday mornings a worship service is held in the auditorium. While Crossings is definitely a worshiping community, the Sunday service is hardly the main thing. The overall goal of the church is to engage relationally with its community and help its members learn how to live missionally in their everyday lives. As a coffee shop/church, it engages its community seven days a week in ways that very few traditional churches do. By being intentional about welcoming its community into its space, authentic relationships have been formed and people from all walks of life have come to faith or begun a journey that may someday lead them into a relationship with Christ.[12]

Both of these examples demonstrate the potential of new initiatives when an established denomination is willing to look outside the box and support new ideas of how the church can configure itself in postmodern, post-Christian culture.

A somewhat more mainstream initiative is found in traditional churches that develop a "church-within-a-church." This means that a

---

[12]See www.crossingscommunity.ca to learn more about Crossings Community.

new congregation is begun from within an established church. The new congregation still employs the resources of the mother church but is given a significant amount of autonomy to develop its ministry in unique, contextually relevant ways. On one hand it remains connected to the mother church, but on the other it develops as a separate entity. The mother church provides financial, staff and spiritual support to the new initiative, with the realization that it will develop fresh expressions of ministry for people the mother church itself may never be able to reach. This can be a risk for the mother church, as the new initiative may be more of a drain on its resources than a contributor to them. However, visionary leaders realize that left on its own the established congregation will likely die, as it is unable to change in ways that meet the challenges of contemporary ministry. These leaders are committed to seeing that the mother will give birth to a new baby before her demise, in this way ensuring that her witness to the gospel lives on for future generations.

Recently, when meeting with an established church experiencing a season of overall spiritual health and modest growth, I listened with interest as they described their goal to double their Sunday morning attendance within ten years. This would mean them growing from an attendance of 250 to five hundred in that ten-year time frame. As we met and discussed a number of issues about culture and mission, I asked the forty or fifty people gathered for the meeting whether in ten years it would be OK if they only had two hundred people in their Sunday worship service but also had a gathering of seventy people who met in a storefront coffee shop for an alternative worship service. In this scenario the church had released some people with a vision to start something very different in the downtown area of its town, and it was now connecting with a small crowd whom the established church might never connect with on its own. I went on, asking the people gathered whether it would be okay if in ten years there was a network of house churches that had grown out of the congregation and met in seven or eight homes, including over one hundred people who gathered weekly for Bible study, prayer, accountability and fellowship. Perhaps none of them ever came inside the doors of the church building, but the network existed because the church had empowered its beginning and encouraged its continuation. And, I continued, what if there were several other groups gathered throughout town and formed around shared interests: a group for moms and their babies, a book club, a group that met to serve in the homeless shelter for the evening. The possibilities are endless, but in each case they would be gatherings where people shared life, perhaps prayed together, maybe studied Scripture, and they supported one another and were all somehow an offshoot of the established church. What if all these groups encompassed another eighty people? Finally, I asked what if the church developed some kind of online community to connect with people on the Internet. This could make it possible for the church to reach out to people all around the world, encompassing who knows how many. I asked the group, would it be okay if in ten years attendance at the worship service held in this building were less than it is today, but the overall amount of people ministered to as a church on a regular basis was five hundred or more, only they were spread out over a variety of new initiatives? Most in the group seemed to think that would be just fine, and many of the leaders made it clear that they were ready to help the church think about ways to approach their future differently.

These examples demonstrate the kind of exilic leadership that is necessary in a post-Christian culture. This kind of spirit will carry the church forward despite the many challenges we face.

CONCLUSION

While many traditional churches will never be able to make some of the radical shifts necessary to thrive in the new cultural reality, they can participate in the renewal of the church by supporting these kinds of initiatives. This kind of collaborative interaction moves us past the lament of loss and failure and into the hope of new formulations of the faith and its practice.

It may be that the hope for the church in the West is found in initiatives that drastically break with traditional models of church life. Determining the shape of new models will take creative theological reflection, fueled by a prophetic imagination that tackles ideas about the church's very identity. These are key practices that address the fact that many traditional models are struggling in many (most) places, and the hope of the future flows out of a missional identity that finds new shapes for the church and allows it to form in unique, Spirit-directed ways. This will take an openness to creativity and innovation in our theological thinking about the nature of the church. It will mean we will have to be theologically responsive to our ministry context so as to generate a renaissance in contextualization that facilitates a missionary engagement.

In these exilic times leadership in the church calls for an appropriation of the prophetic imagination demonstrated in the time of Babylonian and Persian captivities by Isaiah and Nehemiah. This imagination provides us with an indispensable theological resource and a practical example of resistance to the ways of the empire. This is central to constructing a vision to nourish the faith of a distinct and effective exilic community. Exilic leadership will seek to help engender hope in the life of a congregation by cultivating an imagination within them that fuels a missional vision for its future existence. This kind of leadership is crucial for the future of the Western church.

9

Thinking Like Exiles

A RESPONSIVE THEOLOGY

After becoming a Christian in my late teens, I was spiritually nurtured in a vibrant and theologically conservative church. In that tradition, not atypical of many evangelical churches of that era, divorce was in most cases considered to be a great sin that carried major consequences. While divorce between two Christians might not be an unforgivable sin, it certainly meant disqualification from any kind of significant leadership role within the church. As a new Christian I absorbed this teaching as the faithful interpretation of Scripture and as God's will for his people.

In my first year of Bible college I met a fellow student who was several years older than I. As I got to know him, I was deeply impressed with his character, knowledge of Scripture, passion for the Lord and concern for others. I had no doubt that he would be a great pastor once he finished his studies. One day we were having coffee together in the student lounge, and he revealed to me a shocking fact: he was divorced! This revelation threw me for a loop, as it cut against many of my embedded theological assumptions. Suddenly I was confronted with two competing beliefs that lay within me: one that my friend was eminently qualified to serve as a leader in the church, and the other that people who were divorced, like him, were disqualified from leading in the church. This dilemma was exacerbated later that semester when one of my professors, who I had come to deeply respect, brought up the subject of divorce in class. He questioned the idea that divorced people should be barred from Christian leadership and offered some reflections on key biblical passages that sought to understand this teaching in the contemporary context. His thinking jarred the assumptions that I had developed from the teaching of my home church. I was having my theological foundations shaken, both by the experience of meeting a godly and gifted divorced person who felt called to Christian leadership and by some honest exegesis of Scripture that offered an alternative view. For me, these were catalysts that led to a revised theological position on divorce and on the role of divorced people in the church.

An experience like this is not uncommon for most of us at some point in our Christian journeys. Revising our theology, our understanding of God and our practice of the faith may occur many times as we mature as followers of Christ. This can be prompted by any number of circumstances, including something like a drastic shift in the role of the church in culture just like what we have experienced in the West over the past several decades. The experience of exile is one that causes us—just as it did ancient Israel—to think about God differently. Our theology must always be willing to consider new discoveries and new ways of understanding what it means to live faithfully. The work of church leadership in a time of exile is to help congregations think theologically about their identity as God's exiled people and consider what the implications of these circumstances are for the practice of their faith. This entails several specific practices.

A THEOLOGY OF CONTEXTUALIZATION

Being in exile requires the post-Christian church to develop a theology that responds to its culture in a way that embodies the biblical ideals of *accommodation* without *compromise*. As we have seen, these twin ideals are represented in the stories of Esther and Daniel and are clearly sketched out in 1 Peter. So too the contemporary church must define its core identity effectively so that it can accommodate itself to its culture without compromising those things that are intrinsic to its nature.

The current Western church desperately needs to recover its distinct identity and catch the vision of Jesus, who made himself at home as an exile, that is, as one who was not really "at home." Similarly, the church must find ways to live fully in the world without being assimilated into all its ways. Jesus did this without compromising his core identity as Son of God, and the church needs to do this without falling into some of the perspectives and behaviors that have accommodated it to the host culture in the past. A responsive theology is one that seeks to help the church find the appropriate response to the culture in which it finds itself. Responsive Christian theology recognizes that if the church is going to be relevant to its surroundings it must discover how to practice its beliefs in a way that allows it to integrate, as much as possible, into the life of the dominant culture. Furthermore, it also recognizes that interaction with that culture may in fact help the church to understand its theology more fully.[1]

We have seen how Israel responded theologically to its new surroundings in Babylon and also in Persia. Response was also intrinsic to the development of Judaism in the Second Temple period.[2] An example is how the early church employed a responsive theology (although perhaps in an unconscious way) as it emerged within first-century culture is Acts 10–11, as Peter is summoned by God to bring the gospel to a Gentile context. The story begins with a God-fearing Roman centurion named Cornelius who has a vision from God to locate Peter and bring him to his home. Peter also has a vision that calls him to rethink his ideas of what is religiously clean and unclean. Messengers from Cornelius's house bring Peter to Cornelius. Finding a large group gathered, Peter says to him, "You are well aware that it is

---

[1]This is a key part of cultural engagement, that the church can actually have its own understanding and practice of the gospel enhanced by engaging with the culture around it. For a further exploration of this see Craig Van Gelder, "How Missiology Can Help Inform the Conversation About the Missional Church in Context," in *The Missional Church in Context: Helping Congregations Develop Contextualized Ministry* (Grand Rapids: Eerdmans, 2007), pp. 39-40.

[2]This can be seen in the development of certain doctrines during the Second Temple period. See Anthony J. Tomasino, *Judaism Before Jesus: The Events and Ideas That Shaped the New Testament World* (Downers Grove, IL: InterVarsity Press, 2003). Notably Tomasino writes regarding Judaism's interaction with Zoroastrianism, the religion of Persia: "Through interaction with priests and scholars of different faiths, the Jews undoubtedly learned a thing or two about their own God" (p. 74).

against our law for a Jew to associate with Gentiles or visit them" (Acts 10:28). Despite this, in response to the vision, Peter enters Cornelius's house and addresses the crowd, saying, "I now realize how true it is that God does not show favoritism but accepts those from every nation who fear him and do what is right" (Acts 10:34-35). Peter then announces the good news of Jesus and watches as the Holy Spirit falls powerfully on the assembly. Those "circumcised believers" who had accompanied Peter are astonished that "the gift of the Holy Spirit had been poured out even on Gentiles" (Acts 10:45).

This story is perplexing in certain ways, as it would seem that after working so closely with Jesus and watching him cross many boundaries in order to reach out to a variety of people, including Gentiles, Peter should well know that God does not show favoritism. However, it seems the message had not fully penetrated Peter's thinking and that his theology still needed to grow and respond to what God was doing. As the story continues, we see that Peter was not the only one in this position.

Immediately following the scene at Cornelius's house, we read that the church leaders in Jerusalem hear that the Gentiles have received the word of God (Acts 11:1), so when Peter goes up to Jerusalem to discuss the matter, we are told that the circumcised believers "criticized him and said, 'You went into the house of the uncircumcised and ate with them'" (Acts 11:2-3). Then Peter carefully explains what had taken place at Cornelius's house. The leaders in Jerusalem are forced to cease their objections and praise God, saying, "So then, even to Gentiles God has granted repentance that leads to life" (Acts 11:18).

Here again it is somewhat hard to understand why the early church struggled with this issue in light of their experience with Jesus, but on the other hand it demonstrates how deeply cultural and theological traditions can run. For our purposes, the primary lesson embedded in this story is one of Jesus' disciples responding theologically to what God is doing in a crosscultural or countercultural context. They are learning how to accommodate themselves to the cultural demands of contextualization while at the same time remaining uncompromised in their embodiment of the gospel. This clearly had major theological ramifications, as well as practical ones. It is not that their theology had to change as much as it had to grow in response to God's new working. This meant that their understanding of the gospel had to grow so that they could continue to embody Jesus' ministry in their new circumstances. On the issue of first-century Jewish believers learning how to understand the role of Gentiles in the church, N. T. Wright observes, "Jesus did not intend to found a church *because there already was one*, namely the people of Israel itself. Jesus' intention therefore was to *reform* Israel, not to found a different community altogether."[3] The leadership of the first-century church had to discern that this was true theologically, which it clearly was, given the prophets' words that Gentiles would be included in the final gathering of God's people (Is 56:1-8). As their theological understanding of the gospel grew, they could then adapt their practice to their context. What is important to note here is that the cultural context actually aided the church in its understanding of the gospel. This is quite antithetical to how the church often does theology. In many sectors of the church we have been taught that we should be suspicious of culture because culture so often runs counter to the ideals of Christian ethics. Here in the Cornelius story we see how God was active in what was for many Jewish Christians a less-than-ideal context. However, engaging with this context actually helped the early church get its gospel right. At its core a responsive theology of contextualization actually anticipates reciprocity between church and culture. That is, both will benefit from engagement with the other.[4]

The willingness and ability to discern and adapt to God's working in our day is crucial to developing a contextualized theology for our circumstances. The same approach to doing theology today that the early church took will enable the church to contextualize itself in a way that accommodates to its exilic circumstances without compromising its core theological identity.

---

[3]N.T. Wright, *Jesus and the Victory of God* (Minneapolis: Fortress, 1996), p. 275, as quoted in Michael Goheen, *A Light to the Nations: The Missional Church and the Biblical Story* (Grand Rapids: Baker Academic, 2011), p. 84.

[4]Craig Van Gelder, *The Ministry of the Missional Church: A Community Led by the Spirit* (Grand Rapids: Baker, 2007), p. 64.

In order to aid in this work, a key activity of church leadership needs to be leading their church in sound theological reflection. This means inviting reflection on the full meaning of the gospel and its interaction with culture today. The art of theological reflection is often lacking in Christian leadership and must be revitalized if a responsible responsive theology is to be developed within the life of congregations. We must think of theology not as some esoteric set of propositions that have little to do with the actual work of ministry, and we must also resist the idea of thinking about theology as a static set of ideas that cannot be touched or reconsidered. Theology is the ongoing task of trying to improve on our interpretation of God and his Scriptures. This is particularly important when the message of the gospel ceases to attract. At that time it is important to refocus and seek to reanimate the ideas that give the gospel its power to influence men and women for Christ.[5]

Theological reflection intentionally brings the realities of our lived experience into conversation with key theological resources such as Scripture, tradition, reason, previous experience, culture, prayer and conversation. As we intentionally process our new experiences, particularly those that challenge our traditional understanding of the gospel, through these established theological lenses new appropriations of the faith emerge. This allows us to respond responsibly and appropriately to our context in a way that honors the past but is engaged with the present reality.

A responsive theology will incorporate new insights into the gospel that are gained from cultural circumstances and thus help the church to be more faithful to its core identity and message.

---

[5]Clark H. Pinnock and Robert C. Brow, *Unbounded Love: A Good News Theology for the 21st Century* (Downers Grove, IL: InterVarsity Press, 1994), p. 7. For full explorations of the art of theological reflection see Howard Stone and James Duke, *How to Think Theologically*, 2nd ed. (Minneapolis: Fortress, 2006), and Elaine L. Graham et al., *Theological Reflection: Methods* (London: SCM Press, 2005). For a concise overview see Don Payne, "Field Education and Theological Reflection in an Evangelical Tradition," in *Preparing for Ministry: A Practical Guide to Theological Field Education*, ed. George M. Hillman (Grand Rapids: Kregel, 2008), pp. 55-71.

A THEOLOGY OF PRACTICE

The work of contextualization is ultimately a work of ministry practice. This is why an emphasis on practice over doctrine needs to become the key factor in determining authentic expressions of church and faith. This does not mean neglecting the content of Christian faith, but it does mean practice must become more central to theological leadership than constructing "correct" doctrine. In previous generations it has been assumed that proper belief should be given pride of place in determining faithful Christianity, whereas in times of exile praxis must be given priority.

First Peter is deeply concerned with practice as the defining mark of faithfulness. The central command is "Be holy in all you do" (1 Pet 1:15), which colors everything else about the letter. A central feature of the epistle is the household code (1 Pet 2:11–3:7), which expounds faithful behavior as a sign of genuine belief. This is not to deny that Peter is also concerned with the theological identity of his churches; in fact, the practice of the church flows out of its theological identity. However, for Peter it is the practice of faith that ultimately demonstrates the faithfulness of the church.

Similarly, in the Old Testament stories that we have been considering faithful practice is what makes Daniel and Esther heroes. Esther is a model worthy of canonization because despite some "nonkosher" behavior she acts faithfully for her people. Her heroism is not in her theological fidelity—the book does not even name God—rather, it is in her sacrificial behavior toward her people. Daniel may have been theologically pure, but it is his actions as a faithful Jew that win him favor with his captors and demonstrate the potential results of faithful behavior in captivity.

Exile calls for action, and a theology of practice is necessary. While Christianity in general and evangelicalism in particular have always emphasized piety, correct belief has most often been seen as the essence of true Christianity.[6] Orthodoxy is treated as a series of propositional truths to be believed in order to entitle one to the mantle of

---

[6]Roger E. Olson, *Reformed and Always Reforming: The Postconservative Approach to Evangelical Theology* (Grand Rapids: Baker, 2007), p. 23.

"Christian." In Christendom, intramural arguments about doctrine could be joined and understood by large swaths of the church and even much of the nonchurch population. Doctrine united and separated various Christians.

In our fragmented, post-Christian culture, by contrast, what is demanded is a theology of orthopraxy more than orthodoxy. Again, this is not to dispense with the need for orthodoxy as a foundation for faith. It is, however, to make the practice of the Christian faith the ultimate concern of theology. What really matters now is how the church is able to articulate and demonstrate a transformative spirituality. If people are going to consider Christianity as a religion, the first text they may read is not the Bible but the church. What the church needs in order to be a text fit to be read is a theology that emphasizes practice as the primary indicator of genuine faith as opposed to a content-centered faith that prioritizes adherence to certain doctrines.[7]

This observation brings together the strands of identity, mission and theology that we are considering in this section. These are all crucial to the church in exile. The three must remain in conversation with one another in order for a full-orbed understanding of Christianity to emerge in these unique days of exile. Each strand finds its ultimate expression in the praxis of the church; this is why a theology of practice is crucial for the church today.[8]

An emphasis on practice is showing up in new expressions of communal living such as those characterized by the new monastic movement. These movements include small communities of Christian people who move into needy neighborhoods, live communally and seek to bring the presence of Christ to these communities by serving their neighbors in any way they can. They reflect a deep commitment to reproducing the

---

[7]See ibid., pp. 73-79, for further discussion on the need for this kind of theological emphasis.
[8]See Ray S. Anderson, *An Emergent Theology for Emerging Churches* (Downers Grove, IL: InterVarsity Press, 2006), especially chap. 6. Anderson posits that theology in the current era must emerge out of the ministry practice of congregations. Discerning the work of the Spirit through the work of the church as illuminated by the word of God becomes the key shaper of theological thought in the post-Christian era. This approach places the emphasis for theology on how the faith is practiced.

ministry of Jesus and are an attempt to take seriously what it means to put Christ's teachings into practice. While in many cases these communities are grounded in a classical, orthodox, even evangelical theology, the primary characteristic that unites and defines them is their emphasis on practicing the faith among the poor.[9]

Another example is a downtown church in Toronto in which a semi-regular "coffee house" event takes place and artists from the community are invited to come and share their work. Artists are invited to talk about their work and what inspired it, whether a painting, sculpture, song, poem or other type of artistic expression. In many cases the artists who present their work are not Christians, and their explanations often do not reflect anything close to an orthodox theological view of the world. However, the church engages in this activity as a way of showing hospitality to its community and supporting its artists. The people are committed to developing friendships and showing God's openness. However, they take a risk of being perceived as theologically compromised because of their willingness to allow unorthodox ideas to be shared under the auspices of a church-sponsored event. Despite this risk, the congregation is more committed to practicing God's love and acceptance among its neighbors than it is to being perceived as "doctrinally pure."[10]

In a slightly different vein, churches need to take non-Christians seriously as full participants in the life of the church. Traditionally non-Christians are just observers in the church until they become believers themselves. Their opinions carry little official weight, and their ability to serve in the church is limited to tasks like helping at a church cleanup day or volunteering in the nursery. Deep engagement with the life of the body is largely withheld because they are not seen as spiritually ready (or able) to be too involved. There is an unspoken mantra that to become a

---

[9]For an explanation of these communities see Scott Bessenecker, *The New Friars: The Emerging Movement Serving the World's Poor* (Downers Grove, IL: InterVarsity Press, 2006), and Shane Claiborne, *The Irresistible Revolution: Living as an Ordinary Radical* (Grand Rapids: Zondervan, 2006).

[10]The church is Toronto Alliance Church, and it is highly committed to an orthodox, evangelical faith but less concerned about whether they are perceived that way by the evangelical constituency.

member of the church one must follow a particular progression of experience that looks something like the following:

Believe→Behave→Belong

This assumes that before one could "belong" to the church, one has to first believe the right things, then demonstrate a degree of genuine Christian behavior (as defined by the local church). Then one can be accepted as someone who belongs to the body and can be trusted with ministry responsibility.

Increasingly the order of conversion is changing. In this postmodern, post-Christendom era the order can often look more like the following:

Belong→Behave→Believe

For some people conversion occurs only after the chance to belong to a church community that truly invites them to be a part of its inner life and to participate in a genuine way. Slowly they begin to adopt the lifestyles and ideals of the community, until they realize that they have become a true convert to what the church believes.[11]

This is illustrated in the research done by Jim Henderson, Todd Hunter and Craig Spinks in their book *The Outsider Interviews*. They traveled around the US interviewing young adults who were not Christians in order to understand their perceptions on the church and Christian faith. One of the significant conclusions that they came to as a result of their numerous conversations was that people both inside and outside the church want to serve. One of their interviewees states clearly, "Don't invite me to church—invite me to serve."[12] By inviting those currently outside the church to become genuine partners in various aspects of our ministry, we include them in a way they want to be included, and this may ultimately be what allows them to connect with the church and, more importantly, with Jesus.

A theology of practice is committed to offering people patience, space

---

[11]The concept of believe→behave→belong; belong→behave→believe, is not original to me. However, I do not recall where I was first introduced to it.

[12]Jim Henderson, Todd Hunter, Craig Spinks and David Kinnaman, *The Outsider Interviews: A New Generation Speaks Out on Christianity* (Grand Rapids: Baker, 2010), p. 135.

and opportunity so that they can seek and explore Christian faith in a way that does not keep them at arm's length but welcomes them to enter into the life of the church as they continue on their journey toward God. Such behavior reflects a theological priority on the practice of the faith over belief in the right doctrines.

A THEOLOGY OF THE SPIRIT'S ACTIVITY IN CULTURE

We have already briefly considered the role of culture in helping the church do theology, but to take these initial ideas further, cultivating a responsive theology requires that we fully embrace a theological perspective that perceives God's Spirit as active in our culture, that is, secular culture. The church has had a mixed record on this particular issue. In some quarters of the church there is a deep resistance to the idea that God may dwell or even work in certain sectors of society. In some realms of church life the "world" is a place to be avoided, because associating too closely with popular culture and the people who enthusiastically participate in the "world" will have a corrupting influence on spiritual life. In this view, because culture is largely godless, involvement with it should be for the purpose of evangelistic engagement only. This view is epitomized in the writings of Oswald Chambers, whose devotional book *My Utmost for His Highest*—while written in a bygone era (1935)—has nonetheless influenced many with a form of piety that emphasizes personal experience with God over incarnational ministry in society. Chambers writes, "The central point of the kingdom of Jesus Christ is personal relationship with him, not public usefulness to men."[13] Such attitudes dismiss the world as a place where God can be found.[14]

---

[13]Oswald J. Chambers, *My Utmost for His Highest* (New York: Dodd, Mead & Co., 1935), p. 293. This reference came to my attention in a quote from Doug Pagitt in *The Post Evangelical* (El Cajon, CA: Emergent, 2003), p. 123. This is not to completely devalue Chambers's contribution to Christian spirituality; rather, it is to point out an inherent flaw in the approach that Chambers represents.

[14]For interaction on the plausibility of God being active in popular culture see Craig Detweiler, *Into the Dark: Seeing the Sacred in the Top Films of the 21st Century* (Grand Rapids: Baker, 2008), pp. 29-32. Detweiler's focus is on movies, but his comments in this section argue for a broad appreciation of the possibility that God can appear in and work through various forms of popular culture.

Others in the contemporary church take a slightly less cynical approach, believing that culture can be coopted and used for sanctified purposes; a Christian (often evangelical) subculture has been created that offers music, movies, books and video games for Christian entertainment. This allows for Christians to enjoy the same kind of activities that are offered through popular culture but in a way that keeps the world at arm's length and still—subtly—sends a theological message that the Spirit is more likely to be present in a song produced by a Christian artist than one produced by a non-Christian artist.[15]

There are, of course, other models that equate Christ with culture in such a way that he is so watered down that any form of cultural expression is considered appropriate. Yet, to live in exile is to appreciate the fact that God is present in the host culture in ways that transcend our Christendom-shaped views and ideals. Acts 10–11 reminds us of the Spirit's working in a cultural setting that Peter and the Jerusalem leaders previously thought unthinkable. Yet when Peter shows up at Cornelius's house, he clearly senses from his vision and his initial engagement with Cornelius that the Spirit is at work, and so he crosses the threshold of Cornelius's front entrance and enters the home of a Gentile. God had, of course, been there long before. If one is willing to read the book of Esther from the vantage point of faith and look for the activity of God in the story, one may discern the signals that God is already at work even before Esther arrives on the scene. Mordecai's words that Esther has come to her position "for such a time as this" (Esther 4:14) signal the prior working of God, as do the various reversals and "coincidences" spread throughout the story. God's concluding open-ended question at the end of the book of Jonah, "And should I not have concern for the great city of Nineveh . . . ?" (Jon 4:11) is a haunting reminder that the reason God called Jonah in the first place was that he is present in Nineveh, concerned about its behavior and wanting it to repent. Unlike Jonah (Israel), he had no intention of staying separate from the people for whom he was concerned.[16]

---

[15]Dave Tomlinson, *The Post Evangelical* (El Cajon, CA: Emergent, 2003), p. 124.
[16]Christopher Wright, *The Mission of God: Unlocking the Bible's Grand Narrative* (Downers Grove,

A key perspective in the view that God works in and through culture is the idea that human culture bears the imprint of God himself. Culture is rooted in the divine, trinitarian culture and in the ongoing dialectic between the transcendent God and temporal humanity.[17] God is the ultimate culture maker and the one who superintends all human culture in the sense that he is in creative partnership with human beings as they steward creation (Gen 1:27-28). If we take this perspective from the Genesis account seriously, then it is not difficult to embrace the idea that God is involved in intricacies of human culture and its ongoing development.

Thus in exilic conditions we can expect that God is in the midst of the culture in which we find ourselves. He will be working in places we may have previously thought unlikely. His grace is active in the lives of people, whether they know it or not. Some are already actively seeking grace, even though they may not know exactly what they are seeking for (Cornelius); others are not obviously seeking, but that does not mean that God is not seeking them (Nineveh). A responsive theology embraces this reality and emboldens the work of active cultural contextualization because it assures us that God is at work in that context.

Musician Lucinda Williams expresses a theology of God's activity in the everyday realities of life in her song "Blessed." Williams introduces us to a variety of characters who potentially offer us a glimpse into how the divine presence can be seen through the everyday lives of regular people. She sings about being blessed by people such as the minister who practiced what he preached, the neglected child who knew how to forgive, the teacher who didn't have a degree, the homeless man who showed us the way home, the hungry man who filled us with love and many more like them.

Williams's song offers a vision of the world that anticipates God's presence in every vista of life. God is active in the circumstances of people's lives and the events that surround them. A responsive theology em-

---

IL: IVP Academic, 2006), p. 461. For other biblical examples of ways that God works in culture and through nontraditional means, see Detweiler, *Into the Dark*, pp. 15-16.

[17]Brad Harper, "Response to John Franke," *Cultural Encounters* 6 (2010): 35-36.

braces this truth as a core reality in understanding God's work in this world and equips us to live in exile with a view that God is right here in the midst of it with us.

Art is a primary example; movies, television, literature, music, painting and sculpture are all media in which people engage the mysteries of life and seek to understand or express truth. God is often an explicit or implicit topic in these forms of expression, and it should not surprise us to find that God's Spirit is in them, drawing us to himself. We should embrace and not dismiss the spiritual conversation that often takes place in art and the testimonies that some people offer regarding the connections with the divine that they have made through various forms of art, even when a particular piece of art may not explicitly honor God.[18]

A recent example of this can be found in director Terrence Malick's film *The Tree of Life*. Not only is the movie's title a clear reference to the story of the fall in Genesis 3, but also the movie explores the reality of life in a fallen world where beauty and ugliness, life and death, signs of the divine and unspeakable evil, all exist together. The movie begins at creation (or at least the origin of the planet) and explores the richness and delight of birth, love, family and faith. It also explores the devastation of human cruelty, parental abuse, the death of a child and the questioning of God that accompanies such things. While the movie is open-ended in its interpretation of these things, leaving the audience to come to their own conclusions, it is a sincere expression of spirituality and the search for meaning. Is it not possible that God's Spirit is pleased to engage with such art and invite us into a conversation with him through it?

Christians can acknowledge God's work in culture by wholeheartedly participating in it as artists. It may be that the arts can become an increasingly viable way for Christians to express themselves and their faith to the world. The arts, whether graphic, literary or dramatic, can both facilitate an engagement with culture so that the gospel can be proclaimed and be a vehicle for Christians to express the realities of their

---

[18]As an example of this, Detweiler, *Into the Dark*, p. 15, points to the R-rated movie *Raging Bull* as the catalyst to his own Christian conversion.

exilic experience. The various forms of artistic expression that both dialogue with culture and provide encouragement for Christians resemble the diasporic advice tale in its own address to the theological and historical circumstances of its original audience. Perhaps Christian artists can create similar narratives, whether through writing novels, composing music or making movies that tell hopeful stories of Christian exilic life that can serve the church in the same way that the stories of Esther, Daniel and Jonah served Israel.

On another front, certain places once thought to be venues that God avoided, such as bars, rock concerts and tattoo parlors, can be gathering places that provide opportunities for shared expression, experience and relationship. They can facilitate the Spirit's work in culture and human life and remind people that moments of transcendence occur in everyday events.[19]

Also, religions and people's own personal experiences, even ones that do not explicitly honor Christ, can be places where the Spirit is at work. Our theology must accommodate the fact that God may choose to work in people's non-Christian religious experience and even the most unusual of life's circumstances. To dismiss the hints of divine life that people identify in their own stories is to miss the potential for the expanse of God's work in a culture that is increasingly distant from him. It is also to forgo the potential for dialogue that may help to produce greater clarity and truth.[20]

A friend of mine, who was raised in a committed and loving Christian home and spent many years of his life as a drug addict living on the streets of a major Canadian city, tells the story of going to a crack house to meet one of his dealers. Stepping over bodies of fellow addicts passed out on the floor, he spotted the woman who often sold him his drugs sitting on a couch across the room. As he approached her, she fixed her

---

[19]For an exploration of tattooing as a source of religious meaning see Tom Beaudoin, *Virtual Faith: The Irreverent Spiritual Quest of Generation X* (San Francisco: Jossey-Bass, 2000), pp. 77-78.

[20]Clark Pinnock agrees when he writes that the Spirit's work is "guiding, luring, wooing, influencing, drawing all humanity, not just the church" (*Flame of Love: A Theology of the Holy Spirit* [Downers Grove, IL: InterVarsity Press, 1996], p. 216).

gaze directly on him. Before he could speak, she said to him in a questioning voice, "Bobby, what are you doing here?" He had met her in the same crack house many times, but the question and the look on her face made him pause. He would tell you that in that moment Jesus was speaking to him. The question "What are you doing here?" took on a deeper proportion. In some mystical way the question took on an existential quality, as it seemed like Jesus was sitting on the couch and asking him the question. In that moment he felt the conviction of the Spirit for the way he was squandering his life, and suddenly he wanted to change. He didn't answer the question; all he could do was turn around and leave the house. Could it be that Jesus was present in that crack house? Could it be that Jesus somehow manifested himself in a female crack-using drug dealer? My friend would tell you he could. Can our theology of God's working in and through culture and human experience bear such possibilities? A theology of exile shaped by the reality that God is in the land calls us to affirm such possibilities and celebrate them, because they offer us assurance that God is active and in control even when his people seemingly have little control of their own.

When the dominant culture all around us can appear to be disengaged from our God, and we perceive a declining openness to explicitly Christian faith, the responsive theology demonstrated in the stories of previous exiles is important to recover. It calls us to look for God's work even in places that we may have previously thought were not the domain of God's presence. It reminds us that the Spirit is ever present and that he "can foster transforming friendship with God anywhere and everywhere."[21]

CONCLUSION

A. W. Tozer said, "What we think about God is the most important thing about us." Rather paradoxically, based on some of the things covered in this chapter, it is true that our conception of God will ultimately direct how we decide to journey through the reality of the church's exile in these days. The theological need for us is the same as it was for Israel and the

---

[21]Ibid., pp. 186-87.

early church—that is, to recognize that our current circumstances will inevitably reveal new things about who God is and how he works in this world. Thus we need a theological vision able to respond to the things God reveals about who he is and who we need to be, and then to put these insights into practice effectively while anticipating that further insights will be given as we interact missionally with our new context. In guiding the church through exile, this kind of theological leadership is necessary. We cannot batten down the hatches and think that what we once "knew to be true" was an infallible interpretation of the faith that cannot be deviated from, and that if anyone should dissent then their condemnation is required. Rather, like our ancestors in the faith, we must openly—even eagerly—look for new and appropriate ways to revision and reorient our faith as Christians to the emerging reality of post-Christendom. In such a posture is the hope that our faith will remain as vibrant and lasting as the faith of Israel and the original disciples.

10

Holiness

AN EXILIC IDENTITY

Erik Erikson was a developmental psychologist renowned for his theories on the development of personal identity. Erikson postulated that among other things personal identity includes a sense of personal consistency and awareness of how one is unique. One's identity is the way one is known and recognized and how one establishes reputation among others. Identity formation is crucial to all human beings, especially in the move from adolescence into adulthood.[1] This move toward maturity is crucial to groups as well as individuals especially when that group finds itself on the margins of a society and is striving to establish itself as a community within a cultural hegemony that is quite different and much more powerful.

Identity formation for God's people in exilic situations is foundational to their survival. We have already touched on aspects of identity for the church in exile, but more must be said about this topic because it is a defining issue for exiles of all kinds—whether political, religious or socio-theological.

For the church a core tenet of its identity is the understanding that it is called to represent Christ in this world. In all of its imperfections, the church is called to somehow demonstrate the life of Jesus. Put another

---

[1]For a full exploration see Erik H. Erikson, *Identity, Youth and Crisis* (New York: W. W. Norton, 1994).

way, by embodying the gospel message in its life together the church makes the gospel make sense. The church is itself the logic of the gospel, as it demonstrates the difference that Jesus can make when he is taken seriously and his teachings are followed, even imperfectly. In this sense the church is created to make the gospel plausible to those outside it, and this self-understanding is increasingly necessary for both the church and the world. This is because the culture no longer helps the church make disciples; it has largely ceased dispensing any snippets of the biblical story or reinforcing forms of biblical morality once taken for granted.

I did not grow up participating in or attending any church. From time to time an occasion arose that would bring me and my family to a church, but this was rare. My parents were good people who were Christian in their religious orientation and certainly not opposed to faith in any way, but I did not grow up regularly imbibing the wisdom of Sunday school teachers or fidgeting in the worship service while the pastor passed on the wisdom of Scripture. Nonetheless, as a child and young person I knew the Lord's Prayer, I knew that Moses delivered the Ten Commandments, I knew that Jonah was swallowed by a whale, and I knew that Jesus died on the cross for my sins. How did I know these things? I'm not exactly sure. What I do know is that somehow the culture delivered them to me. I did not get it from the church because it was not a place that I frequented.

My story is not one that many young people today would relate to because the culture no longer helps them learn Christian ideas. Where once it may have made a contribution to Christian formation, it cannot be counted on to fulfill the same function today. The church is largely on its own in helping people to learn about and experience the reality of Jesus. This calls us to embrace our identity as his people and to see that our life together is where people will see that the gospel makes sense as an alternative story to the other stories that are guiding their lives.

Intrinsic to the development of this aspect of the church's identity is the idea that it is called to be a holy people. As we have seen, the impetus toward holiness became a central response for Israel to its exile in the same way that it plays a central role in Peter's first letter. Holiness is an identity issue for the people of God at all times; however, in times of exile it becomes the category under which boundaries are explored and in which distinct behaviors are described and defined. The biblical idea of holiness is characterized by the idea of being set apart. The Hebrew word often used for holiness is *qâdôš*, which connotes being selected and consecrated. In Greek the word for holiness is *hagios*, which has a similar meaning, literally "to be set apart or consecrated." Being set apart calls for behaviors that reflect the ethics of Christian faith by engaging the world in constructive ways that contribute positively to the overall life of the community in which we live. It also calls us to disengage from behaviors we deem to negatively affect ourselves and the community in which we reside. By practicing these things consistently, we define what makes us distinct as those who seek to live as followers of Jesus.

It is somewhat natural for us to shy away from calls to holiness, in part because we fear the kind of austere, mandated legalism that is often a part of movements associated with holiness as a core value. We recognize that holiness can lead to self-righteousness and to divisions between those who are "holy" and those who are considered not to be. Nonetheless we cannot avoid the fact that the biblical authors did not hesitate to call their communities to lives of holiness. The church must live into this key piece of its identity if it is to truly be the body of Christ in this world and somehow embody his life in a way that gives credence to the wisdom of the gospel.

In order to do this it is important for us to understand what true biblical holiness is and how it might function in a world like ours.

RELATIONAL HOLINESS

What is holiness? In some contexts the answer to this question is relatively simple: there are a handful of things you do (e.g., attend church, tithe your money, volunteer in a ministry, pray, read the Bible, live a morally upright life as defined by the group) and a handful—or two—of things you don't do (e.g., skip church, drink, smoke, have sex outside marriage, go to certain places that the group disapproves of, ask too many questions about the beliefs and practices of the church). As long as you do your best to fit into the formula, you are considered holy even though no one may actually call you by that term.

While certain items on these lists of behaviors may indeed reflect the wisdom of Scripture, holiness cannot be defined by a simple formula. At its core the biblical vision of holiness is relational. It sets out the way people can live in reverential relationship with God and enjoy the benefits of that relationship as a community separated for his worship.[2] At its heart holiness is about communion with God, but because this communion takes place in the realities of the physical world, it is an embodied holiness, not a totally abstract concept that eludes any specific definition about what it looks like in practice. Furthermore, it is assumed by the authors of Scripture that living a holy life and embodying the God who is holy will not occur by happenstance. God's people, however well intentioned, will not simply wander into holiness without some direction; they need specific practices that will direct and empower them in the pursuit of holy living. Walter Brueggemann reflects on the traditions found in Leviticus as representative of this reality. He writes, "The tradition of Leviticus urges disciplines of holiness, concrete bodily ways whereby life is knowingly directed toward the holiness of God that comforts even as it demands."[3] The practices of holiness make the church into a place where God's wisdom and his intentions for this world can be displayed. The practices, however, are not simply the following of certain rules; they are the practices that cultivate a relationship of love and obedience. They are practices deeply rooted in a responsive relationship. This relational holiness is intrinsic to the biblical vision for life in this world. First Peter also captures this idea, as the author ties his call to holiness to his audience's connection to God through Jesus Christ and its need to embody that relationship in specific, concrete ways.

As we have seen in the Old Testament, exile prompted Israel to renew its commitment to holiness as a way of boundary maintenance and cul-

---

[2]Jill Middlemas, *The Templeless Age: An Introduction to the History, Literature, and Theology of the "Exile"* (Louisville, KY: Westminster John Knox, 2007), p. 133.

[3]Walter Brueggemann, *Deep Memory, Exuberant Hope: Contested Truth in a Post-Christian World* (Minneapolis: Fortress, 2000), p. 63.

tural distinctiveness. If, as we maintained earlier, the priestly injunctions of Leviticus were finalized during the time of exile, we cannot miss their clarion call to Israel to imitate its God by living lives that reflect his intentions for them (Lev 11:44-45; 19:2; 20:7). In writing to his first-century audience, Peter uses the same language to remind his readers that the life they are to live must be separate from that of the broader culture and will define them as those who are attached to Christ. Holiness in 1 Peter constitutes a means for the church to live out its identity as a saved people. That is, as those who are now in Christ and are designated as God's people (1 Pet 2:9), their calling is to be holy as God is holy (1 Pet 1:15-16). As a holy community God's people are called to lives of engagement, not retreat from the world. Yet, their engaged lives must also reflect their relationship with Jesus in a way that shows themselves as distinct from those with whom they rub shoulders on a day-to-day basis. In the Western church a renewed idea of what it means to be holy as God's people today is necessary for effectiveness in these days of exilic existence.

LIVING A LIFE OF NARRATIVE HOLINESS

The church's life together is designed to be a text that tells an alternative story to the world, specifically God's story.[4] This is reflected in 1 Peter 2:4-5, where Peter describes the church as "living stones" connected to the "living Stone," Jesus himself. Thus they are "being built into a spiritual house to be a holy priesthood, offering spiritual sacrifices acceptable to God" (1 Pet 2:5). This language unambiguously connects Peter's church with the Jerusalem temple of old, the place where God dwelled in a unique and powerful way. Now, however, the presence of God is not primarily in a place but is in a people, and that people is Peter's audience and by extension the church wherever it is found.[5]

---

[4]To clarify, my use of the concept of the church as a "text" is not to imply that the Bible is insufficient as a text or that the church supersedes the Bible as a text. It is to acknowledge the important role that the church plays as a testimony to the truth of God and his word, and thus how it can be understood as another text that people can "read."

[5]As we noted in chapter three, this theological proposal, that God's presence dwells with a people more than in a place, begins to appear (albeit indirectly) in the book of Esther.

This invites us to think of holiness as an ongoing expression of the biblical narrative embodied in the ongoing life of God's people. This makes holiness an act of narrative, of living within the story of Scripture and dynamically interacting with that story so as to faithfully embody it in a contemporary context. This understanding of holiness is different than a static approach that takes the Bible as a book that was written and finished years ago and now must be applied and obeyed as an external law that has been handed down to us. Narrative holiness is guided by the idea that we are called to live by our story, not by a set of rules, to live according to a narrative that orients us in a way that runs in harmony with the story of God but may often run counter to the narrative of our culture. When we see Scripture as external to us, not something that we are a part of, it functions as someone else's story that we are now trying to learn from. When we understand it as our own story, we can enter it as those who are heirs of a tradition that we are attempting to faithfully perpetuate. Put another way, narrative holiness thinks about holiness as continuing to write God's story. It is an attempt to conscientiously participate in the ongoing expression of God's life in this world. This makes holiness deeply relational, as it is the outflow of our connection to God and is ultimately expressed in our connections with one another. Thus we enter into the biblical story, the story of who God is and how he relates to our world, and we seek to express that story in the way we live.

This changes the motivation for holiness from the idea of obeying God—or the Bible—to the idea of participating in the life of God and seeking to express that life faithfully. This deeply relational approach to holiness is not only more in keeping with the story of the Bible but also invites us to know God in relationship as the core value in what it means to be holy.

Thus holiness is the art of faithfully living out God's ongoing story in new times and new contexts. Holiness is artful faithfulness that seeks to appropriately live the way God has called his people to live at all times but also understands that holiness is always expressed in the time and place that God's people now find themselves. The practice of artful faithfulness is guided by the narrative of Scripture, but it is a great challenge because Scripture is not always clear on everything we face in our pursuit of holiness. Thus it calls for great courage and great discernment to live in a way that is faithful to God's ongoing story. In fact, at times we may even discern that our context can determine what it means to be holy. This of course raises questions about the timelessness of biblical truth and the transcultural application of its teaching. If holiness is an art more than a science and its expression can change in different times and places, how do we ever know whether we are getting it right? Some will reject this kind of subjectivity out of hand as unhelpful at best and unbiblical at worst. However, the biblical story—our story—addresses this tension and demonstrates that it is possible to live a holy life in different contexts. By looking briefly at two biblical examples, we can find the key to the art of living out narrative holiness.

The two biblical examples present the art of holiness in an interesting juxtaposition because while they offer different visions of what it means to be holy, they appear right beside each other in the canon of Scripture. The exilic narratives of Ezra and Nehemiah (treated here as one unit) present a vision of holiness that is highly separatistic. A key feature of their message is the idea that for Israel to truly be holy it needed to deal with and turn away from the practice of intermarriage with people from other nations. Ezra 10–11 reports on Ezra's confronting Israel on its need to repent from intermarriage with foreigners and then to take the extreme step of sending its mixed-race families away from the land in order to make things right before God. Nehemiah 10:30 reiterates this command. In both cases the people commit themselves to it. This epitomizes the vision of holiness that emerges from these two books, which calls Israel to express its uniqueness as a people through practices that keep it apart from other nations and radically emphasize its separateness from others.

Nehemiah is followed canonically by the book of Esther. In Esther we get a very different vision of holiness from that of Ezra–Nehemiah. As we explored in an earlier chapter, Esther is a controversial figure because of her complete immersion in Persian culture, including her marriage to the king, a Gentile. Esther is certainly not a poster child for the kind of holy life Ezra and Nehemiah had in mind. Esther's holiness, as we have

seen, is found in her faithfulness to her people and her willingness to act
on their behalf at a time of national crisis, even at the risk of her own life.
While she immerses herself in the ways of a foreign land, she expresses
her uniqueness as a representative of her people by putting their welfare
before her own in an act of great heroism.

It can be argued that both models exhibit artful faithfulness in their
own given contexts. For Ezra–Nehemiah the context is of return to the
land, where the reestablishment of things is paramount and the need to
return to original ideals is a necessary part of that project. In Esther we
find a situation in which extreme marginalization is occurring and in
which Israel's clear distinction from Persian customs is problematic, so
much so that its existence as a nation is in jeopardy (Esther 3:8 indicates
that Haman's appeal to the king for Israel's extermination is rooted in its
peculiarity as a people). In that context, holiness is a delicate dance between cultural engagement and fidelity to God's story for his people. In
both Ezra–Nehemiah and Esther the main characters are holy because
they live in a way faithful to the unfolding story of their God as it is
embodied in the life of his people.

The reality is that true holiness is found by living in the tension between these two ideals: living separate from the world and living fully
engaged with the world ("in" but not "of"). It is in the midst of this
tension that we recognize that in many ways these are competing callings,
and yet they must be held together creatively by those determined to live
faithful lives. This is the art of a relational, narrative holiness.

HELPING THE CHURCH TO BE HOLY

If the church is going to live out a relational, narrative holiness, then it
must be familiar with the story it is supposed to tell through its life together. Put another way, the church must be able to answer the question,
what is it that marks the church as "alternative"? As we have seen, 1 Peter
suggests that the mark is the church's being formed into a community
that reflects God's holiness as described in the law of Israel in general
and in Leviticus 19 in particular. In this sense, Peter's call to his audience
is that it continue to exist as a people in the world in the same way that

Israel was constituted to function as an embodiment of divine life for the world to see. Accordingly, the contents of a text like Leviticus 19 still retain their formational power for contemporary congregations who face challenges of personal and communal holiness similar to those of ancient exiles. A text such as Leviticus 19—as mediated via 1 Peter 1:15—is highly suggestive for the church in contemporary Western culture and can serve as a resource for an unfolding dialogue on communal life.

A New Testament text that continues the textual tradition of Leviticus and offers further aid in this important pastoral work of defining the exilic identity of the church today is the Sermon on the Mount (Mt 5–7). Here we find the clearest, most concise exploration of Jesus' vision for his community. Embodied in this text is a blueprint for a community that looks drastically different from what is normally found in the world of our common experience. Beginning with the Beatitudes (Mt 5:3-12) and covering topics such as adultery (Mt 5:27-32), dealing with enemies (Mt 5:43-48), care for the needy (Mt 6:1-4), financial stewardship (Mt 6:19-24) and judging others (Mt 7:1-6), this text sketches a defining picture of what a holy community looks like. Forming communities of engaged nonconformity will require understanding this text in a way that informs the daily choices of its members.[6]

Leadership in exile helps the church define its story and understand how to live out that story so that it can establish itself as a community that, through its life together, both critiques the establishment principles of the empire in which it finds itself and also offers another way of living that is demonstrated by the life of the church itself. In these exilic times it may be that an especially faithful act of pastoral leadership would be to lead a congregation in a protracted study of Leviticus 19 and Matthew 5–7 with thoughtful consideration given to the implication of these words on communal life. In the various venues in which preaching and teaching take place, texts become foundational for the casting and ex-

---

[6]For further consideration of the Sermon on the Mount as having formative power for shaping the church into the "hermeneutic of the Gospel," see Mark L. Branson, "Ecclesiology and Leadership for the Missional Church," in *The Missional Church in Context: Helping Congregations Develop Contextualized Ministry*, ed. Craig Van Gelder (Grand Rapids: Eerdmans, 2007), pp. 94-125.

ploring of God's vision for his people as distinct from their culture. This is not only an act of community building but also an act that is infused with missional possibility. For as the church lives out the communal vision offered in Scripture, it will become a place that increasingly has something truly different to offer to the world around it.

A further act of pastoral faithfulness in exile is to lead the church in prayer for a fresh anointing of the Spirit on its life together as God's people in this world. As 1 Peter conceives of its audience as a people formed by the Spirit, the contemporary church needs to ask God for new power from his Spirit, since it currently functions from a place of genuine weakness within a culture in which the power resides in the secularizing forces that are active in shaping it. The Scriptures provide the right knowledge for the church to develop as a countercultural community, but the Spirit is necessary to empower our obedience. In exile, public declarations of dependence on God are necessary for both the formation of the church and the appropriation of the Spirit's empowering in the life of the church. The act of leading the church in prayer for the Spirit's renewal places the locus of hope directly in God's hands and recognizes that without the formational work of the Spirit the church can never be what God has designed it to be.

New Testament scholar Morna Hooker tells the story of working with a group to prepare the *Methodist Service Book,* a liturgical resource for Methodist churches. When working on some of the intercessory prayer sections of the book, she noticed how liturgies in all traditions placed prayer for the church at the forefront of the sections on intercession. Hooker thought that this was a misguided way to pray, that the church should demonstrate love for others first by praying for the needs of the world before finally turning to internal needs. However, the committee she worked with refused the changes that she suggested. On reflection, Dr. Hooker came to understand their logic: "The Church is Christ's body, carrying on his work. We need to pray for the Church, *in order that* we may pray and work for others."[7]

---

[7]Morna Hooker and Frances Young, *Holiness and Mission* (Norwich: SCM Press, 2011), p. 12 (italics original).

To lead the church effectively we must make prayer for the Spirit's anointing on the church a matter of regular prayer in our public, pastoral prayers. Organized times of prayer, which are always crucial to the life of the church, take on new urgency when we are working from the margins because we realize that any help we received from the public square is either waning or all but gone, and God is now our only real source of help. Exile invites us to once again return to the source of our life as Christ's body, the Spirit himself, and prayer is our way of addressing him.

The centrality of the Scriptures and the Spirit are certainly not new ideas in the church or for approaching exile. Certainly Second Temple Jews understood the need for a written record that would guide and inform their lives, and thus, as we have already considered, in exile the Hebrew Scriptures took definitive shape as the Hebrew people determined those documents that were critical to the understanding and practice of their faith. The corpus of a holy writ that emerged would serve as a foundation to their religious identity. Scripture must be emphasized if the church is to grow into its identity as a "royal priesthood, a holy nation" who "declare[s] the praises of him" to the world (1 Pet 2:9). The biblical Word is always central to guiding the church into obedience. Faithfulness to the Word directs the creation of an alternative community. At the same time, the church must rely on the work of the Spirit, who enables its obedience and guides its life as an engaged, nonconformed community. As we do both of these things, we will be able to live into the tension of a narrative holiness that helps the world read the story of Scripture through us.

LIVING A LIFE OF ENGAGED NONCONFORMITY

Exilic holiness is fully engaged with culture while not fully conforming to it. Living as a Christian exile in Western culture calls the church to live its life constructively embedded within society while not being enslaved to all of its norms and ideals. Sometimes holiness has a personal cost and demands taking a stand that draws attention to oneself. At other times holiness is not defined by dramatic action but by the day-to-day choices we make. This is not a new idea, for it is what the church has always been called to. However, the exilic situation is always ambiguous for those placed within it. When one has autonomy and the power to make the rules, life is slightly less complex. When one is the one who determines what is "right," it is much easier to do what is right. Exile takes away such power and leaves one in a situation where what one thinks is right may be different from what the prevailing culture thinks is right. In such circumstances decisions must be made about how to do right and about which formerly held beliefs and practices can be reshaped so as to fit a new context. For Christians living in Western culture, holiness will entail trying to live a biblically directed life in a continually shifting moral climate. Once more, this is not new; however, as the culture of Christendom continues to recede, the challenge of holiness increases. The work of leadership is to help the church learn how to engage culture effectively and build discernment so as to decide when and how it must disengage from cultural ideals so as not to conform to them in inappropriate ways.

As we have seen from our study of Esther, one of the marks of her character and her success as a Jew living in Diaspora was that she lived a life of proportionality in contrast to a culture of excess. While those around her were given to displays of grandeur, Esther displayed a more modest approach. This is crucial to helping the church understand our own engagement with our culture. Proportionality requires that cultural participation occur not mindlessly but with discernment and a sense of morality that flows from an appreciation of a biblically informed identity as Christ's church. While most Christians will choose to participate in the mainstream culture of materialistic consumerism, our participation is best marked by a proportionality that reflects a commitment to things beyond material acquisition. Spending will be balanced by joyful giving in ways that benefit the work of the church and the needs of the surrounding community. In a consumer culture, consistent, generous giving is a countercultural practice that can demonstrate proportionality in our citizenship.[8] Furthermore, many Christians will choose to participate in

---

[8]In my home country of Canada, for example, according to a comprehensive 2007 study done under the auspices of Statistics Canada, 84 percent of Canadians fifteen and older reportedly

the political process by critiquing, even protesting, important social and political issues. Such involvement is appropriate yet also demands proportionality. This means that not only will our discourse be respectful and modest, but we will also refrain from the inflammatory, uncharitable and unfair rhetoric that often marks current civic discourse around controversial issues. Just as Esther worked within the system and lobbied for her preferred positions, when given opportunity she spoke and acted with decency and proportion.[9]

Engaging the process even further, some will choose to run for public office and participate in various levels of government. Daniel's example legitimates this response to exile and provides a model for those in power to follow. His entering fully into the corridors of power reminds us that just because one is in exile does not mean that one should not take advantage of the possibilities for influence that come as a result of participation in the power structures of society. Serving in government offers Christians an exilic strategy that should not be neglected as long as it remains an option.

Esther modeled a positive cultural engagement, but she also took a nonconformist stand when the future of her nation was at stake. She acted on behalf of her people even though her own life was at risk.[10] Daniel, who also embodies full cultural engagement, clearly demonstrates holiness as a cultural act of nonconformity in a number of his actions. Whether regarding his refusal to not eat nonkosher food (Dan 1:8), his friends' refusal to bow to the king's idol (Dan 3), or Daniel's own commitment to praying to Yahweh in the face of a royal edict that no

---

give to charitable organizations. However, the top 10 percent of givers, defined as those who give over $1,002 per year, give almost two-thirds (62%) of total donations. See "Caring Canadians, Involved Canadians: Highlights from the 2007 Canada Survey of Giving, Volunteering and Participating," www.givingandvolunteering.ca/files/giving/en/csgvp_highlights_2007.pdf.

[9]Carol M. Bechtel makes the point that even when Esther asks for a counteredict from the king that will see the slaughter of many Persians within the city of Susa, her request is not out of proportion to the degree of hatred that still prevailed against the Jews there (Esther 9:13-15). See Bechtel, *Esther* (Louisville, KY: John Knox, 2002), p. 9.

[10]In addition to noting that the example of Esther is problematic even in her own day, this continues to be the case in light of Christian ethics and the cultural values of our own era. Accordingly Esther's example raises difficult questions about how we apply scriptural examples—questions that we cannot fully explore here.

such prayers should be offered in Babylon (Dan 6), there are times when engagement with culture is trumped by faithfulness to holiness as defined by God's standards. At times like these, holiness becomes a form of nonviolent protest against the ways of the host culture. It is not simply a negative rejection of certain cultural practices but a positive affirmation of our own beliefs as the people of God.

First Peter positions its overarching call to holiness in 1 Peter 1:15 on the practicality of ongoing life choices that would have allowed for the church to remain engaged with the mainstream of its culture. However, we also know that in the early years of the church Christians were known for their repudiation of some of the mainstream cultural pleasures for which the Roman world was famous, such as the theater, pagan religion, gladiatorial contests and races. Rejection of these cultural practices sometimes brought persecution.[11] This may have been the case for some in 1 Peter's audience who were being persecuted as a result of their commitment to Christ (1 Pet 2:20; 3:16). This persecution may be inevitable when one seeks to live a holy life in an exilic situation; at times it will draw attention, and on some occasions that attention may come at a high price.

If the church is to remain faithful to God in a time of exile, it will have to practice holiness in everyday living by making proper moral choices on things like being honest in the workplace, being faithful in our marriages, being kind to our neighbors and being willing to serve in our communities. At other times outright rejection of cultural norms will be necessary. This will inevitably be the case for young people and single adults who reject the cultural norm of sexual activity outside marriage. Such a stance may provoke quizzical looks at a minimum and could also draw ridicule of one type or another, but this practice acts as both a critique of the hegemonic culture and as an affirmation of God's ideals. In other circumstances the church's attempt to adhere to doctrinal purity may bring it into conflict with the mainstream of current cultural thought. It may mean being featured unfavorably in the media for taking a clear position on right-to-life issues or for refusing to let a Hindu group

---

[11]D. A. Carson, "1 Peter," in *Commentary of the New Testament Use of the Old Testament*, ed. G. K. Beale and D. A. Carson (Grand Rapids: Baker, 2007), pp. 1032-33.

advertise its meditation classes for young people in our church bulletins. A stand for the uniqueness, even exclusivity, of Jesus can bring charges of intolerance and bigotry; expressing the faith with integrity will mean that sometimes such a stance will be required. Exile inevitably brings those affected by it into conflict with the powers that make exile a reality.

As Bryan Stone describes it, the church must exercise a "holy and evangelical eccentricity" that will not always be tolerated not only because it behaves differently but also because it exposes the folly of prevailing systems.[12] This is at the heart of a missional holiness that bears witness to the life of God embodied in an alternative community of faith. Loving our enemies and refusing to seek revenge cause the world to see the emptiness of its own violence. Sharing resources and caring for the poor reveal the artificiality of accumulation and competition. Welcoming the stranger offers a positive critique of the fear and suspicion that so often govern human interaction. Reconciliation and forgiveness stand in contrast to the hostility and division that typify opponents in many parts of the public square.

For church leaders, developing a doctrine of holiness that reflects an engaged nonconformity will not only allow the church to be effective in the world but will also remind it that at times it must protest the ways of the world by refusing to conform. The next proposal is central in directing that effort.

LIVING A LIFE OF LOVE

Too often as Christians when we think of holiness we think of all the things that we should be against or should not do. Holiness can largely be cast in negative terms, and as a result the church is often known more for what it is against than what it is for. When opinion polls are taken that seek to get a sense of how the church is perceived, people most often express their understanding of the church as being against things. They see the church as being against gay people, against people who live in common-law relationships, against people of other religions, against

---

[12]Bryan Stone, *Evangelism After Christendom: The Theology and Practice of Christian Witness* (Grand Rapids: Brazos, 2007), p. 315.

people who vote Democrat, against people who like to party and so on. In a course that I teach on mission, one of the assignments I give to my students is to interview two people who currently do not attend church and would not consider themselves to be practicing Christians. One of the questions they ask those they interview is why they think most people don't attend church. The answers are usually very similar and predictable. They see the church as cold, detached and judgmental. Sometimes they specifically identify the kinds of issues listed above as indicators of the church's unwelcoming nature. Without clearly saying so, they understand the church to have a certain moral code that isolates it from outsiders and vice versa. In other words, the church's practice of holiness is not seen as a benefit but rather as an encumbrance to its effectiveness.

Of course, there is a sense that whenever a group of people is guided by a story that in places runs counter to the story of the predominant culture, they will at times stand apart from the crowd and will be perceived negatively. However, this inevitability notwithstanding, could it be that one of the reasons why the church is perceived the way that it is is that we have a misplaced emphasis on what it means to live a holy life? In emphasizing certain behaviors and lifestyles as "wrong," perhaps we have missed emphasizing the way that holiness is genuinely expressed.

Ultimately nothing is more central to expressing God's holiness than love. This is at the heart of Jesus' words to his disciples regarding how love would be the clearest indicator of their relationship with him (Jn 13:34-35). The love of the disciples' community would reflect Jesus' love for them and also reflect their connection to the God of love (1 Jn 4:7-8) and thus be a demonstration of his nature to the world. Jesus also taught the fundamental truth that a life pleasing to God is rooted in a relational holiness centered in love for God and for our fellow human beings (Mt 22:37-40). As we have already considered, Peter fully understands that love is at the heart of holiness when he calls his churches in the first century to live lives of holiness (1 Pet 1:22; 3:8; 4:8). Whether our engagement with the world is positive or leads us into conflict with the power structures of our society, it must be an expression of love for the world that compels us, because that is what compels God to engage with the world (Jn 3:16).

The reality is that many Christians and the congregations that they populate do their very best to live this way. In my experience the church is a very loving place, filled with genuinely loving people. Unfortunately, this is not the way that we are perceived by the world. Perhaps some of this perception is unalterable because unless love is experienced it can be hard to believe. Love has to be embodied, and if people only see Christians on TV acting unloving or standing up for an unpopular moral position, then their perceptions will be formed by those things alone. In order for the holiness of true Christian love to break down those barriers, it must be experienced, and this can only happen when a person is a recipient of that love. This can only occur as we move out of our churches and allow the holy love of God to flow through our lives in relationship with others.

Charles Colson, a former aide to President Richard Nixon and a Watergate conspirator who turned into an advocate for prisoners and prison reform as well as a noted Christian author and speaker, tells the story of taking a group of volunteers to visit inmates on death row at a prison in Indiana. The group's time at the prison was drawing to a close, and Colson had an important meeting with the governor of Indiana that he had to get to. Time was of the essence, and one of the volunteers was holding everything up while he remained in conversation with one of the inmates, James Brewer. Colson recounts the scenario in his book *Loving God*:

> "I'm sorry, we have to leave," I said, looking nervously at my watch, knowing a plane stood waiting at a nearby airstrip to fly me to Indianapolis to meet with Governor Orr. The volunteer, a short white man in his early fifties, was standing shoulder to shoulder with Brewer. The prisoner was holding his Bible open while the older man appeared to be reading a verse.
>
> "Oh, yes," the volunteer looked up. "Give us just a minute, please. This is important," he added softly.
>
> "No, I'm sorry," I snapped. "I can't keep the governor waiting. We must go."
>
> "I understand," the man said, still speaking softly, "but this is important.

You see, I'm Judge Clement. I'm the man who sentenced James here to die. But now he's my brother and we want a minute to pray together."

     I stood frozen in the cell doorway. It didn't matter who I kept waiting. Before me were two men: one was powerless, the other powerful; one was black, the other white; one had sentenced the other to death. Anywhere other than the kingdom of God, that inmate might have killed that judge with his bare hands—or wanted to anyway. Now they were one, their faces reflecting an indescribable expression of love as they prayed together.[13]

This story is an example of the way love can eloquently express the holy "otherness" of God and his people. It crosses boundaries of many kinds and touches the core of our true humanity, awakening us to the possibility that the message of life in Christ may in fact have potential as a guiding narrative for our lives. For this possibility to be created, Christians must embody that love outside their comfortable Christian circles.

     A life of love that is outward and engaged will consistently challenge us to be open hearted toward all people. It will cause us to see the beauty of all people and affirm the work of God in them, even if they themselves are unaware of it or reject it. In fact, this is how we can cultivate love in our lives: by intentionally giving ourselves to being in relationship with others whose spiritual commitments are different from ours. If you want to grow in love, the way to do it is not likely going to be by attending more Bible studies or prayer meetings; it will happen by getting close to people who are not like you. It is there that we discover the reality of God's image in everyone and that we put a face to things we may not like or agree with.

     It is easy to be against homosexuals when you don't know any homosexual people. When you become friends with a gay person, your thoughts on the issue are invariably challenged, and you are forced to develop more grace and nuance in your approach to someone different from yourself. More often than not, your capacity to love grows, and thus so does your ability to reflect God's holiness.

     Vincent Donovan was a Catholic missionary to Tanzania from 1957–1973. In his work with the Maasai people, he saw numerous men and

---

[13]Charles Colson, *Loving God* (Grand Rapids: Zondervan, 1997), pp. 193-94.

women come to faith in Jesus, and the church become visibly established in an otherwise unreached part of the world. In his work with this warrior people, who had absolutely no acquaintance with the Christian gospel before he got there, he learned that the holiness of love was the core of faithfully bearing witness to Jesus. Taking time to be present with the people and genuinely engaging them in love was the foundation of his ministry to them. In a letter to family and friends at home in the United States he wrote:

> I had been encouraging the people of this village—men, women, and warriors—to talk and tell me what they thought about the world and life and death and God. One cannot but be moved by listening to people of another culture, a culture more ancient than one's own, speaking their deepest thoughts about such things. And I was moved. Here was a way of looking at the world, and a whole world picture entirely different from anything I had known.[14]

Donovan's unique ministry was fueled by a love for the people of Tanzania that grew up from being among them. Through him people came into contact with God's love personally, and this offered them a positive experience of the gospel that opened them up to further dialogue and eventually acceptance of it as their own story. Donovan's experience can inform our own as we learn to live among people far different from ourselves. We too must love in a way that invites people to tell us their stories, share their true thoughts and repeat their experience of life in this world. An open heart toward them is an expression of relational holiness that embodies God's holy love for them as his children.

Love is the essence of holiness because it is the essence of God. Our own experience of God's love and being in fellowship with him is the relational fusion that leads us to love others. This is how relational holiness works, as we allow our own experience of God to be expressed in our relationships with others.

---

[14]This is an excerpt from a letter Donovan wrote in July 1969, in John P. Bowen, *The Missionary Letters of Vincent Donovan: 1957–1973* (Eugene, OR: Pickwick, 2011), p. 141. For a clear expression of Donovan's love for the people he worked with see Bowen, *Missionary Letters*, p. 119.

LIVING A LIFE OF GRACE

Churches rarely err on the side of being too gracious. Sometimes within church circles one encounters people who are wary that the church may be guilty of offering too much grace to people in and outside the church. The idea is that if too much grace is offered people will abuse it. They will live in ways that are not faithfully Christian, and if the church "lets them get away with it" not only will the grace-abusing sinner be lost, but also the church will also be on the hook before an unhappy God. While it is certainly possible to abuse grace and thus cheapen it by not emphasizing our obligation to be obedient to God as a response to his grace, rarely can the church be accused of being too gracious. When one considers the lavishness of God's grace depicted in Scripture and as experienced by humans, it is not hard to conclude that the church can still do better when it comes to extending God's grace to others.

As we touched on in chapter five, one of the themes running through the book of Jonah is his refusal (or lack of desire) to believe that God would extend the same grace to the Assyrians that he does to Israel. Jonah reminds us of how we can become hostile to those who are antagonistic toward us and forget that God longs for them to experience his grace, too, and that he has chosen his people to share that grace with them. First Peter's emphasis on love (1 Pet 1:22; 3:8; 4:8) intrinsically emphasizes grace as necessary among the members of his exilic community.

If the church is to be a community of holiness, then it will also need to be a community with a robust doctrine of grace. There are at least two reasons for this. First, in order to pursue holiness we need a doctrine of grace that will allow room in our lives for inevitable failure. This occurs personally when we fall short of being the persons we know Christ wants us to be, and it occurs communally when we fall short as a collective body. Without a good theology of grace, we can easily become discouraged. We are well aware of our own shortcomings, and if we don't have a clear sense that God is gracious to us in our failings we can easily become discouraged and feel defeated, even to the point of wanting to give up because we have come to believe we are perpetually unworthy and displeasing to God. This is a tough way to life. Collectively, if our theology of grace is lacking, we can become cynical about the overall lack of perfection in the church. We begin to see the failings and focus on the gap between what the church is supposed to be and what it actually is. Without a good grasp of grace, people can start to believe that the whole venture is a lost cause. The result is we either give up or live in perpetual cynicism, criticizing the church because it is never good enough, and having an overly harsh attitude that can be oppressive in both our own lives and the life of the church. The appropriate function of grace helps us to cope with the personal and communal shortcomings that are inevitable in the lives of human beings trying to represent something divine.

This is not to say that we do not take the pursuit of righteousness seriously. The epistle of 1 John reminds us that a life of perpetual sin does not reflect a genuine connection with Jesus and is not the way Christians are called to live (1 Jn 3:3-6). Earlier in the same letter, the author tells his audience that he is writing so that they will not sin (1 Jn 2:1); however, he assures them that if anyone does sin Jesus is available as their advocate to atone for their failings (1 Jn 2:1-2). In his attempt to help develop a community of holiness, John recognizes that an assurance of grace, rooted in the doctrine of the atonement, is necessary if his church is going to realistically live out this vision of holiness.

Second, and more positively, a proper doctrine of grace can act as a motivation toward holiness. Grace allows us to make room for the reality of sin and offers the hope of forgiveness and a new beginning. As this happens in the life of a congregation, a culture is created that acknowledges that sin is going to happen, but when it does the church is a place of grace that offers many chances to try again. This motivates us to keep going and to remain open to God's word operating through his Spirit, forming the church and bearing with it as it struggles toward the fulfillment of its calling. This does not eliminate the call to obedience but enhances it by reminding the church that when failure occurs and we do not behave as God's holy people, we will learn to forgive and start again. In no way does this deny the possibility of the need for church discipline in certain circumstances, as this too can be an expression of grace and must function appropriately in the body. However, what is needed for a church to become holy is a theology of grace that allows for failures to occur in a way that nonetheless empowers the continued pursuit of a more perfect holiness.

The theological vision for such practice is of course rooted in the very nature of God himself. In a powerful declaration of self-revelation, God discloses to Moses his true nature when he says to him in Exodus 34:6, "The LORD, the LORD, the compassionate and gracious God, slow to anger, abounding in love and faithfulness." These words and others like them in Scripture (cf. Ps 103:7-12) are central to our understanding of who God is and what this then means for the church to embody his life collectively. If we are to show who God is to the world around us, then we must demonstrate the immensity of his grace.

On occasion I have encountered people who think that their church is "too gracious," as I briefly mentioned at the beginning of this section. By that they mean too tolerant of sin or lax on calling people to account for their supposed shortcomings. I was once told by a church leader that in his church "we hear a lot about grace." From there he went on to say that he thought it was spoken about too much at the expense of other important doctrines such as God's judgment. My response is to wonder whether it is possible to be "too gracious." Has any church ever fully offered the extensive grace that God offers to us? Has any church completely embodied the gracious, compassionate, patient nature of God to its community? It seems to me that far from being too gracious the church has not been gracious enough. We are connected to a God of grace, and part of demonstrating his character is embodying his grace faithfully and fully. While the failures of the church often compromise its witness to society, what we need is to not be more condemning of those who fail but more gracious in the same way that God is gracious. This will enable the exilic church to more fully reflect the true nature of God and, perhaps, to offer the world a community of holy grace that truly is an "alternative" to the world's ways and thus is inviting to others.

In order to accomplish this, church leaders must develop a biblical theology of grace, and faithfully teach and seek to model it in their leadership and through authentic living in order to help the church become such a community. The challenge in doing this will always be great, but it is at the heart of holy living in a time of exile.

CONCLUSION

As we considered at the outset of this chapter, the development of identity is crucial to maturity. Furthermore, developing identity helps to define a community and imbues it with a sense of its own distinctiveness within the larger society. For the church, this is always a crucial aspect of its life together as it seeks to embody its call to be God's people in a particular context. As exiles living on the margins of Western society, discerning what God's call to holiness looks like is part of the church's calling. Perhaps in the days of pseudo-Christendom the church sought to be faithful to a moral code that was broadly accepted, if not practiced, by large segments of the culture. This ethos allowed the church to take the position of a kind of conscience in the culture, reminding people of what was right and making them feel guilty for their lack of adherence to it. Today, an application of God's holiness that respects the change in our world is called for. It is a holiness that emphasizes living engaged but nonconformed lives that are guided by love and exercise genuine, abundant grace that will enable the church to distinguish itself as an alternative, holy people and thus serve the culture from the margins.

11

Exilic Mission

ENGAGING THE CULTURE AS EXILES

For Israel, exile brought about a rediscovery of its missional nature and a reminder that it was still commissioned to be a "light for the Gentiles" (Is 42:6). In the same way, the marginalization of the church in the Western world is awakening a new missional focus that is both a response to the new relationship between church and culture and a rediscovery of the church's true nature.[1] Once again the biblical resources we have been employing offer a template for exilic living as they provide a missional perspective for their audience. First Peter in particular is relevant in terms of how the church is to function in a cultural situation of exile. Just as Israel needed to see that despite its exile God was still calling the people to be his witnesses, the recipients of 1 Peter are also invited to see that their social marginalization in no way negates their calling to fulfill the commission that Jesus gave to the church to be his witnesses. Therefore it is not surprising that the decentering of the church and the challenges of a post-Christian culture provide an impetus for the church

---

[1]For representative literature that reflects the contours of this discussion, see Darrell L. Guder, *Missional Church: A Vision for the Sending of the Church in North America* (Grand Rapids: Eerdmans, 1998); Michael W. Goheen, *A Light to the Nations: The Missional Church and the Biblical Story* (Grand Rapids: Baker Academic, 2011); Craig Van Gelder, *The Ministry of the Missional Church: A Community Led by the Spirit* (Grand Rapids: Baker, 2007); and Michael Frost, *Exiles: Living Missionally in a Post-Christian Culture* (Peabody, MA: Hendrickson, 2006). Many of these authors see the loss of a missional identity in the church as the core reason for the decline of Christendom.

to rediscover its true identity and rethink how it can fulfill its mandate to mission.[2] Inevitably reflection on this reality will cause the church to reconfigure its approach to mission in some necessary ways.

MISSION THROUGH RELATIONSHIPS

As we have seen, the missional identity of the church as described in 1 Peter is played out primarily in the context of social relationships, particularly as they are characterized by mutual submission, one to another. What does this mean in a twenty-first-century context?

First, it means that the church is intentional in forging relationships with its community. This requires the church to find ways to engage its community that build relationships. This calls the church to truly be present in the community, to live with the people it is called to serve. Practically speaking, it means that a local congregation must determine where it can connect with the people of its community so it can understand and help meet the community's needs as it builds relationships. In one place, this could mean providing affordable daycare; in another it could mean an afterschool program for children; in another it could be a monthly Saturday night dance that allows people to connect socially and build relationships.

Of even greater importance is how these relationships function. First Peter teaches the importance of submission in relational life, which will mean that the church seeks to live unselfishly, giving preference to the needs of others and not insisting on getting its own way. This is a perennial problem within the church and often leads to church fights and splits, and it diminishes the witness of the collective body in the world. In a post-Christian culture, transformed relationships are necessary to facilitate the testimony of the church. Missional relationships call us to be listeners and caregivers in a way that embodies the care and compassion of God himself. It asks us to, like Jesus, be willing to be found with the "sinners" and the unlovely so that the relational priorities of God are found in our lives too. In extreme circumstances it may mean

---

[2]Elaine Heath, *The Mystic Way of Evangelism* (Grand Rapids: Baker, 2008), p. 27.

not seeking retribution on those who persecute us but instead giving up our right to justice. This kind of humility offers a testimony to our affiliation with Christ and his power to transform not only individual lives but also culture when his model is sincerely followed.

Furthermore, this kind of relational evangelism means that the church itself will function as a place that demonstrates the power of Christ to transform human relationships. This requires the development of many practical habits, such as learning how to share our resources and how to open our hearts and lives so that we live authentically, remaining committed to one another in the midst of relational struggles and communal strife, and even learning how to open up the life of our immediate family so that newcomers and "strangers" can be included.[3] This kind of countercultural community is what identifies the church as God's people, confirms his work among us and helps to give the church its evangelistic potency.

A family I know embodied this kind of relational witness when they took in a young, unwed mother from a very difficult background and home life. When the young girl found herself pregnant but wanting to keep her baby, my friend and her family stepped in and made a place for her in their home. They did this despite the fact that they already had children of their own and lived very busy lives. It has not been easy, but their commitment to serve this young woman in this way flows from a deep commitment to express God's love to others. This is not to insinuate that Christians have the corner on the market when it comes to this kind of hospitality, but this kind of commitment to others is an extension of Christian holiness that is lived out in deeply relational terms. It carries great potential for giving witness to the gospel in a post-Christian age.

MISSION AND PROCLAMATION

In the story of Jonah our reticence for missional engagement is challenged. The story clearly implies that God's people must be willing to engage ("go," Mt 28:19-20) the world and offer the good news God has

---

[3]For an extended exploration of these ideas and the concept of the church as a family, see Joseph H. Hellerman, *When the Church Was a Family: Recapturing Jesus' Vision for Authentic Christian Community* (Nashville: B & H, 2009), especially chap. 6.

for all people. Even more importantly Jonah's story confronts us with the reality of God's great concern for all people (Jon 4:11). This challenge makes remaining aloof from people outside the church a nonoption for those who are a part of the church.

While the primary evangelistic strategy offered by Peter involves non-verbal action, in 1 Peter 3:15 he counsels the use of words to offer a "reason for the hope that you have." This call to proclaim the faith leads us to consider two specific applications of ancient exilic missional thinking in the postmodern Western context.

Church-based, community-centered evangelism. Appropriating the wisdom of 1 Peter and the exilic models of Esther, Daniel and Jonah requires adopting a dual focus in our approach to mission that can appear contradictory on the surface. On the one hand, mission is exemplified in these models (discounting Jonah for the moment) by a quiet, nonintrusive engagement with the broader culture. On the other hand the New Testament command for the church to go into the world (and here we can reengage Jonah) requires some kind of outward orientation to the church's life. In the models we are employing as our exilic advisers, we can see the importance of a particular distinctiveness of life as central to the effectiveness of one's witness. Esther behaves with loyalty; Daniel remains faithful to the laws of his faith; Peter calls for holiness in his churches as a sign of their commitment to Christ. This reminds us of the importance of the inner life of the community in mission.[4] Yet we also see how there is an outward orientation in these books. Esther depicts the conversion of many Persians to Judaism; Daniel depicts the foreign kingdoms in which Daniel serves as coming to recognize Yahweh as the true God; 1 Peter casts a vision to his community that their goal for living faithfully is the conversion of their oppressors; and Jonah clearly calls for its readers to have a missional vision for all people. This reminds us that our vision can never be exclusively inward or exclusively outward.

---

[4]As discussed earlier, in taking Esther, Daniel and Jonah as "advice tales" we are assuming that as characters they in some way are designed to embody the life of Israel as a nation. Therefore what they do or don't do is instructive to the nation as a whole. Thus we can rightly apply their model to the "community" as a whole.

The proposal offered here is that mission must be rooted in the life of the church but also include an outward thrust that takes seriously the missional nature of God's people and Christ's call for his church to be a people who go into the world. Traditionally it has been understood that in the Old Testament Israel's primary call, or "strategy," for mission was *centripetal*, that is that it was called to give testimony to the greatness of Yahweh through its internal life as a nation. By Israel's worshiping and practicing the law faithfully, other nations would see the quality of its national life and be drawn to worship Yahweh themselves (Deut 4:5-8). In the New Testament, we come to the book of Acts and read Jesus' vision for the church to ultimately go to the ends of the earth with the gospel message (Acts 1:8). As the story of the early church transpires, we see the church intentionally going into new areas with the express intent of bearing witness to the work of Christ. This approach to mission has been called *centrifugal*, that is, the inner life of the church actually spread outward so that it is brought to places with the hope that people there would receive the message and enter into the new life of Christ that was lived out by the church. What is necessary for mission in a post-Christian culture is a commitment to both of these approaches.[5]

Evangelistic methodologies employed in Christendom have largely been based on what is commonly called an attractional model of evangelism. In this model, evangelism is often centered on a program or an event that was potentially attractive for people to attend. As an example, perhaps one of the most outwardly successful evangelistic methods for many years was the evangelistic crusade epitomized by Billy Graham's ministry. These events were often large spectacles that met in hockey arenas, football stadiums or large tents. They employed contemporary music, multimedia presentations and interviews with famous celebrities who testified about their faith in Christ, and they featured a "famous" preacher like Graham. While Billy Graham's organization, like those of many other evangelists, sought to work with local churches in order to promote the crusade and follow up on new converts, the events were

---

[5]Goheen, *Light to the Nations*, pp. 129-32.

nonetheless largely independent endeavors. Their success was to a large degree predicated on the name of the preacher, the size of the event and the quality of the program offered. The crusade was result oriented, with its success measured largely in terms of how many people "made decisions" for Christ. This was usually indicated by how many people responded to an altar call. Evangelism was usually centered on the event itself. While relationships may have been important in terms of Christians inviting their non-Christian friends, the "real" evangelism would have been perceived as happening at the crusade meeting itself.

Another example of an approach to evangelism reflective of Christendom is the local church outreach program in which churches offer a program designed specifically for nonbelievers. It might be a children's vacation Bible school program, a concert featuring a Christian artist, or an Alpha program, all of which would contain a message of Christian truth and offer an invitation to believe the message. These programs are usually highly utilitarian in that they are designed to offer something perceived as useful, relevant and ultimately helpful to the everyday life of a nonbeliever. Whether they provide a fresh, simple approach to Christianity, a night of entertainment (with a message) or an inexpensive program for children (and maybe a break for busy suburban parents), they are depicted as something with practical value for the user but also serves as a vehicle for the church to reach out to people with the gospel message.

These methods serve a purpose and have led many people to a genuine relationship with Jesus. However, they are approaches that work in a culture that has some predisposition toward Christianity and even to the church itself. To test this theory, one only has to ask how these methods would work in a different age—Peter's, for example? It is quite unimaginable to consider Peter suggesting to his churches that they should host an outreach concert or start a seeker service, not just because these are later-day innovations but because the pagan population that surrounded these churches in Asia Minor would have in no way been predisposed to attend anything of the sort. Just as these were not options for Peter's church, so they are increasingly less appropriate options for a marginalized church in an increasingly un-Christian Western culture today.

What was Peter's strategy for mission? It was for the church to act as a witness to the surrounding community through the quality of its life together, then to go outside the church and live in a way that continues to bear witness to the people encountered in everyday life. This was the foundation of the church's mission: the church as a witness through its common life, and Christians as witnesses as they proceeded into their world to live out their faith. Bryan Stone reflects the New Testament idea of church as witness when he writes, "Baptism was far more than a symbolic nod to tradition or a quick initiatory rite, but rather one's commissioning into a missionary existence."[6]

The temptation and often the pressure on church leaders is to always be devising a new evangelistic strategy or promoting the latest program that is working in other settings. This is not wrong in itself; in fact, evangelistic strategy can be part of missional effectiveness. However, it is not the core idea of mission in 1 Peter (or the New Testament as a whole). Peter's instruction to the exilic church is that faithful evangelistic witness comes in the form of the simple, daily obedience of Christian people living together in authentic New Testament community and going into their world as ambassadors for Christ.

Such a "strategy" encounters resistance in the church because it can be perceived as insufficiently direct or aggressive, particularly so in a consumer culture that is nurtured on products being marketed strategically. Also, such an approach may not appear to some to be sufficiently "result" oriented. In a culture that likes to quantify things so as to measure their efficiency, an approach that places the emphasis on community formation and mission through simply being intentional about involvement in the wider society may not deliver easily measurable results. However, while crusade evangelism and user-friendly programs may have been highly viable forms of public witness in a culture of Christendom, in exile they are far less effective. While they may still have a marginal place in the overall mission of the Western church as Chris-

[6]Bryan Stone, *Evangelism After Christendom: The Theology and Practice of Christian Witness* (Grand Rapids: Brazos, 2007), p. 104.

tendom wanes, it is the life of an alternative community, demonstrating a distinct quality of life that is ready to give an answer about that life when asked, that will prove most evangelistically effective in the current cultural reality.

As we will see, this calls the church to become a community that is intrinsically missional as opposed to being one that "does" mission. The difference between the two may be subtle, and it does not eliminate the possibility that a missional church might decide to develop a strategy for mission or to organize a mission project, but a truly missional church may be described using the following four characteristics that are adapted from the work of Michael Frost:[7]

1. A missional church understands that we, in the West, live in a post-Christian culture and that the church now functions from the margins as opposed to being at the center.

Many of the influential church models of recent decades come from the *Field of Dreams* model; they operate on the principle of "build it and they will come." Whether the emphasis was on contemporary worship, charismatic manifestations, seeker services or Bible teaching, the idea was consistently that people would come to the church if we provided them with something that related to them and met their needs.

The missional church understands that the church has lost its place in Western culture and now finds itself on the margins of culture, with declining attendance and diminished influence.

2. A missional church takes seriously the call to "go" and make disciples.

The missional church understands that it can no longer run programs and expect people to respond. The church must go to the people and seek ways to demonstrate the gospel through actions and words outside the confines of the church building and community. This, as we have discussed, is intrinsic to the church's identity and does not negate the undergirding need for community formation in the church and for our "going" to be culturally appropriate in the

---

[7]Frost, *Exiles*, p. 55.

forms of mission that are undertaken. However, any church that takes its missional identity seriously realizes that engaging with "the world" is a necessity.

3. A missional church is organized around mission as opposed to being a church that does mission.

Missional churches start with mission. Missional churches are driven by a theology that believes that God is by nature a missional God. The church is itself an expression of God's mission (*missio Dei*). Some churches "do" mission. They include mission in their list of church activities, but it is not necessarily at the heart of what they do. Rather, "building up the body" is given priority as the purpose for the church. Missional churches, by contrast, see mission as the core of their identity and live out this identity in all they do. Put another way, missional churches primarily understand themselves as being sent (like missionaries) into the world for the sake of those who do not currently know Christ. The work of building the body is crucial but only to the extent that it serves the purpose of mission.

4. A missional church sees itself and its ministry as an expression of the incarnation of Christ.

The incarnation of Christ informs the theology of the missional church. Missional churches believe that as God entered the world in human form, adherents enter (individually and communally) into the context of the culture and society around them, aiming to transform that culture through local involvement in it. This holistic involvement may take many forms, including social activism, hospitality and individual acts of kindness, as well as verbally proclaiming the message of Christ's saving work. Missional living makes the church part of the culture while still acknowledging that it is an outsider who ultimately lives on the margins. Missional churches take seriously the idea that God is at work in this world and that the church is called to participate in that work.[8] This approach is reflective of the models we have been considering in this

---

[8]Torrey Seland, "Resident Aliens in Mission: Missional Practices in the Emerging Church of 1 Peter," *Bulletin for Biblical Research* 19, no. 4 (2009): 568.

study (Esther, Daniel, 1 Peter). In each case there are high levels of integration with the broader culture, combined with deep commitments to the distinctiveness of the church's identity as God's people. This reflects the goal of the gospel, to enhance and enlarge the kingdom of God by reaching out to others and seeking to touch their lives regardless of their lifestyles or beliefs.[9]

Ultimately being "missional" is an identity issue. It is about how we understand the true nature of the church. Church leaders in the post-Christian West will need to help orient their churches to a missional way of thinking and being if they are to engage the culture in meaningful evangelism.

Ironically, the way to engender such an orientation is by helping churches actually get involved in mission. Missional communities will not develop out of doing more Bible study and adding more prayer meetings; they will develop out of actually doing mission together. This does not contradict the fact that a distinction can be drawn between churches that only include mission as a part of their overall program and truly "missional" churches. Missional churches prioritize mission at their core and then get busy actually "doing" mission, because they know that to be a missional church means a vigorous engagement in activities that accomplish mission.

This does not mean that ongoing Bible study and prayer are not essential parts of community formation, discipleship and mission, or that theological reflection on mission is not necessary. It is to say, however, that missional passion comes out of doing mission more than it comes out of studying passages about mission or praying for it. Leaders who understand the need for missional community will create that community most effectively by simultaneously teaching about alternative community while helping the church to engage in practical missional endeavors. This primarily means helping the people in the church to see

---

[9]For further thoughts on what defines a church as being missional, see Michael Frost and Alan Hirsch, *The Shaping of Things to Come: Innovation and Mission for the 21st-Century Church* (Grand Rapids: Baker, 2003), in particular chaps. 2–4. Also Van Gelder, *Ministry of the Missional Church*, especially chap. 4.

the missional potential of their own lives and encouraging them to seek to engage their own world missionally in creative ways. It also means seeing ways that the church as a whole can potentially engage its broader community with initiatives that can bring blessing to it. As people participate in mission in all its forms, the church community will be formed in a healthy, biblical way.[10] While ministry done within the body of Christ is essential to the ongoing life of the church, it is the things done for the sake of those outside the body that have a particular potency to form the church. If the life and mission of Christ is our model, then we should not be surprised to find that we experience the renewing power of the Spirit when we follow Jesus into mission. It is when we go to the places that he already is, in the world with the "sinners" and outcasts, that we encounter him most profoundly and find that the church becomes what our Lord intended it to be.[11]

Michael Frost borrows the term *communitas* to describe the radical dimensions of belonging and social togetherness that should define the life of the church. He writes about the need for a group of people to have an experience of *liminality* in order for true *communitas* to be experienced. This means that people need to have a shared experience of being pushed to their limits or out of their normal comfort zones so that they are tested in a meaningful way. The result will be a shared bond that transcends the bonds experienced in most human relationships. This kind of experience often occurs, for example, when people share in a short-term mission trip and are forced to deal with a new culture, less-than-ideal conditions and a challenging work project that they undertake together. Such an experience pushes people beyond what they are normally comfortable with, and when done with others this forms communal bonds that a year's worth of small group Bible study will not. Frost proposes quite rightly that the experience of belonging to the majority of suburban churches is hardly "liminal." He suggests that only by

---

[10]For further exploration on how engaging in mission is central to forming missional, disciple-making congregations, see Jeffrey D. Jones, *Traveling Together: A Guide for Disciple-Forming Congregations* (Herndon, VA: Alban Institute, 2006), pp. 89-92.

[11]For a very helpful discussion of these ideas, see Ray S. Anderson, *An Emergent Theology for Emerging Churches* (Downers Grove, IL: InterVarsity Press, 2006), p. 186.

engaging in challenging, missional living can a group of people truly become the kind of church that is missional in its orientation and is a reflection of the kind of church that Christ had in mind. This church is one that is radically devoted to one another and radically oriented to the world in terms of its commitment to mission.[12]

As individual Christians increasingly understand that their life in Christ is designed to be missional, a heightened need for Christian community will develop as the church becomes a necessary support network for missional living. This means that churches will need to read their contexts effectively and decide what they can do to go into their communities with a vision for serving them and bearing witness to the person of Jesus Christ. In some contexts, this will mean getting involved with new immigrants by hosting English as a Second Language classes and helping to prepare job resumes. In other contexts it will mean providing meals, shelter, clothing and simple health care for the poor. Others will offer counseling services for individuals, couples and families in trouble. Still others will recognize the need to begin something radically different as a new expression of church in their community: perhaps initiating a weekly gathering in a local bar, opening a coffee shop as a place of hospitality and relationship building, or developing a collective for artists in the community for mutual creative stimulation, conversation and support. Each local church has to identify its own unique gifts and calling, but actually getting involved in mission outside the walls of the church is critical to the formation of authentic, missional community.

While the missional potential of the church is rooted in the life of the church and the church "being" the church, that life cannot become what it is intended to become without actual missional engagement. Churches that only focus on their internal life become inwardly focused and ultimately inert. The church is designed to be missional by nature and thus can never opt for an orientation that lacks an outward focus.

A dialogical proclamation. The prescription for proclamation in 1 Peter 3:15 offers the same kind of wisdom to the contemporary church as

---

[12]For Frost's exploration of *communitas* and *liminality*, see *Exiles*, pp. 103-29. Frost draws from the work of sociologist Victor Turner in his use of these terms.

it did for our first-century counterpart. While 1 Peter's wisdom is not the only New Testament approach to evangelism, in a culture that rejects the idea that one person alone can know the truth and that is averse to those who would try to preach in a way that seems to force faith, former methods of witness must be replaced by more dialogical approaches. This is where the approach that 1 Peter offers to its readers can help contemporary congregations learn how to engage in approaches to proclamation that include the following characteristics.

Listening versus telling. Can listening be evangelism? Evangelism is generally perceived as a form of telling or sharing of the gospel message from one human being to another. While the proclamational aspect of evangelism can never be lost, in the current age listening itself needs to be understood as a highly evangelistic act. Evangelism in exile begins not with our mouths but with our ears. We begin by listening to people's stories and seeking to understand their lives. In an age of detachment, individuality and postmodern homelessness, it is in the act of listening that evangelism truly begins to happen. Listening is not simply a pre-evangelistic act of relationship building, not something that we must do in order to gain credibility so that we can get to the real business of telling people what we know they need to hear. We listen in order to hear people's stories, to understand their lives, to identify where God is already at work and to discern signs of spiritual hunger. Listening is the place where authentic relationship is forged.

Listening is the evangelistic act of genuine presence and authentic relationship that mirrors the incarnational activity of Christ and is the essence of mission. If proclamation does take place in a way that offers an "answer with gentleness and respect" (to paraphrase Peter) it flows out of a deep, genuine listening.[13]

An offering apologetic versus an apologetic of certainty. At one time a particularly popular type of apologetics was largely "proof" oriented in its content and approach. For instance, certain lines of traditional apologetic thought offer "five arguments for the existence of God" or "four

---

[13]For further exploration of listening as an evangelistic activity, see Frost and Hirsch, *Shaping of Things to Come*, pp. 97-99.

reasons why we can believe that Jesus really did rise from the dead."[14] This kind of approach, as helpful as it can be, when delivered with a strong dose of certainty is rooted in a modernistic and Christendom mindset that believes in rationality above all and often assumes a certain amount of predisposition to theism in general and to Christianity in particular on the part of the listener.

Instead of providing four reasons why one should believe the resurrection to be true, an offering apologetic will engage in a mutual exploration of ideas that offers some reasons why we personally—and Christians generally—believe the resurrection to be true. While the content may be similar, the tone is drastically different. Rather than presenting a case, we are inviting a dialogue that explores the mystery of Christian faith and offers to our conversation partners our own testimony of belief as the foundation for further exploration, rather than appealing to a (supposedly) rational theory. This does not mean that cogent thinking and well-articulated arguments are not important; however, postmodern uncertainty calls for this kind of humble offering as opposed to an overly confident telling. A central characteristic of this apologetic is a focus on Jesus as the content of faith. Evidence points to the fact that people like Jesus; they just don't like Christianity.[15] In light of this, our proclamation of the gospel should seek to focus on the person of Jesus rather than our views of creation, the afterlife or even the viability of the resurrection as a historical event. While these important ideas cannot be bypassed, they are generally not the most germane issues that people are working through in their respective spiritual quests. Perhaps what people need is to be brought into contact with the person of Jesus, the Jesus of the Gospels, as much as we are able to describe him—the Jesus who played with children, ate with sinners, touched lepers, walked the dusty roads of

---

[14]A classic example of this kind of apologetic approach is found in Josh McDowell, *Evidence that Demands a Verdict* (San Bernardino, CA: Here's Life Publishers, 1979).

[15]As an anecdotal illustration of this, Seattle pastor Karen Ward reports that in a survey done in their Pacific Northwest community 95 percent of respondents affirmed their appreciation for the person of Jesus. Their appreciation of the church, however, was far less overwhelming. See Eddie Gibbs and Ryan Bolger, *Emerging Churches: Creating Christian Community in Postmodern Cultures* (Grand Rapids: Baker, 2005), p. 48.

Palestine and embraced the cross. This is the Jesus whose story compels people and needs to be told. Therefore the power of exilic apologetics rests in making the person of Jesus the focus of our faith-sharing conversations.

Pastor-teacher evangelism versus evangelist-preacher evangelism. The model of the evangelist-preacher is not used here necessarily to describe someone who stands in front of a group of people and preaches an evangelistic message. It is chosen to depict an approach to evangelism that emphasizes the need to deliver a message to a person or group of people. It conveys the idea that evangelism gets the message out and that "getting the message out" is ultimately what is important, even if it has to be forced and offends. What matters is that people hear the gospel one way or another. Again, while there is tremendous importance in delivering the message of salvation so that people can understand, consider and respond to it, the evangelist-preacher model assumes many of the same things (a predisposition to belief and a basic familiarity with the message) that are resident in a Christendom culture but are not characteristic of a post-Christendom culture. These new cultural realities make the goal of "getting the message out" much more difficult and complex.

The pastor-teacher model reflects more of a shepherding style of evangelism that takes the long view and seeks to journey with people on their road toward Christ, or on their road away from Christ as it may be. Pastor-teachers are those who stick with a congregation for the long haul, who speak truth but also build relationships, who befriend, care, counsel and preach, but always with a view to having an arm around the shoulder of and walking beside the one they are serving. In exilic contexts, evangelism is much more like shepherding than delivering a message, because in a post-Christian age evangelism takes a long time. Increasingly people are coming to the gospel from a long way away. The lack of a basic understanding of the Christian message, latent unbelief and a cultural milieu that does not help develop Christian disciples anymore mean that mission is a long-term process in most cases. While proclamation of the message is always a primary goal, successful evangelism should be measured by our ability to walk with people on their journeys: listening, answering questions and staying the course.

CONCLUSION

The church needs to embrace these ideals for evangelism if it is to be effective in its mission in exile. Church leadership is charged with the responsibility of helping a church embrace such a vision.

The preceding proposals are necessary for missional engagement in exilic circumstances and will allow the church to adapt its mission to its current and to continually shifting Western context. The church must remain in dialogue with an increasingly secular society. However, the challenges of cultural engagement can also serve to remind us that exile is not meant to be our permanent state.

12

The Hope of Restoration

A New Home for Exiles

Michael Jinkins in his book *Invitation to Theology* uses the analogy of a rope to help describe the Christian doctrine of eschatology. Jinkins imagines God's working in history since the coming of Jesus as a rope that is attached at one end to the historic work of Christ and is anchored at the other end in the "dim future" when God will act in a way that culminates human history as we know it.[1] To develop the analogy further, the rope is a guide that we grab on to as we journey through our section of human history as it connects us to God and his work in the past, the present and the future. For the contemporary Western church, our journey has led us into the valley of exile, and as we traverse through it we are guided by the belief that this is not our final destination. We live in the knowledge that there is a future that, while mysterious in its details, is still ahead of us. Though we currently live away from our ultimate home, there is a hope that one day we will no longer be strangers and aliens in the world, that there will be a homecoming to end our exilic journey and bring us to the place where we were ultimately created to live.

The hope of restoration, of once again being home, is at the heart of living in exile. This hope is in keeping with the hope that ancient Israel

---

[1]Michael Jinkins, *Invitation to Theology: A Guide to Study, Conversation and Practice* (Downers Grove, IL: InterVarsity Press, 2001), p. 248.

had of one day having its land restored to it. As the hope of physical return began to diminish, the eschatological hope of the Second Temple period emerged, and as we saw in our examination of 1 Peter it was sustained in the early church. It remains a legitimate and necessary motif for the church today in the sense that it reminds us that as God's people the ultimate end of exile is always eschatological, and until then we live in a time when we are never fully "at home."

On the surface this kind of encouragement may not seem necessary for the church in the West. Perhaps it is here that the drastic difference between the exilic experience of the first church and our own becomes clear. As Christians in Western nations, for the most part, life is not full of trials in the same way that it was for our early ancestors in the faith. We face little to no state-sponsored persecution, little physical violence and for the most part only mild derision from some people for our faith. In the majority of cases, people may not share our faith, but they do not begrudge us holding to it. Our lives are generally quite comfortable, successful even. Why do we need to hope for the world to come when this one has actually been pretty good to us? Furthermore, in trying to apply 1 Peter's eschatological emphasis to our day, there is built-in resistance to such views because of the cultural context in which postmoderns have been nurtured. We live in a culture that is not given to deferred gratification any more than it is interested in heavenly glory, and thus a teaching that calls us to focus on a reward that will not come in this life does not seem overly relevant. Our culture expects that immediate personal fulfillment and improvement will be a byproduct of—if not the very reason for—any commitment that we make. We feel entitled to this, so if we make a commitment to something, the benefit should come to us quickly, not after we die or in some long-awaited return of Christ. Finally, we live in a culture that seeks to avoid pain and suffering at all costs. We use medication, therapy or just flat-out giving up on things that take too much effort as ways to alleviate any suffering that we may experience. So when Peter encourages us to embrace suffering and persevere under it so as to identify with Christ in his sufferings until he returns— we do not embrace such a message too readily. These culturally conditioned responses make Peter's message a tough sell in today's church, let alone in the broader culture.

This trend has led to and been exacerbated by the fact that eschatological themes have largely vanished from the Christian pulpit. Along with the instant gratification mentality of Western culture, there seems to be an overall intellectual embarrassment over belief in the doctrine of the second coming. There is also an inclination in some quarters towards belief in the liberal ideal that human progress is the ultimate answer to what ails the world. For some, the contemporary expressions of eschatological belief as found in the literalistic fanaticism of the Left Behind series have led to an overall leeriness of being lumped in with that set if we take eschatological hope too seriously or become too enthusiastic about it. The result of all of these factors is that we have experienced an almost complete absence of eschatological themes in the teaching of the church in the past several decades.[2]

Yet the New Testament is clear that the church is established as a thoroughly eschatological people who "live the life of the future in the present as they await the consummation."[3] Indeed if we truly live as an alternative community, embracing the countercultural norms of the gospel in an ever-growing pluralism, it may be that Peter's message of future hope and perseverance will become ever more relevant to the exilic experience of the church in the Western world. Such a message is one that can buoy God's people with hope when faced with occasions in which the cost of practicing our faith is high. If the church in exilic times embraces a full-orbed exilic strategy, it will indeed need an eschatological component to strengthen it against the forces of the world that continually come against it in both subtle and aggressive ways. John Drane observes correctly that "no Christian tradition seems to have any sort of serviceable eschatology for the twenty-first century world in

---

[2]For a brief but well-considered overview of how this trend began and why it continues, see Thomas G. Long, *Preaching from Memory to Hope* (Louisville, KY: John Knox, 2009), pp. 112-17.

[3]Gordon D. Fee, *Paul, the Spirit and the People of God* (Grand Rapids: Baker Academic, 2011), p. 49. Fee asserts that the greatest difference between the early church and today is the eschatological vision that guided the early Christians in contrast to our almost complete lack of the same.

which we live."[4] He further comments that we need to overcome any embarrassment that we may feel about this doctrinal component of Christian faith and work on developing a meaningful eschatology for our time.

First Peter's eschatological hope can contribute to such a conversation and provide a key piece of exilic theology for today's church as well. The eschatology of 1 Peter makes relevant connections with today because it is a hope-based vision that includes both future and present dimensions. The book uses more than one metaphor to articulate the nature of eschatological hope. This is in keeping with the New Testament as a whole, which offers several different ways of thinking about ultimate eschatological hope. Eschatological hope includes both temporal (end of time as we now experience it) and spatial (new heaven and new earth) dimensions. As we have noted, in 1 Peter there is a clear vision for the world to come that offers a place of rest from whatever struggles this life presents. However, this is coupled with a current mission that makes our lives in this world meaningful as we seek to live out the ways of the kingdom so as to attract others to it. This mission and the suffering that is potentially part of the faith journey are sustained by the abiding presence of Christ, with whom we identify and whose presence we experience not just as a future hope but as a current reality through the abiding presence of his Spirit (1 Pet 1:3-5). Therefore 1 Peter's eschatological theology includes both present and future dimensions, both of which are highly relevant to the life of the church.

Perhaps the most appropriate way for us to understand the nature of this hope is through the lens of restoration (or return). This paradigm captures both the present and future aspects of eschatological hope in a way that honors the idea that there is a future homecoming for God's people tied to a decisive act of Christ returning and restoring fallen creation, along with the perspective that what we do in the world right now matters and contributes to the day of ultimate homecoming.

---

[4]John Drane, *After McDonaldization: Mission, Ministry and Christian Discipleship in an Age of Uncertainty* (Grand Rapids: Baker, 2008), p. 27.

A Vision of Restoration and Return and Its Implications

The picture of a renewed creation is different from what many contemporary Christians hold to. For them heaven is a nonmaterial space occupied by purely spiritual beings. The biblical vision, however, seems to be something different from this, as in both Testaments we read of a future vision that includes a renewed earth. The prophet Isaiah declares, "See, I will create new heavens and a new earth. The former things will not be remembered, nor will they come to mind" (Is 65:17). From here he sketches a vision of people laboring and enjoying the bounty produced by the work of their hands, and the wolf and the lamb feeding together (Is 65:25). This correlates with the vision of John in Revelation 21:1: "Then I saw 'a new heaven and a new earth,' for the first heaven and the first earth had passed away." Rather than this being a place that people are taken up to, it is a place where God comes down to dwell (Rev 21:3). God's ultimate eschatological hope is not the creation of an otherworldly sanctuary that has no resemblance to the world that we currently inhabit; rather, it is a new earth that provides a place for true homecoming. It is where exiles return to their native land.

This is the culmination of the biblical story, the story that we are all a part of that began with the exile of the original couple from the land that God created as their true home. Their exile from the Garden provides an archetype of subsequent exiles of God's people, including our own as contemporary Christians. In various ways our history is one of living away from the good creation that God has provided for us and intended for us to enjoy. Eschatological hope is found as we once again enter into a restored creation that is the home we have longed for. This idea is rooted in a perspective that this world is intrinsically good. This is in opposition to the view held in many quarters that understands creation as "evil" and heaven as "good."[5] This latter view is a dualistic one that leads to the mistaken understanding of Christian hope as rooted in an otherworldly idea of heaven, having nothing to do with our current

---

[5]N. T. Wright, *Surprised by Hope: Rethinking Heaven, the Resurrection, and the Mission of the Church* (New York: HarperOne, 2008), p. 95.

world. This understanding regards this current world as of little value in the present and no value in the future.[6]

In the view of an eschatology based more on an understanding of the restoration of creation, salvation is ultimately about redeeming all things in creation, not just human souls, and thus it is an act of repairing what went wrong with creation, not scrapping it altogether.[7] This view offers hope that what we do now is part of the overall eschatological future that God has in mind. It is based on God's promise that he will make all things new, not that he will destroy all things and begin again with another *ex nihilo* creation. This hope even includes the possibility that the best of human culture will flow into God's new world (Rev 21:26).[8]

This theological vision is the foundation of an eschatological hope for contemporary exiles because it values the idea that God created us for life in this world but, as a result of the fall and subsequent failures on the part of humanity, the experience of home that God intends for us is elusive. The view that this world must ultimately be done away with and a new, nonmaterial one created devalues the reality of our exilic experience, since it takes the real-world experience of living away from home and offers that instead of restoring us to our original—and genuine—home, God will replace it with a new home. This is akin to being asked to resettle in a new land that may indeed be a fine land but is not one's true home. A renewed creation is the home we exiles long to go back to. However, as 1 Peter makes clear, this new creation is a home that is distinct from our original one in at least one clear way. It is an inheritance that will not "perish, spoil, or fade" (1 Pet 1:4).

The revelation of this inheritance is rooted in God's work of redemption, which brings with it the restoration of God's original intent for his creation.[9] With the return of Christ, human history culminates and a new creation begins, where once again God is present and his will is done. It is a place where both the first-century exiles to whom 1 Peter

[6]Richard Middleton, "A New Heaven and a New Earth: The Case for a Holistic Reading of the Biblical Story of Redemption," *Journal for Christian Theological Research* 11 (2006): 75.
[7]Ibid., p. 90.
[8]Stanley Grenz, *Theology for the Community of God* (Grand Rapids: Eerdmans, 2000), p. 646.
[9]Middleton, "New Heaven," p. 76.

is addressed and contemporary exiles can once again find themselves at home, because it is the place where Jesus Christ is ultimately revealed (1 Pet 1:7) and where God dwells. It is the restoration of the experience that the original couple had in their Garden home, where God walked with them and sought their company (Gen 3:8-9). It is God's participation in the new creation that makes it a genuine return home for those who have lived as exiles far away from the place they desired to be.[10]

The idea of our eschatological hope being the renewal of creation also fits 1 Peter's view of eschatology as a motivation for engaging in the world right now. The language of the epistle does not speak of salvation as escape from or abandonment of this life; instead, Peter's focus is on the promises that God offers for the future. Peter wants his audience to understand that what is to come in the future now casts its shadow backward, affecting the life and work of the church in the present and thus offering a way of shaping its current identity. The fact that what we do now has an impact on what will come in the eschatological future inspires continued faithfulness (1 Pet 1:9) and joy in the midst of the current challenges the church faces (1 Pet 1:6, 8).[11]

This eschatological vision strongly influences the letter's view on the function of the church in this world. First Peter 4:7 reminds readers that "the end of all things is near." This leads the author to list several practices that his readers should therefore engage in as a result of the coming culmination of this age. The things listed are unmistakably this-worldly: alertness, sober-mindedness, prayer, loving one another, offering hospitality, serving others and speaking God's word. These activities improve the audience's immediate circumstances and are intended to bring praise to God (1 Pet 4:11). For the author of 1 Peter, eschatological hope was not dissociated from a life engaged in the pursuit of making this world better. This may in fact be because he understood the link between the current creation and the renewed creation to come. Future hope is inextricably linked with present hope. New creation is rooted in old creation. Exile is a time to work toward restoration.

---

[10]Grenz, *Theology for the Community of God*, p. 647.
[11]Joel Green, *1 Peter* (Grand Rapids: Eerdmans, 2007), p. 28.

This vision of future hope legitimizes all other actions that living in exile calls for and that we have explored in the previous chapters, such as leadership, holiness, theological faithfulness and mission. In fact, without such a vision, it may be impossible to sustain these activities for any length of time.

Preacher and homiletics professor Thomas Long tells a story about when he sat on a chaplain's advisory council for campus chaplains at Princeton University. One day, while hearing yearly reports from the chaplains, one advisory board member asked the chaplains, "What are the students like morally these days?" After a bit of a pause, a Methodist chaplain tried to answer the question:

> "Well," she said, "I think you'd be pleased. They are pretty ambitious in terms of careers, but that's not all they are. A lot of them tutor kids after school. Some work in the night shelter and the soup kitchen for the homeless. Last week a group protested apartheid in South Africa . . ." As she talked, the Jewish chaplain began to grin. The more she talked, the bigger he grinned, until finally it became distracting. "Ed, am I saying something funny?" she said, slightly miffed. "No, no, I'm sorry," he replied. "I was just sitting here thinking. You are saying that the university students are good people, and you're right. And you're saying that they are involved in good social causes, and they are. But what I was thinking is that the one thing they lack is a vision of salvation." We all looked at the Jewish university chaplain. "No, it's true," he said. "If you don't have some vision of what God is doing to repair the whole creation, you can't get up every day and work in a soup kitchen. It finally beats you down."[12]

Living as exiles calls for a vision of what God is doing to repair the whole creation. It is only as we live with such a vision that we can do so with hope, because that vision provides us with the eyes to see our efforts in ministry as a collaboration with God's eternal work of restoring his fallen creation and providing a new home for his people who have lived these long years as exiles, far from the home they were created for.

With this as a foundation, there are at least two other tasks of ministry that an exilic eschatology calls for from church leadership.

---

[12]Long, *Preaching*, pp. 123-24.

FORMING AN ESCHATOLOGICAL IDENTITY IN THE CHURCH

We have already considered how an eschatological perspective on life will not necessarily be easily embraced by Western people in the twenty-first century. This is not to imply that the church does not need to be formed in a way that also emphasizes the current hope and meaning that the gospel provides and that kingdom living engenders. As we have seen, such a perspective is of course foundational and also vital for the church in exile. However, the eschatological identity that 1 Peter seeks to engender is not only a vital backdrop for exilic living, but it also reflects a broader New Testament perspective that can at times be lost in a cultural context like that of Western society.

In this perspective exile becomes particularly potent as a way of understanding the church in today's culture, as it is from an eschatological perspective that the church can most vividly see its life as a matter of living "away from home," indeed far from the ultimate home for which we are created and destined.

It is here that the pastoral use of prophetic imagination comes into play once again. Leadership must help the church to see how its life in its immediate social context is designed to be a foreshadowing of the age to come. This means that leaders must teach the church that the immediate work of building an alternative community has ramifications that go beyond simply the building of a better world, for they speak to the kind of world that is ultimately to come. The renewed creation that we wait for can be found in embryonic form in the church's life in the present time. As the church, we are pointing beyond our flawed experience in this world to a better one to come, so that ultimately the church is not just a group of "resident aliens" but also conveys a foretaste of renewed creation. Stanley Grenz illuminates some of the characteristics of eschatological community: peace, harmony, love, righteousness and fellowship.[13] While these qualities are sometimes elusive in human community, we are called to cultivate them in the church as a sign of the age that is to come. As leaders it is our task to invite the church to envision our life

---

[13]Grenz, *Theology for the Community of God*, p. 647.

together in light of the experience of the new creation to come.

Thus the church must be called to imagine what God has in mind for the future by participating in its emergence today, all the while anticipating that our experience now is only a foretaste of the future. Furthermore, this vision can be cast in highly countercultural terms, since the church is a place where the immediate is not the only reality to be pursued. This can become a highly subversive act of alternative community as the church rejects the common view that immediate gratification is what one should expect from life and offers an alternative view that lives with a vision for a renewed creation as our inheritance to come.

Finally, this eternal perspective is crucial to sustaining faith and hope in the face of a culture disinterested in the Christian message. Since living as a Christian can cause one to feel less and less at home in this world, the hope of a future world where we will once again "be at home" becomes a faith-sustaining vision that the church must hold to and promote as an aspect of its core ethos, just as Peter did, in exilic times. It must come out in our preaching and teaching regularly. Our public prayers should often express the language of eschatological hope. The idea of this eternal hope needs to be written into our mission statements and church values. This language of eschatological hope should be part of the evangelistic proclamation of the church. In a world where, despite the many material comforts enjoyed by most Westerners, many in our culture struggle with personal pain and despair, a message of hope that responds directly to the fallenness of this world with the promises of a renewed creation can offer hope to those in need of it. Finally, it must flavor our discourse as we encourage one another with reminders that our faithfulness to Christ and perseverance under the various trials that do surface in our lives will ultimately be rewarded.

The pastoral act of developing an eschatological identity in the church directly addresses the reality of an exilic context, as it acknowledges the distance that we live from our true home, but it also offers the key exilic resource of restoration hope and return to home that enlivens congregations for their ongoing journey. This act of prophetic imagination is necessary for the life of exilic people. Although it does not guarantee that despair and doubt will never creep in, even in those times our vision of future hope is necessary.

DEALING HONESTLY WITH DOUBT

Exile is a doubt-producing experience; it leads us to wonder why we should stick with the identity that led us into exile and whether it may not be better to choose another identity to live by. For ancient Israel, doubt that Yahweh was the true God was addressed by the prophets and psalmists not as an abstract theory but as an act of pastoral care. It was a response to the allure of Babylonian opulence and religious hegemony. In Asia Minor, 1 Peter's audience was experiencing marginalization and trials due to their faith, which led some to doubt. When one finds oneself ostracized because of one's Christian faith, or if one's commitment to the faith incurs criticism or even mockery, it is natural that one may begin to doubt the truth of the gospel of Jesus Christ. After all, it is not usual to believe that the body of a dead man was raised to life, or that a man could truly be God, or that God actually lives in one's heart. Ancient people were no less skeptical than modern people of these outrageous claims. Thus, Peter's assuaging the doubt of his readers concerning their faith in Christ in light of society's response is one clear purpose of the letter.[14]

For contemporary Christians, exile in a post-Christian era can definitely create a (high) degree of doubt regarding their faith. Exile calls core beliefs into question because they are no longer commonly held and, as with Israel of old, it appears as if other "gods" have overcome the power of Yahweh, pulling back the curtain and exposing his weakness as a deity.

Like the psalmist, today's post-Christian exiles can say, "Awake, Lord! Why do you sleep?" (Ps 44:23) and "Why do you hide your face . . . ?" (Ps 44:24). Indications that doubt is a reality in the psyche of the culture and among Christians today are found in both statistical data and on bestseller lists.[15] Doubt is an inevitable reality of exile and a genuine expe-

---

[14]Karen Jobes, *1 Peter* (Grand Rapids: Baker, 2005), p. 42.
[15]The statistics presented by Reginald Bibby on the religious identity of Canadian young people

rience within the church today. Thus, pastoral leadership has to address the reality of doubt in the church through three key movements:

Admit doubt. Pastoral honesty about the reality of exilic doubt is the beginning point. Just as Peter directly confronts the reality of first-century suffering, church leadership must name the reality of how exile produces doubt and admit that it is in fact a common experience. This is the beginning of being able to disable its persuasive power in personal and congregational life. Doubt should be acknowledged in exilic times. It is here that the power of biblical lament, which was an important component of Israel's processing of its exile, can be experienced, as it offers the proper liturgical vehicle to express the doubt we feel as an exiled community. The resources offered by the book of Lamentations demonstrate that Israel genuinely doubted the presence and power of Yahweh when Babylonia overtook it. Spiritual struggles and doubts are not something we should cover up as if they do not exist among the faithful. For many, doubt is a natural part of the life of faith. Exilic circumstances provoke the impulse to doubt because the culture no longer reinforces Christian belief by telling us that those outside the system are wrong and most likely lost. Now, those who embrace Christian belief are told that their faith is not accepted by the mainstream, and its veracity is questioned at numerous points. Thus we need to acknowledge the reality of the situation and that doubt is a real issue among Christians living on the fringes of an increasingly secular culture.

When we name doubt honestly and specifically, we can begin to work with it and constructively address it not as a faith-disabling reality but as a faith-building possibility.

Offer the community of faith as a place of sustaining faith. The

---

offer some indication of this. Thirty-two percent of fifteen- to nineteen-year-old Canadians identify themselves in the category of "no faith" in Bibby's 2008 survey, up from 13 percent in 1984 (*The Emerging Millenials: How Canada's Newest Generation Is Responding to Change and Choice* [Lethbridge, AB: Project Canada Books, 2009], p. 176). While this does not mean that they are atheists or agnostics per se, it does indicate a reluctance to identify with an established tradition, particularly Catholic or Protestant. See further the popularity of books such as Richard Dawkins's *The God Delusion* (Boston: Mariner, 2008), and Christopher Hitchens's *God Is Not Good* (Toronto: Emblem, 2008), which have demonstrated the current cultural openness to religious doubt.

church functions, in sociological terms, as a plausibility structure. That is, it is a place where people with common beliefs come together to support one another and reinforce their shared commitments. The group is structured to help its members continue in their beliefs by making them plausible, even when others outside the group tell them they are wrong. This function becomes even more vital when the culture at large plays less and less of a role in reinforcing core Christian beliefs. Because of this the church community must play an even more central role in the believer's life as it reminds us that we are not "crazy" to pursue faith in Jesus and invest our lives in God's kingdom. Thus the ongoing cultivation of biblical community and an ongoing emphasis on the believer's need to participate in it become central to pastoral work.

Recently in my own church, one of our members went through a tremendously difficult time of testing in which he questioned everything about his faith. At one point he was sure that the whole thing was a "crock" and that his commitment to Jesus was a completely misguided way to live. Throughout this period of time he remained in contact with a number of people who listened sympathetically to his struggles and offered encouragement to him. They allowed him to express his doubt, lament his situation and rail against God without judgment. In the end, as he slowly moved back to faith, a more mature and robust faith at that, he testified that it was the support of his church community in the midst of his doubt that made it possible for him to once again confess Christ as Lord and determine to engage in the mission of Christ with a new-found enthusiasm.

This kind of story is not and will not be uncommon in the church in exile. The church must be open to this kind of struggle but must remain as a place that asserts faith in Christ no matter what the cultural contours indicate or the media pundits have to say.

Present the hope of future glory. As we have already explored in this chapter, the nature of the church needs to be shaped by an eschatological perspective that calls its members to believe that their faith will ultimately be vindicated in an age that is to come. Pastoral leadership in exile responds to the latent temptation to doubt by constantly reminding its members of this fact. This is not to imply that we should just hang on and hope that someday it will all work out; rather, it is to consistently root the faith of the church in the core teaching of Jesus and the apostles that this life is not all there is and that faith is the act of believing this assertion is true. In exile people need the encouragement that a future hope provides not to keep them "hanging in there" but to remind them of the true nature of Christian faith both within this world and beyond it. Perseverance in exile calls for leaders constantly to stimulate this hope so as to combat the temptation congregations experience to give in to the kind of doubt that leads to the abandonment of faith.

In the small church plant I am involved in, this philosophy led us to undertake a preaching series on the book of Revelation. I have always been intimidated by this particular book, but our pastor felt strongly led to pursue this course. I am a part of our church's teaching team, so I had to take my turns preaching on various texts from the apocalyptic vision the apostle John offers. The goal of this series was that by offering a vision of the end we would have motivation to live in the present. Indeed, as a fledgling church plant in an affluent, educated, religiously disaffected community, this text functioned as an identity-shaping word that reminded us that the ways of the world in which we find ourselves are not ultimately the prevailing ideals of history. God has something else in mind. This is a vision that congregations need to have as a touchstone for their lives, as it keeps them aware that our current experience in this world is not our home. There is a future hope that trumps the power structures and wisdom of this world and offers us reason to reject the temporal victories of the prevailing belief system.

CONCLUSION

The eschatological hope of the gospel reminds us that exile is not our permanent state. There is a future home offering that long-awaited experience of restoration that is always the hope of exiles. Nurturing this hope supplies the church with a key resource for remaining faithful in the midst of the impermanent experience of being away from our true home. Just as this was a foundational perspective for the first-century church, its recovery as a living doctrine within the church today will add sustaining passion to the church's mission and message in a world that longs to know there is genuine hope beyond experiences in this broken world. Church leaders today must develop an eschatological vision that will help local churches and ministries to live into a hope that includes a future beyond the limitations of our current experience. Living as an eschatological people is one of the main tenets of exilic life because it reminds us that our story as God's people is larger than the here-and-now story we find ourselves in.

Conclusion

CONVERTING THE CHURCH

The trouble . . . is not moving mountains,
But digging the ground that you're on.

JAKOB DYLAN,
"SOMETHING GOOD THIS WAY COMES"

Miracles of deliverance must be wonderful things to experience. Unfortunately, for most of us and by their very nature, miracles are rare, and deliverance usually comes as a result of hard work and everyday routines. These routines flow out of patterns that develop consciously and unconsciously and become ways for individuals and communities to function effectively in their particular circumstances.

For Israel, a miracle of restoration would have been a nice resolution to Babylonian exile, but it did not come. Instead the nation developed new ways of living as God's people under foreign rule. These new patterns of life and faith enabled it to survive its various captivities and emerge intact as a people. Similarly, the early church—while the recipient of more than a few miracles—did not enjoy a place of power in the world. The early church also had to develop patterns and habits that enabled it to fulfill its calling as a distinct people in the Roman world. In both cases,

God called his people to do the theological work necessary for them to contextualize their faith and serve his purposes in the midst of their exilic circumstances.

This book has largely been devoted to considering the patterns and habits necessary for the church in the West that will enable us to faithfully follow in our ancestors' footsteps and serve God's purposes in our own exile. While a miracle of deliverance might be welcome, it is more likely that God is also calling us to determine what it means to be his people in our particular context. This consideration of some specific exilic resources and their potential application to the church is intended to aid an ongoing conversation. Going even further, it calls for a conversion of the church. It invites the church in the Western world to see itself as in exile so that the specific resources of an exilic theology can be applied in ways that will enable it to thrive in generations to come.

Employing the motif of exile could be a tremendously helpful move for the contemporary church. It will potentially enable the church to understand more clearly the reality of its cultural circumstances and provide resources to help it not to be overwhelmed by those circumstances. Walter Brueggemann notes the potential of the exilic motif to accomplish this when he writes that accepting an exilic identity "is an act of polemical theological imagination that guards against cultural assimilation."[1] Exile, as we have seen, calls for a definition of identity that engages new cultural realities but also acknowledges that we have an identity distinct from them.

Furthermore, exile also offers potential for the church as it rediscovers its true identity because, contrary to being a disaster, the exilic experience of losing cultural power and finding ourselves marginalized may indeed be needed to restore the church to its true identity and missional calling. Perhaps we will discover that on the margins of society the church will once again find its God-given vocation to engage the dominant culture in subversive ways, resisting the powers and principalities

---

[1]Walter Brueggemann, *Hopeful Imagination: Prophetic Voices in Exile* (Philadelphia: Fortress, 1986), p. 111.

and finding ways to offer an alternative message and way of life.[2]

The potential of exile as a motif to enable the rediscovery of true identity, as well as renewed effectiveness, commends it as good news for the church to be "converted" by. The biblical and Second Temple materials we have explored are resources that can inform and nurture this conversion so that it becomes a robust vision to guide the church in its current milieu.[3] As we have seen, the church in the West developed in a context that welcomed its participation in the shaping of culture and provided the church with a sense of privilege that shaped its identity in society. As the culture began to shift and the process of secularization began, the church slowly lost its place at the center of national life. This shift was exacerbated by the postmodern fracturing of culture that has continued to unfold in the past forty-five years. The immense change that has resulted from this ongoing shift has left the church on the margins of Western culture. On the whole the church has been slow to adapt to the new cultural situation in which it finds itself. While few Christian leaders labor under the old paradigm of Christendom, many have not grasped how drastic the implications of cultural changes are on the ministry of the church.

Our experience of displacement as Christians in places such as the United States, Canada, the United Kingdom and other European countries is not completely unlike that of ancient Israel in its sociological realities. In both cases the people involved experienced a move from the center to the margins; in both cases those who understood/understand the implications of this shift had/have to enter into creative theological reflection on how to translate the faith into these new circumstances. The efforts of our Old Testament ancestors provide a template for our own reflections; as the preceding chapters demonstrate, their response can continue to direct us as Christian exiles. The specific aspects of hope found in a responsive theology, a renewed identity as

---

[2]Elaine Heath, *The Mystic Way of Evangelism* (Grand Rapids: Baker, 2008), p. 26.
[3]An example of how a biblically informed motif of exile can be applied to a people group so as to help it thrive in adverse circumstances can be found in Gregory Lee Cuéllar's work on Mexican immigrants, *Voices of Marginality: Exile and Return in Second Isaiah 40-55 and the Mexican Immigrant Experience* (New York: Peter Lang, 2008).

God's holy people, and a reawakening to our call to be God's missional people give clear direction to the life of the church today, just as they informed Israel in the past.

The example of Second Temple Jews, who continued to reflect theologically on how their faith functioned in their culturally changing circumstances, demonstrates to us how the ongoing challenges of exile can be met as the cultural setting continues to be reshaped.

Finally, the New Testament church, particularly as it is epitomized in 1 Peter, offers further direction for the church today as it continues to embody the exilic ideals of the Old Testament by applying them in a new context. The first-century church also built on the Second Temple idea that deliverance from exile would be an eschatological experience, and their vision of ultimate exilic hope can continue to inform our exile as Christians today.

This heritage offers an orienting perspective to the church, if it is willing to agree that its marginalization is ultimately an exilic experience that demands an exilic theology in response. As we adopt this perspective, the church can embrace all the hope that an exilic theology naturally delivers, because we will then be walking in the same steps as ancient Israel and as the first-century church, which each found its way through exile and flourished.

Embracing such a paradigm will not be easy, because it will ask us to break with some standard theological conventions and traditional views of ministry. This challenges the ways of Christendom and its long-standing norms. As the late theologian Stanley Grenz wrote regarding the propensity of evangelical theology to be fearful of exploring new ground, it may be accurate to say that the guiding dictum has been (parodying *Star Trek*) "to cautiously go where everyone else has gone before."[4] However, exile challenges such conservatism, because it pronounces judgment on it. It tells us that everything is not okay, that the old ways of doing things no longer work and that sticking with them is not an option. Things have changed and, by once again allowing his people to

---

[4]Stanley Grenz, *Renewing the Center: Evangelical Theology in a Post-Theological Era* (Grand Rapids: Baker, 2000), p. 7.

experience exile, God is placing a fresh call on the church to rediscover its true identity and be renewed by it. For Christian leaders, this is a challenge to help the church understand its place in contemporary Western culture so that it can respond effectively just as ancient exiles responded to their own unique circumstances.

As mentioned, this is a hard transition for some to make. Christians who largely insulate themselves from the larger culture may not think things are all that dire; for them exile is a far too extreme idea to embrace. For those still in the grips of an eschatological triumphalism that fuels their faith and allows them to only live in perpetual future victory, exile may seem an overly gloomy prognosis. For others, the idea may not immediately resonate because it carries with it ideas of physical displacement and incarceration. However, if exile is to offer the church a hopeful and helpful vision to live into, then the work of converting the church to such a paradigm is an important part of helping the church find its postmodern, post-Christian identity.

The motif of exile is necessary for the church today in order to help it fully understand and honestly name its true cultural circumstances. Only then can it begin to respond to them in a way that will enable it to reject assimilation and recapture its true identity as God's distinct people in this world. Brueggemann reflects the need for exiles to be "converted" to the true nature of their cultural reality when he comments on the ministry of Isaiah to Israel: "The central task of 2 Isaiah is to invite people home, to create a sense of that prospect and hope. But in order to do that, the poet had to *convert* Babylonian Jews into exiles, to persuade displaced people that after two generations, this is still not home."[5]

It is my hope that this paradigm for understanding the church's place in contemporary Western society might present a vision of a hopeful demise—that as the Western church embraces its true place in contemporary culture as a decentered people now on the margins, it will see that exile is the motif that offers the most hopeful resources for it to draw from in order to resist cultural assimilation. Furthermore, it will

---

[5]Walter Brueggemann, *The Prophetic Imagination* (Philadelphia: Fortress, 1978), p. 111 (italics added).

strengthen the church's determination to be what God has called it to be: an alternative community that proclaims the good news of God to a world that desperately needs to see and hear it. Then, just as personal conversion brings the indwelling of God's Spirit into our lives so that we are transformed and empowered by him to live as followers of Christ, so too will the Spirit of God empower us collectively to be transformed by his grace and enabled to be Christ's exilic people in the world today, just as Christ's people have been in the past.

> I, the LORD, have called you in righteousness;
>   I will take hold of your hand.
> I will keep you and will make you
>   to be a covenant for the people
>   and a light for the Gentiles,
> to open eyes that are blind,
>   to free captives from prison
>   and to release from the dungeon those who sit in darkness. (Isaiah 42:6-7)

Author Index

Subject Index

Scripture Index